Children, Film and Literacy

Becky Parry
University of Leeds, UK

palgrave
macmillan

First published 2013 by
PALGRAVE MACMILLAN

Palgrave Macmillan in the UK is an imprint of Macmillan Publishers Limited, registered in England, company number 785998, of Houndmills, Basingstoke, Hampshire RG21 6XS.

Palgrave Macmillan in the US is a division of St Martin's Press LLC, 175 Fifth Avenue, New York, NY 10010.

Palgrave Macmillan is the global academic imprint of the above companies and has companies and representatives throughout the world.

Palgrave® and Macmillan® are registered trademarks in the United States, the United Kingdom, Europe and other countries.

ISBN 978-1-349-45150-0   ISBN 978-1-137-29433-3 (eBook)

DOI 10.1057/9781137294333

A catalogue record for this book is available from the British Library.

A catalog record for this book is available from the Library of Congress.

Typeset by MPS Limited, Chennai, India.

For Jon, Sam, Jake and Dan

Contents

List of Figures and Tables

Figures

Tables

Foreword

The relationship between film and literacy is a rich and promising one, yet literacy researchers have not explored it extensively in recent years. This book, therefore, makes a significant and highly informative contribution to this field. It is puzzling as to why film has been so neglected in contemporary studies of children's multimodal practices. Perhaps the lure of the internet, with its potential to link film to a range of related texts, and its extensive social networking opportunities, has marginalised the study of film as a medium. It may be the case that the grammatical complexity of film is just a little too challenging, even for the most expert of multimodal analysts. Whatever the reasons, this lack of attention to film has left a lacuna which Becky Parry's book comfortably fills.

The importance of this book for the study of children, film and literacy lies in the careful attention it pays to three areas. The first major contribution is its exploration of the place of film in children's cultural, emotional and social lives. No doubt all of us can still remember iconic films from our childhood days and the powerful effect they had on us. Like many others born in the 1950s, my earliest memory of film was sitting in a darkened cinema, crying despondently at the death of the mother of a deer named Bambi in the Disney animated film of that name and squeezing tightly onto the hands of my two younger brothers, just in case they were as upset as I was (however, being little more than toddlers at the time, the intensity of the story somewhat passed them by and it was their older sister alone who sat staring at the screen in a somewhat traumatised state). The high-quality animation, rich colours and poignant music worked together to wrench every drop of emotion out of the film's audience, and the intense experience was enough to create a lasting love of film for me from that day (although I still find most death scenes too heart-wrenching for words). Becky's analysis of children's response to film includes a sensitive appraisal of Disney's portfolio and, while critiquing the ideologies underpinning many of the films, many of which are racist and sexist in nature, she acknowledges the affective impact of the animations on children and recognises the appeal of Disney for childhood audiences. It is this sensitivity to children's responses to film which is a great strength of the book. Becky avoids simplistic judgements and, instead, offers a nuanced appraisal of the complex, contradictory and culturally bound place of film in children's lives.

The second strength of the book is that it makes clear the relationship between engagement with film and children's understanding of narrative, demonstrating how the study of moving image should be central in literacy teaching. Children learn much about plot and structure from film and they can transfer this understanding to print-based texts. Becky offers a detailed analysis of children's writing based on their film viewing and production and demonstrates the way in which they had internalised a complex set of conventions and rules through film viewing that was then embedded into their writing. Unfortunately, the skills the children demonstrated are not always recognised in a literacy curriculum that is focused on the acquisition of knowledge and understanding related to alphabetic print, and Becky's work presents a direct and powerful challenge to this orthodoxy. It is the case that work on film within the literacy curriculum has led in some projects undertaken in the past to a use of film that serves primarily to support the reading and writing of print-based texts, privileging the latter. Becky's work contests this approach and she emphasises that, while there is little doubt that a focus on film can enhance traditional literacy skills, children should have opportunities to learn about film as a valuable medium in itself. Drawing on Margaret Meek's contention that 'texts teach what readers learn', Becky argues that children develop the skills to decode and make meaning from film by watching films. This is a powerful message that should lead to curriculum approaches that enable children to analyse and produce films as valuable and significant texts within themselves, and not merely as ways of enticing reluctant children to engage with printed texts.

Finally, a further strength of the book is that it presents a series of engaging vignettes of children who are both consumers and producers of film, tracing children's meaning-making in a way that places creativity at the heart of the curriculum. Becky's methodological approach is genuinely participatory, and the children are engaged as active agents in the research process, their voices at the very centre of the study. This offers a model for all who wish to work with children to draw out aspects of their meaning-making for analysis and reflection. There is a deep authenticity to this approach and Becky does not shy away from addressing the challenges to such work. In drawing attention to the powerful role that popular culture plays in children's productions, she also reminds us that children's experiences are not homogenous and that for some, popular culture may not be as attractive as other cultural forms, while for others, it is their key passion and we ignore it in the classroom at our peril.

This is a book that goes to the heart of some of the critical debates in literacy education in the current era. As this book goes to press, we are in the midst of a curriculum review in England led by a Minister for Education, Michael Gove, who wishes children to return to the golden age of a mythic past in which popular culture has no place, forced out of the curriculum by an emphasis on high cultural forms and low-level decoding skills. It is up to the education profession to respond to this outright attack on some of the fundamental principles of child-led provision by re-asserting the cultural and educational value of texts and forms that are prevalent in children's everyday, out-of-school lives. Becky's book provides a touchstone and moral compass for this endeavour, pointing both to the educational value of such work and, as importantly, to its social and cultural worth, giving, as it does, greater voice and agency to children by valuing their everyday encounters with films and texts of all kinds.

Professor Jackie Marsh
University of Sheffield

Acknowledgements

Many thanks to Jackie Marsh and Julia Davies for their rigorous and inspiring supervision. Thanks also to my partner Jon who, on too many occasions, held the fort and to my boys who knew losing my memory stick was not the end of the world. Thanks too to my family, in particular my younger sister who as a child I named 'Looby Loo', in honour of the character in *Andy Pandy*, and who has put up with my obsession with popular culture ever since. To my dad who always had a new computer or camera for me to try to get my hands on, to my mum and older sister who were and are great teachers and to my grandparents who ensured my love of stories and film.

I am grateful to friends (Kathy Loizou, Tracy Owen-Griffiths, Alison McKenzie and Soo Boswell) and colleagues (John Potter, Cary Bazalgette, David Buckingham, Allison James, Penny Curtis and Andrew Burn) who have asked how it was going and listened to the answer and from whom I like to think I have learnt a great deal. I also greatly appreciate the welcome I was given by the head and staff at my research school who, in what are increasingly difficult and constrained circumstances, supported and took an interest in the fieldwork.

A special acknowledgement is needed for the role of all the young people I have worked with in my years in education whose engagements with film and media have prompted me to undertake this work. The six children involved in this research, and their class, shared their experiences with me so readily, I am particularly indebted to them. I also acknowledge with gratitude the consent given by the children and their parents for the inclusion of their drawings and storytelling in the sharing of this research.

1
Introduction: A Narrative on Narrative

Narrative is ubiquitous and takes many forms, from written and oral language to still and moving images. Barthes (1975) observes that in every culture narrative is ever present:

> Like life itself, it is there, international, transhistorical, transcultural. (Barthes, 1975, p. 1)

As Barthes describes, the earliest philosophers, including Aristotle, turned their attention to defining the characteristics of narratives and this has been the subject of debate as new forms of storytelling emerge. Regardless of innovations in medium and form, narratives continue to be highly important to the lives of children:

> When we are born we enter into a world of stories: the stories of our parents, our generation, our culture, our nation, our civilisation. (Goodson, et al., 2010, p. 2)

As parents we teach children how to be, how to think, how to imagine, how to feel, how to remember, using stories in many different forms. Bruner (1986) describes narrative as a mode of thought and the work of Vygotsky (1978) and Elkonin (1978) demonstrates that it is make-believe or playing stories which form the richest context for young children's learning. Hardy (1975) describes narrative as a primary act of mind:

> Narrative is crucial in life and in literature. Our ordinary and extraordinary day depends on the stories we hear. One piece of news, a change of intention, even a revision of memory, a secret, a disclosure, a piece of gossip may change our lives. (Hardy, 1975, p. 16)

Although the primacy of narrative has been contested in relation to very young children's experiences of reading (Pappasa, 1993), there can be little doubt that

1

narrative is highly significant to their engagements with texts. Robinson (1997) demonstrates that with each encounter with a new text, readers draw on previous experiences to make sense of them. As a result, as readers we develop repertoires of experience of narrative from print, film, television and other media, which help us engage with new texts. However, literacy has conventionally been taught through the telling and re-telling of print-based stories.

The importance of narrative was acknowledged in strategies to support the formal teaching of literacy in the UK:

> The promotion of children's understanding of narrative texts, and opportunities to create them, are core aspects of children's literacy development. (DCSF, 2006 Year 1 Literacy Planning)

Fictional books are used to teach children not only how to decode alphabetic text but also how to infer meaning from the combined uses of language, font, layout and images. Through narratives we learn literacy (Dyson and Genishi, 1994), we construct identities (Marsh, 2005) and we become storytellers (Brice Heath, 1983). The importance of narrative is ingrained in school practices in written, oral and dramatic form. Learning about narrative is a critical aspect of becoming a reader and accessing education:

> Narrative is primary in children, but it stays with us as a cognitive and affective habit all our lives long. (Spencer, 1982, p. 288)

Despite the clear significance of narrative to the teaching of literacy in schools, film and other popular media narratives are often treated with suspicion (Lambirth, 1994).

Meanwhile, at home children's early experiences of narrative are likely to be visual (picture books), moving image (children's television and film) or screen-based texts (computer games and websites). Attention has been paid to the role of media forms of narrative in children's lives such as television (Hodge and Tripp, 1986; Buckingham, 1993; Robinson, 1997; Messenger-Davies, 1997, 2001), games (Buckingham et al., 2006; Bearne and Wolstencroft, 2006) and websites (Marsh, 2010; Merchant, 2005a, 2005b); however, the relationship between children's film as a narrative form and children's emerging literacy has not been fully explored.

This monograph, therefore, presents a study of children's experiences of film and the significance of children's film as an aspect of a shared children's culture. The work contributes to a growing field of study that acknowledges the relationship between popular media and children's literacies and identities. It is important to make clear at this stage that I am not claiming a greater significance for film over other media or popular forms. I do however, demonstrate, in subsequent chapters, the benefits of examining in close-up a specific media form. I recognise that film is just one element of a wider constellation of other media and activities that constitute children's popular culture and indeed children's lives. Furthermore, that the different forms of children's popular culture converge and interrelate in interesting ways that it is also important to pay attention to. The same narrative can now appear as a film, television programme, book, console or computer game and website. However, children's films are narrative texts with their own formal affordances, codes and conventions and, as such, they contribute to what Robinson (1997) describes as children's developing repertoires of narrative.

The research was motivated by a desire to situate film alongside other media as a form through which children learn to read and create their own narratives at home and potentially at school. The data described in this work seeks to understand what children learn about narrative from their engagements with children's films. The ways in which children participate in and engage with children's film are examined alongside an exploration of the extent to which children's films are sources of ideas about narrative in the classroom. Finally, the processes through which children draw on children's film when creating their own moving image narratives is analysed in detail.

Narrative learning

Goodson et al. (2010) describe narratives opening up spaces for learning:

> Narrative learning is not simply learning **from** the stories we tell about our lives and ourselves. It is learning that happens **in** and **through** the narration. (Goodson et al., 2010, p. 2)

I present narratives of six children's literacy identities in relation to film at home, at the cinema and at school. My perceptions of the children's identities, informed as they are by fieldwork data, are also informed by a narrative of my own – the cumulative experience of participation and engagements with film at home, at the cinema and at school. As a result I begin with six vignettes, storied accounts, of my own experiences of film as a child, a teacher, a parent and a film educator. The process of reflecting on these telling moments contributed to the formulation of my research. Goodson et al. (2010) point out that narrative learning as part of the life course often occurs implicitly and that making it explicit is associated with learning:

> For all those interested in education as a route to self-development and social purpose narrative learning would seem to offer a promising gateway. (Goodson et al., 2010, p. 132)

I therefore present a reflection on some key personal and professional experiences, which provoked questions and enabled me to arrive at an appropriate starting place for my research.

Hollywood tales

When I was a child my gran used to tell me stories. There is not anything unusual about a granddaughter listening to the stories of her grandmother but the stories I listened to were not from books. The stories she told me were intricately woven plots and they were based on Hollywood melodramas and the lives of the Hollywood stars. Bette Davies, Olivia de Havilland, Vivien Leigh, Audrey and Katherine Hepburn, Jane Russell, Ingrid Bergman and Joan Crawford became the brooding, pouting, earnest, heroic stuff of my imaginings. Whether they played an insolent and feisty heiress, a martyred downtrodden sister, or the classic femme fatale, I came to love hearing their stories. My gran had a particular way of telling stories, building up gradually to a key line such as, 'Why ask for the moon when we have the stars?' from the film *Now Voyager* (Rapper, 1942). She would mingle the film plots with snippets of juicy information from the private and public lives of the stars. According to my gran's wonderfully digressing narratives, on and off screen these women had terrible difficulties to overcome including poverty, heartbreak and public misunderstandings.

It was many years later that I actually got to see any of the films she retold. No video or DVD copies of old films were available then. Sometimes I would find myself watching a 'half-way through' film on a Saturday afternoon on BBC Two and realise that the story was oddly familiar to me. As a consequence of this experience I always believed that film was a significant source of stories. It did not occur to me that films were of any less value than books, television, comics or songs. I did not become a film 'buff', I had no interest in how films were made and did not imagine I could make films, but just as some children become habitual book-readers, I did go to the cinema or watch films at home whenever I had the chance, especially those films with strong female characters and with a high likelihood of being a 'weepie'.

Alien invasion

I have two particularly significant childhood cinema memories. The first was going to see *Star Wars* (Lucas, 1977). I cannot remember being especially excited before going but all the same there was a buzz about it and as a result I found myself, with my siblings, in a long queue for tickets. When we finally got into the cinema, the tickets had been oversold and there were no seats. I look back and imagine the usherettes taking pity and letting us sit on the floor at the front (something that surely would not happen now in times of more health and safety rules). However, this was an important part of the whole experience. We were caught up in the excitement that was *Star Wars* the cultural phenomenon. It wasn't long before we were using large sticks, broom handles and any other tube-shaped objects as light sabres and, although none of us ever wanted to be the only female character, Princess

Leia, we made up our own girl *Star Wars* characters or took on the roles of the boys.

I also recall with great emotion watching E.T. (Spielberg, 1982), the story of a stranded alien. During the scene by the river where E.T. is found close to death my sisters and I wept noisily. I was distraught, but I loved the film. I loved the fact that the children kept things hidden from the grown ups. I loved the humour of the connection between Elliott, the main character (and middle child!), and E.T. but most of all I identified with Elliott. I responded to the fact that his family did not listen to him, believe him or take him seriously and for me the denouement of the film was that everyone had to stop and listen to Elliott; he was right and they were wrong.

My love of the film E.T has become a family narrative. Like children today keen to collect toys, cards and experiences linked to a favourite text, I was delighted to find, in a charity shop, a model of E.T., which still lit up and said, 'Phone Home'. On a recent trip to the Florida theme parks I was more excited than any of the children when I got to ride on a BMX bike over the night sky to John Williams' evocative music. Perhaps some films become 'always' films – significant memories of a shared experience.

Tread softly

After completing my Communication Studies degree in Sheffield I trained to be a secondary school English and Drama teacher (there were no courses for teachers of Media) and took up my first teaching post in 1992. During my training we spent just one day exploring the possibility of teaching Media Studies, despite the growth of this area and the high likelihood of a teacher of English being asked to teach either the subject or media within English. This session was run by a local secondary school teacher who described what he did in the classroom to explore the film *Pretty Woman* (Marshall, 1990). However, before we even got started, a lively discussion erupted about whether or not this was a text worthy of study. This discussion drew on common discourses about the value of the text, and the film was dismissed, by my peers, as being rubbish. There were also anxieties about the representation of gender in the text, although eventually a consensus was reached that this was a text that could be studied to ensure young people were able to deconstruct it and see its ideological imperfections. Coming from a Communication Studies course which was largely composed of the study of popular texts, whether they were television detective series, representations of race, or the history of the penny dreadful, I realised that my position in the group was distinct from many of the English graduates who would go on to be colleagues. I also realised that my peers were asking fundamentally different questions of popular texts than those applied to literary ones.

There is a moment which I love in the film *Pretty Woman*. As someone who loathes shopping and feels totally intimidated by glossy shops, I love and re-enact this moment with friends. Julia Roberts' character returns to a shop in which she had been sneered at, with a large amount of money to spend. In context this is hardly a feminist moment, the money is her client's, the shop assistant is female and our Cinderella still gets prettily transformed for the ball. However, for me the shopping moment connected with my social anxieties about going into 'posh' places and I loved it. In the classroom this affective response was being trampled on and I worried about the children these English teachers would also encounter whose pleasures they might also trample on (Pompe, 1992b). This experience made me increasingly determined to teach Media Studies.

Monstrous stories

In my early years of teaching I encountered an issue which appears to be a fairly common experience. One boy in my English class persistently wrote extremely violent stories with sprawling narratives and evolving monsters, which I found difficult to respond to appropriately. I discovered on further enquiry that this boy had a particular interest in Japanese anime films and manga. This made me aware of the need to take an interest in the sources from which children draw in their stories, but also left me with a dilemma about how to make the writing compatible with the newly introduced statutory requirements of the National Curriculum. Years later this dilemma also contributed to the formulation of my research.

Chivalric code

From a period of time in which I worked in cinemas and children's film festivals one experience in particular stays with me. I was approached by an education welfare officer at a school who ran a group for children with experiences of bullying, and who wanted to explore if there were any films the children might find relevant to their experiences. We discussed some possible activities and this led to the group taking part in two screenings, one of an Icelandic film called *Benjamin Dove* (Snær Erlingsson, 1995) and one entitled *The Mighty* (Chelsom, 1998), an American film. Both films had male protagonists who were from 'ordinary' not affluent backgrounds and explored issues of bullying. Both films end with tragedy and redemption and some greater understandings, although their moral stance is not didactic. Both also draw on myths of the codes of honour between knights and explored the reasons why people bully and are bullied.

Following the activity we ran a drama activity, which gave the children an opportunity to further explore and discuss their responses to the films. It would be fair to say I was relieved to have an audience for *Benjamin Dove* (Snær Erlingsson, 1995) – few teachers would opt to bring a whole class to a subtitled Icelandic film with its washed out, if achingly beautiful, snowy landscapes and its depiction of such a bewilderingly different rural lifestyle. *The Mighty* (Chelsom, 1998) was more accessible although, by having such a sad ending, it was not the end-of-term treat choice. However, nothing could have prepared me for the children's responses. They took on an ownership of these films and used them to make comparisons with their own experiences. It struck me that this is often what we do with fiction; we relate, we empathise, we distance ourselves, we immerse. And yet it was striking that these children seemed to respond to the films as if they had never seen aspects of their own lives, in this case bullying, at the cinema before. Following the screening the children formed a club which had a code of honour based on the same knights' code explored in the films. I felt that these films had an impact on the children beyond the everyday; the affective responses the children had to the films was important and needed to be valued.

Bugs and baddies

When my middle son, Jake, was four I noticed he always chose to be the baddie in any re-enactments of films he loved. When he came out of a screening of the film *A Bug's Life* (Lasseter, 1998) he didn't say 'I want to be Hopper', the evil grasshopper, or indeed 'I want to be Flick, the hero of the story'. He said 'I am Hopper' and proceeded to hop or rather fly around the cinema, park and house for days and weeks afterwards crying joyfully 'Let's Ride!' What struck me was not just that he was asserting that he would choose to be the baddie, Hopper, but also the particular way he expressed himself. My older son Sam, five years his senior, would always say 'I am going to be Postman Pat, Buzz Lightyear or Luke Skywalker with a much greater consciousness that what he was suggesting was a game, and that he was playing at something. When I talked to Jake about why he chose to be Hopper he grinned, remembering that Hopper could fly, the grin had a hint of mischief in it, recalling the pleasure of transgression.

The trend of quickly identifying the character to 'be' continued, and in every film or television programme Jake watched throughout his fifth and sixth years, he always quickly told me who he was going to be. This was an integral part of our engagement with films. I enjoyed guessing who he was going to be; he enjoyed my reactions. As he grew older he did not always choose to be the bad guy but he certainly chose people at the centre of the action, with super-powers or all the funniest lines. On reflection, I think Jake sought to take on the role of the character who made things happen, who created adventure or acted on decisions. His choices related to his own emerging sense of self as a child encountering a number of new situations – a new baby arriving, moving house and starting a new school.

Through play and the availability of toys and clothes, this film became part of the fabric of home. Jake's liking of *A Bugs Life* became an aspect of his identity, influencing birthday present choices, for example, and developing as a family narrative about his childhood. The pleasures connected with engaging with the film, taking sides, enjoying transgression, and not identifying with the hero, were all responses that contributed to Jake's approach when encountering new texts. His engagement with the role of Hopper, choosing to be Hopper, rather than distancing himself, became a particular way he engaged with stories. Play based on films offered a space in which he learnt to deeply immerse himself into a fictional world while making links with his emerging identity and his fantasies.

In my own experience, then, film played a significant role in my early life as a stimulus of play, an important source of narrative and a shared experience with family and friends. The role of film in my own life helped to inform my decision regarding the focus of my research. As an educator and parent, I had 'lived' experience of the way in which particular films gain in significance in children's lives, enabling them to explore and perform identities. However, this experience raised many further questions, especially relating to the role of film in schools and its potential to connect children's lived experiences with their school literacy experiences.

The study

This was therefore a study of children's engagements with film at home and at school and an attempt to examine the way in which their understandings of narrative based on film manifested in different forms and contexts. Far from being an old media which has already been the focus of considerable study, children's films have been overlooked, especially recently in the hurry to look at young people's uses of newer technologies such as social networking websites (Burn, 2007). Research which focuses on children's participation in contemporary and popular children's films has a strong contribution to make to debates about contemporary childhoods, literacies and identities, and it is this area to which this work contributes.

The research is presented in a chronological structure which attempts to share both the data and findings but also the process through which these were constructed. In the next chapter, Chapter 2, I present a brief rationale for my particular focus on children's film in the context of contemporary studies of childhood and children's culture. In Chapter 3 I examine the significance of children's film as assets or resources in their developing literacy, identity and textual practices and compare this to the role of film in schooled literacy. I go on, in Chapter 4, to consider children as readers of film, I draw on reader response theory and narrative film theory to understand further the role of the reader and the processes involved in reading moving image narratives, by comparison to reading print narratives. In particular, I draw on the notion of the reader in the writer, as a focus and introduce the central focus of the research: what we can learn about what children understand about narrative from their film-related storytelling? In

Chapter 5 I present my methodological approach to my fieldwork, drawing on participative, collaborative and visual methods to engage meaningfully and ethically with the children involved in the research.

In the data chapters I present storied accounts of the developing identities of the children involved in this research with a particular focus on children's film, in the light of recent theory linking identity, literacy and popular culture, Chapter 6. I reflect on the role of children's films in the children's lives as resources for talk and play. Furthermore, I reflect on the different approaches the children take to reading children's films. In Chapter 7 I explore what knowledge and understandings of narrative the children are able to express in written and oral storytelling and the extent to which they draw on their knowledge of film in these contexts and, in Chapter 8, I explore what knowledge and understandings about narrative the children were able to express through film, reflecting on differences between the two contexts. Finally, in Chapter 9 I offer my conclusions regarding the significance of children's films to children's understandings of narrative and make a case for the further inclusion of film and moving image in literacy curriculums and practice.

2
Children's Film: Children's Cultures

Children's films are currently hugely successful commercially and well received critically; many, many films for children are made each year (although less so in the UK). In the past families watched the first broadcast of films at Christmas such as *The Wizard of Oz* (Fleming, 1939). According to research published by the now-abolished UK Film Council (UKFC), of the most successful films worldwide between 2001 and 2008 the top twenty were made for families and accessed by children (UKFC, 2009a), for example the *Harry Potter* (Columbus, 2002) *Lord of the Rings* (Jackson, 2001), *Star Wars* (Lucas, 2002) *Spiderman* (Raimi, 2002) and *Shrek* (Adamson and Jenson, 2001) series of films. Furthermore, children and young people and their parents make up the largest audiences for cinema in the UK:

> The cinema audience for the top 20 films in 2008 was predominantly young, with the 7–34 age group (40% of the population) making up 64% of the audience. (UKFC, 2008, p. 116)

Children today access many more and a much wider range of films at the cinema, on television, on video, DVD, and on the Internet. Viewing can be a solitary or shared experience and children can watch again, pause, rewind and fast-forward to favourite moments and watch the 'making of' content. Related toys, clothes, bedding and books can extend their experience of film narratives (Marsh, 2005). Despite competition from online activities or console games, the significance of film in children's lives has increased in recent years.

Despite this increasing popularity, children's films have received limited attention in studies of culture, media and film:

> Children's culture has been largely ignored, especially the world of animated films. (Giroux, 1995, p. 1)

While there have been studies of children's understandings of television, studies of children's film have been preoccupied with critiques of the

10

Disney Corporation. Sociological research into constructions of childhood, children's culture and children's literature has included a greater interest in children's popular culture. However, in this arena, debates about children's popular culture often focus on the film industry, the films, or representations of children in film (Hanson, 2000) and tend not draw on research into children's responses to children's films. For example, Giroux (1995, 1999) writes extensively about Disney as a global phenomenon rather than taking into account how children respond to any particular Disney texts. Furthermore, the focus on one corporation means that analysis stems from notions of the institution rather than from the child or children in their own context.

In this chapter I explore the ways in which children's films have been differently defined and understood. I situate children's films in the context of studies of childhood and children's culture. I then go on to examine some particular concerns raised about children's films and Disney in particular, including cultural imperialism and global domination, the appropriation of stories and the mis-representations of gender, class and race. In conclusion, I highlight the need for research which attempts to understand children's films in the context of contemporary children's culture and as significant to children's emerging literacy and identity practices.

The construction of childhood

Current debates about the sexualisation (Levin and Kilbourne, 2008) and commercialisation of childhood (Palmer, 2007) have harked back to a time of innocence when children were 'pure and protected'. These nostalgic notions of children and childhood are socially constructed (James and James, 2004) rather than based on detailed research and are, as pointed out by Buckingham (2002), used to present children today as deprived of childhood. Buckingham (2002) demonstrates ways in which the media constructs children as both in danger and dangerous. He goes on to describe the contradictory relationship the media has with children. In one way the media acts as a vehicle for the discussion of discourses problematising contemporary childhood; and in another way the media (currently computer games and the internet) is often blamed for the crises in children's lives. Buckingham (2002) describes the ways in which contemporary accounts of childhood evolve as 'historical narratives' built around 'diverse representations' of children (Buckingham, 2002, p. 61) and argues that notions such as the purity and innocence of childhood are quite recent constructions.

Aries (1998) suggests that sexual innocence, for example, is a relatively recent expectation of children. He describes a range of incidents from experiences of French royal childhood that infer that in the past children were encouraged to be humorous and open with regard to sex and that modesty and decorum were learnt later as part of reaching maturity. Calvert (1998) reviews historical accounts of experiences of children that cite such issues as high levels of morbidity, the need for economic involvement of children in family survival and the presence of children in all aspects of daily life as evidence that, for some pre-industrial children, there was no such thing as childhood as we understand it today. She demonstrates the ways in which early studies of childhood often drew exclusively on boys' experiences and those of children from privileged backgrounds to generalise widely about what was accepted practice for parents. Calvert (1998) identifies the need for sustained further studies of the lives of children from distinct class, gender and ethnic backgrounds. Moreover, Calvert (1998) discusses key changes in relation to child protection, labour, education and the notion of children's rights, which reflect considerable shifts in perceptions and attitudes to children. Experiences and expectations of children and childhood are subject to change and become sites of conflict:

> The concept of childhood has changed dramatically over time, with changes in social structure, cultural assumptions, and technological innovations leading one generation of parents to reject the child-rearing patterns of its predecessors. (Calvert, 1998, p. 74)

Calvert (1998) proposes that it is important to move beyond arguments about whether or not there was indeed a conception of childhood in the past and towards an understanding of the changing conceptions of childhood.

In post-industrial society, against a backdrop of social, economic and technological innovation, changing attitudes to childhood were reflected in the emergence of distinct texts for children such as books, radio, comics and then films, television and games. Negotiations about what childhood is perceived to be, what is suitable for children, children's relationships with adults and what children will enjoy are played out in these cultural texts. Kline (1998) points out, with reference to Western societies, that children's culture has a complex history involving institutions such as the family, the media, the law, the church, the school:

> Culture is, after all, as the repository of social learning and socialisation, the means by which societies preserve and strengthen their position in the world. (Kline, 1998, p. 95)

Kline proposes that children's seemingly autonomous cultural expressions, whether they are nursery rhymes or playground games, 'take shape within a broader cultural framework' (Kline, 1998, p. 95). He argues that adults produce cultural texts and 'urge' them on children, raising questions about what it is that adults are urging on children and how children respond. Clearly, it is the case that, as authors, directors, toy-makers or comic strip artists, adults make texts for children. What is more, adults buy or enable children to buy and access popular culture. Yet children do not simply take up what adults 'urge' on them and children do not always participate in children's culture in ways adults might have expected. The cultural relationship between adults and children can be demonstrated using James' (1998) research on sweets as an analogy for popular culture.

Children's culture: movies and penny mixes

James (1998) indicates that when children eat sweets, they do not simply adopt the practices that adults suggest to them. James (1998) observes that children seek to resist adult authority in their use of language, play and games. Taking the example of 'kets' or 'penny mixes' (unpackaged sweets sold separately), James demonstrates the divide between adults' and children's practices in relation to eating sweets. According to James (1998) adults in the UK attempt to invest sweets with healthy qualities, buying them for children as a substitute meal. Children, by contrast, delight in the sensual, no packaging, hand to mouth experience of gob-stoppers, chews and lollipops. Children decapitate jelly creatures of various kinds and pay little attention to the healthiness or otherwise of sweets. Eating sweets offers transgressive enjoyment despite, and today perhaps partly because of, heightened awareness about healthy eating.

James (1998) argues that adults never buy kets , opting instead for packaged chocolate bars that make claims as healthy snacks. Of course, some adults do buy kets for their children and indeed for themselves. This relationship is a useful analogy for wider children's culture. There is an adult or parental position (that sweets should be healthy snacks) and a child position (that sweets should be fun and sharing them is an act of friendship). Both children and adults can take up each position. Parents can enter into the enjoyment of sweets nostalgically, sharing the sweets they previously enjoyed as children with their own children and recalling the child they used to be.

Parents may equally wish to share the films of their childhood with their children. However, parents may also wish to share newer sweets or films and might attempt to adopt a more child-like position in the way they engage in related contemporary practices, aligning themselves with youthfulness. Many adults read the *Harry Potter* series of books (Rowling, 1997, 1998, 1999, 2000, 2003, 2005, 2007), collect football cards and watch *The Simpsons* (Groening, 1989) for example. However, children may not want to share and at times they seek out sweets, texts, cards and songs which they anticipate will attract disapproval from adults, particularly parents and teachers:

> Children, by the very nature of their position as a group outside adult society, have sought out an alternative system of meanings through which they can establish their own integrity. Adult order is manipulated so that what adults esteem is made to appear ridiculous; what adults despise is invested with prestige. (James, 1998, p. 404)

Popular culture is often a site for establishing a distance between children and adults (Grace and Tobin, 1998), particularly adults in the role of parent or teacher. It would sometimes seem as if children choose to love those things that are the very antithesis of what parents might think is good for them or suitable. There are numerous examples of hugely popular children's films and television programmes which have precipitated adult outrage. The text then becomes a site of conflict and negotiation about which texts are appropriate and ideologically sound for children. Cultural texts such as films for children can be seen to offer both a site of negotiation about children, childhood and parenting and yet are also spaces in which children can distance themselves from adults, developing their own playful, imaginative and transgressive responses. Those who make cultural texts for children have this range of competing issues in mind, sometimes explicitly and sometimes implicitly. As Calvert argues:

> Members of any society carry within themselves a working definition of childhood, its nature, limitations and duration. They may not explicitly discuss this definition, write about it, or even consciously conceive of it as an issue, but they act upon their assumptions in all their dealings with, fears for, and expectations of their children. (Calvert, 1998, p. 67)

Children's culture has two parallel manifestations: that which children engage with as part of social activity with friends and that which adults create for them in the form of books, films, television series, food, sweets, cards and games. These two worlds co-exist and often collide and both children and adults can take up various adult- or child-like positions in relation to the text (Parry, 2009). For example, the long-running TV series *The Simpsons* (Groening, 1989) is enjoyed by adults and children and has humour in it which is intended for both audiences. That is not to say that it is only children who laugh at the physical slapstick humour and only adults who laugh at the ironic, intertextual references. In the characterisation of Homer and Marge as the dysfunctional parents and Lisa and Bart as the clever children who see through their parents' weaknesses and offer them moral or knowing advice, we encounter a blurring of the lines of authority. Exploring the questions 'Who is the parent?' and 'Who is in charge?' is an important aspect of the appeal of the series.

Contemporary film-makers, like their colleagues in the publishing or television industries, demonstrate an ability to recall their childhood and empathise with contemporary children as well as expressing their concerns about parenting. In the animated film *Finding Nemo* (Stanton, 2003) the impact of the over-anxious, over-controlling father on the child (fish) Nemo is explored both from the point of view of the child and the father. Many further recent children's films incorporate adult explorations of changing perceptions of children and childhood. In *Ratatouille* (Bird, 2007) the whole film takes the point of view of a young anthropomorphised rat who wants to be a chef, exploring themes of escaping parental expectations and not conforming to the restrictions of race or class. The way in which relationships between adults and children are explored has been used as a way of making distinctions between films *for* children and films *about* children.

Defining films for children

Children's attempts to resist what is valued by adults and to distance themselves from them is perhaps an aspect of beginning the process of separating from their parents and developing identities that are not inflected by their families. Buckingham (2002) argues that films for children often address the concerns about childhood and adulthood of both the child and the parent:

> Certain kinds of texts – the contemporary 'family' films of Walt Disney or Steven Spielberg, for example – could be seen precisely to unite these two audiences: they tell both adults and children very powerful seductive stories about the relative meanings of childhood and adulthood. As in a good deal of nineteenth century literature, the figure of the child here is at once a symbol of hope and a means of exposing adult guilt and hypocrisy. Such films often define the meaning of childhood by projecting its future loss: both for adults and for children, they mobilize anxieties about the pain of mutual separation, while offering reassuring fantasies about how it can be overcome. (Buckingham, 2002, p. 9)

In *Toy Story 3* (Unkrich, 2010) the mother's sense of loss when her son Andy, the toys' owner, grows up and leaves home is an underlying theme throughout the film. Alongside this theme and portrayed through the toy characters (particularly Woody) Andy's own emotional departure from childhood is represented, although it should be acknowledged that this theme is only one aspect of the narrative. Bazalgette and Staples (1995) offer a definition of children's films which takes into account the relationship between children and adults:

> Children's films can be defined as offering mainly or entirely a child's point of view. They deal with the fears, misapprehensions and concerns of children in their own terms. They foreground the problems of coping with adults, or of coping without them. (Bazalgette and Staples, 1995, p. 96)

This definition describes what the authors perceive to be positive characteristics of films made for children, for example adhering throughout the film to the child protagonist's point of view (sometimes the child is represented as an animal, toy or alien) rather than switching between adult and child perspectives. Children's films are thus perceived to deal with the complex concerns of children rather than offering a simplistic, didactic, adult, moral message. Although they acknowledge the role of adults in children's films to be important, referring to the absence of adults, or the need to negotiate relationships with adults, they make a distinction between these roles and those found in family films.

Bazalgette and Staples (1995) define family films as those films created for wider audiences by the big, commercial Hollywood studios such as Disney and DreamWorks. They suggest that family films do not adhere to the child's point of view and offer instead content that appeals to adults as well as children and feature adult stars as well as carefully selected attractive child actors. According to Bazalgette and Staples (1995) children's films are traditionally made outside Hollywood with low budgets and public subsidy, giving them a distinct aesthetic quality. These distinctions are problematic; the Hollywood family film, *E.T.* (Spielberg, 1982) was innovative in its use of shots, at the height of the child actors, which enabled the director to maintain adherence to the child's point of view throughout.

Using these defining elements the films *The Adventures of Robin Hood* (Curtiz and Keighley, 1938), *Star Wars* (Lucas, 1977), *Indiana Jones: Raiders of the Lost Ark* (Spielberg and Lucas, 1981) and *Shrek* (Adamson and Jenson, 2001) would not be considered to be children's films because they follow the point of view of adult male protagonists. In the *Shrek* films, Shrek's concern with marriage, giving up his freedom and taking on the responsibility of fatherhood are not the immediate concerns of childhood, to which Bazalgette and Staples' definition refers. The focus on love and marriage means the same could be said for many other fairy stories such as *Princess Bride* (Reiner, 1987) and *Snow White and the Seven Dwarfs* (Hand, 1937). All of these films, and others, are adventure films that do not feature children but are included on the British Film Institute list of 50 films children should see by the time they are 14 (BFI, 2005).

By contrast, films about children and childhood that are for adults very often take a child's point of view but, because of the complexity or nature of the content, are not considered suitable for children. For example the films *Slum Dog Millionaire* (Boyle, 2009) and *This is England* (Meadows, 2007) are told almost entirely from the point of view of children. However, because the characters encounter cruelty, poverty and violence, the films were certificated 15 and 18 and are definable as films about children, but for adults. There is a need for a far greater scrutiny of films for children and young people, as there has been with children's print fiction, to produce meaningful analysis and to further debate about defining features.

Although Bazalgette and Staples (1995) criticise family films for including content for both adults and children, historically many children's texts such as picture books, television programmes and comics have often been made with both adult and child audiences in mind (Spencer, 2001). Children's picture books are written and illustrated to introduce children to the world of stories and children make meanings from words and pictures often with an adult. Adults as fellow readers, as narrator and as characters are often to be found in texts which invite complex readings. In *Not Now Bernard* (McKee, 1996) Bernard is a child who is ignored by his parents and eaten by a monster but is also a boy who turns into a monster because his parents ignore him. The pleasure of the book for both adults and children is making sense of the two possibilities and the two perspectives.

In *All in One Piece* (Murphy, 2006) Mrs Elephant gets ready for a night out and her children attempt to help her. Chaos ensues until Mrs Elephant loses her temper. Gran steps in and finally Mr and Mrs Elephant go out for their evening, but in the last image of the book we see the imprint of the paint tray, left out by the children, on the back of her dress. The elephant children and the reader can see this, but Mrs Elephant cannot. The pleasure of these stories is the juxtaposition of the perspectives both of children and adults. The adult and child reader are thus invited to participate in stories which relate to acute observations of everyday family life. It could be argued therefore that specialised publishing or filmmaking for children is an arena for imaginatively exploring both adult and children's perspectives (Spencer, 2001). The inclusion of adult perspectives in children's stories is not, as argued by Bazalgette and Staples (1995), only for the purpose of reaching a wider family market.

Bazalgette and Staples (1995) take particular exception to the way child characters in film are used to express an adult point of view. They give the example of Kevin in the *Home Alone* (Columbus, 1990, 1992) films:

> In Home Alone 2, Kevin (Macauley Culkin) is told by his father to fetch his tie from the bathroom. Kevin replies in close up, that he can't because 'Uncle Frank' is taking a shower in there and he says if I walked in there and saw him naked I'd never grow up feeling like a real man – cut to shot of parental consternation – 'whatever that means'. (Bazalgette and Staples, 1995, p. 96)

This tactic is used in *The Simpsons* (Groening, 1989); in one episode, for example, Lisa and Bart sit in a cinema bemoaning that they never got to see the new 'Itchy and Scatchy' movie and that as a result they would never be properly 'de-sensitised' to media violence. This knowing response expressing an adult position, playfully critiques popular discourses about the effects of media on children and is clearly an example of a child expressing an adult point of view. However, it is also an example of a child rather cheekily observing phrases from the adult world which seem nonsensical. In many of the poems for children by Michael Rosen (1992) adults' favourite phrases are parodied: for example 'Never let me see you doing that again' is ruthlessly exploited in a poem about his dad. Children are thus invited by the text to distance themselves from adults by parodying their parenting. This draws attention to the need to look closely at individual children's films, including those made by Hollywood, to fully understand the constructions of the child and adult and their representations of the relationships between the two. Observations made by Bazalgette and Staples (1995) in terms of the differences between what they describe as children's films and family films raise some highly pertinent questions. However, it is important to ensure that in analysing children's or family films we consider their place in the context of other narratives created for young audiences rather than in isolation.

Absentee parents

Although relationships with adults are a key theme in stories for children, parents are often physically absent. In his analysis of the *Home Alone* films, Kincheloe (1998) situates his critique within a framework of concern about absentee parents. He describes experiences of contemporary childhood affected by divorce and working parents who spend far too little time with their children and states that: 'Childrearing is a victim of the late twentieth century' (Kincheloe, 1998, p. 159). Kincheloe (1998) underpins his critique of the films with the assumption that more children today take care of themselves and are left at home alone than at any other time in history, describing what he perceives to be the ensuing damage to children and society. Calvert (1998) demonstrates that research that perceives children as a homogeneous mass, all subject to the same experiences, is problematic. Kincheloe (1998) does not present comparisons of children's time spent at home now and in the past, or in different contexts, but bases his assumption on statistics relating to higher divorce rates and recent increases in numbers of working parents. The home alone narrative of a child accidentally abandoned by his parents and left to fend for himself prompts a critique of contemporary parenting:

> In Home Alone 1 and 2 not only is Kevin left to take care of himself, but when his parents and family are on screen they treat him with disdain and cruelty. (Kincheloe, 1998, p. 162)

In addition to the questions that can be raised about the underlying assumptions about children's lives in this critique, there is a broader issue about the nature of criticism of children's texts, which is worth exploring further. Kincheloe's response to the films is highly selective, focusing on certain scenes from the films: 'Kevin is banished to the attic upon which he proclaims for his generation: "families suck"' (Kincheloe, 1998, p. 162).

Kincheloe reads the films as a reflection of the postmodern childhood as experienced by children in contemporary society rather than as a fictional text. He focuses on the opening of the film in which Kevin, the protagonist, is being treated unfairly in a busy (and highly affluent) family, resulting in him wishing he did not have a family (surely a narrative device signalling to the audience to expect his forthcoming abandonment). This wish is critical to the moral message of the film ('be careful what you wish for') and the denouement of the story involves Kevin both proving that he can act heroically on his own, but also that, yes, 'flaws and all', he misses his family.

By looking at the *Home Alone* (Columbus, 1990, 1992) films in isolation rather than in relation to other texts for children, Kincheloe's (1998) reading of the film becomes a tool in his critique of society rather than one which places the film alongside other stories of abandonment, escape and independence. In an adaptation of the folk story 'Hansel and Gretel' by the Brothers Grimm in 1815 the two children are abandoned by their parents (although which parent is most at fault and the role of the step-mother have altered with subsequent adaptations). Historically, cruelty to children is a recurrent theme in children's fiction. Harry Potter (Rowling, 1997) is orphaned and treated with contempt by his aunt and uncle. The Baudelaire siblings are also orphaned and then pursued by their evil uncle in the *Series of Unfortunate Events* (Snicket, 1990). In Dahl's (1961) *James and the Giant Peach*, orphaned James similarly escapes his evil aunts on a magical peach full of 'grown up' insects who he befriends and, following an adventure, starts a new life with in New York.

The absence of parents and cruel behaviour of teachers, guardians and aunts and uncles is not only a contemporary phenomenon; 19th century works of fiction such as Dickens' *Oliver Twist* (Dickens, 1838) and Charlotte Bronte's *Jayne Eyre* (Bronte, 1847), both featuring orphans, are clearly influential on children's literature. Children being orphaned or abandoned or escaping tyranny are far from being a sign of contemporary times. In older children's stories adults are rarely represented as caring, patient, tolerant and indeed the actions of adults are often those which the child must react against. The *Home Alone* films then are hardly innovative in their despatching of adults from the scene so that the main protagonist, the child, can take over the direction of the narrative.

Adults in the audience of the *Home Alone* (Columbus, 1990, 1992) films might be uncomfortable with the idea that a mother could forget one of her children, but this is not the linchpin of the story nor the central morality of the film. The moral theme involves Kevin accepting that he has a flawed family, that he sometimes feels like an outcast, but that they are his family after all and he should do what he can to stick with them. This conservative, adult position is offered by the film, but so too is the more playful, transgressive, anti-authority element which might be considered to be the child position. Both of these elements are included by the makers of the film who draw on the traditions and conventions of films for children about including a moral and happy ending and yet understand that the film must also include aspects of fantasy, adventure and challenges to the existing adult world, which children will enjoy. It is possible to imagine that, for children, the film is a comedy generated by Kevin's setting of a series of ingenious traps to outwit and outsmart a pair of grown-up crooks who are trying to steal from his family.

By including this analysis I am neither attempting to debate the issues raised about child rearing, nor am I defending *Home Alone* (Columbus, 1990, 1992) films. Indeed it is easy to why the easy privilege of the family, the con-trived moral ending and the fetishising of McCauley Culkin as Kevin result in adult unease and discomfort. However, I include it here as an example to demonstrate the importance of making space in our interpretations for what children see and bring to children's films. It is also important to consider that both maker and viewer are, after all, participating in texts shaped by previous experiences of children's fiction. The filmmakers might be simultaneously exploring the concerns of contemporary children and childhood, but they will also be concerned with the craft of making a film funny, moving, surpris-ing and scary. Since themes such as cruel adults, absentee parents, empower-ment, transgression and childhood ingenuity are all often found in children's fiction, it is not surprising to find these elements here and not helpful to cri-tique them as if what they represent is indicative of contemporary parenting.

The study of children's literature has moved apace in recent years, consist-ing of analysing and debating the aesthetic qualities of the corpus of chil-dren's print fiction (Nikolajeva, 1996). Children's films are not examined in the same way. As the example above demonstrates, children's films are too often looked at in isolation from other forms of children's culture and are analysed in very different terms from those used to explore children's fic-tion. This can be attributed to the way in which the children's film industry in general and Disney films in particular are perceived. It is therefore useful now to consider some of the criticisms of the Disney corporation.

Global domination: cultural imperialism

Disney is such a strong global brand that it has attracted more criticism than any other film studio. While many still feel nostalgia and affection for Disney films (Forgacs, 1992), as reflected in the continued success of the films, even those made in the 1930s, the commercial activities of the Disney brand have become a major target for criticism:

> If we imagine the Disney Company as a teaching machine whose power and influence can, in part be measured by the number of people who come in contact with its goods, messages, values and ideas, it becomes clear that Disney wields enormous influence on the cultural life of the nation, espe-cially with regard to the culture of children. (Giroux, 1999, p. 19)

Giroux (1999) attributes the power and influence of Disney to its commer-cial success in dominating the marketplace and buying out competitors.

These criticisms could also be levelled at the political and economic structure that enables them to continue to do so. In the USA the commitment to free-market economy sets the context in which film producers have to work so that ensuring their continued success is key to their responsibility to shareholders and a continuation of the company. That Disney appears to do this to an extreme, while also being a company that provides content for children, sits uncomfortably with many. However, accusations aimed at Disney about impositions of morality, ideological messages, cultural imperialism and appropriation of stories (Zipes, 1995a, 1995b), could equally be applied to other film studios (indeed they could be applied to publishing houses or theatres) around the world. Distaste for commercial success is particularly acute in relation to children.

Audiences are uncomfortable with what is perceived as overt commercial activity, such as toy production and the building of theme parks, which position children as consumers. However, in the making of children's films even in such perennially successful studios as Disney, with their strong traditions about what constitutes a children's film, the context of production is more complex than the caricature.

Global domination implies a one-way process of cultural domination of one culture, America, over many others. Marsh (2005) draws on the work of Appadurai (1996) Hannerz (1990) and Hay and Marsh (2000) to suggest that this description over-simplifies what is better described as an international exchange of material resources and human capital (Hannerz, 1990). Appadurai (1996) argues that in modernity globalisation is best described as a series of flows or scapes, that in the case of media include the global distribution of media and the images, ideologies and narratives of media as experienced by the global audience in their own social, cultural and political context:

> Mediascapes whether produced by private or state interests, tend to be image-centred, narrative-based accounts of strips of reality, and what they offer to those who experience and transform them is a series of elements (such as characters, plots and textual forms) out of which scripts can be formed of imagined lives, their own as well as those of others living in other places. (Appadurai, 1996, p. 35)

Although Appadurai (1996) goes on to ascribe a lack of agency to individuals encountering mediascapes, as Marsh (2005) argues, his description is useful to understanding a greater complexity in the production of culture than has been previously described. In particular, Appadurai recognises a shift from a perception of one-way global domination by, for example American culture, described variously as 'Disnification' (Giroux, 1995) or 'Disneyization' (Bryman, 2004) and towards a recognition of the flows between cultures. As Marsh (2005) demonstrates, a nation's culture can, for a variety of reasons, become 'cool' and therefore of value globally.

Marsh (2005) presents the example of Japanese culture for children gaining in popularity, leading to an increased number of alliances between national companies, leading in turn to the production of cultural hybrids. For example, Japanese items of culture are initially repackaged for new markets or territories. Furthermore, as children increasingly access and engage with these Japanese cultural items, such as animations, collector cards, toys and computer games, they become an aspect of wider children's culture. This has the effect that makers of children's texts will draw on ideas from Japanese culture, so that, rather than simply repackaging or appropriating texts, they are adapting and transforming them and the texts can eventually be seen as cultural hybrids (Juluri, 2003) and sites of cultural exchange.

Examination of the process of Japanification (West, 2009) of children's culture highlights some highly interesting differences between the original and the adapted texts. These productive differences (West, 2009) reflect distinct cultural values and ensuing struggles over cultural identity in the field of children's culture. They also demonstrate change and influence, so for example the monsters in American culture are traditionally created as isolated 'baddies' who cannot evolve and must be defeated or domesticated. Shintoist monsters of Japanese culture transform, and can co-exist with humans (West, 2009). Thus two distinct ideas about monsters may flow and become the subject of further change and adaptation. Although American Hollywood films certainly have market dominance, cultural imperialism is no longer an entirely adequate description of the potential for cultural exchange.

The extent to which individuals in the audience or those working for film production companies have agency and can influence how texts are produced and understood is of course not limitless (Morley and Robins, 1995). The context, structures and discourses which surround both maker and audience frame to some extent what films they make and they how those films are understood. I will go on to discuss the extent to which children make resistant and oppositional readings of children's films, however, prior to doing so I will further address some of the specific criticisms, from distinct academic disciplines, of the Disney films as they relate to the notions of global domination and hybridity.

Ideologies in children's films

Within the field of the study of Children's Literature, children's films are often discussed, not as works of creativity or art, but as vehicles for particular ideologies. In the introduction to a special issue of *The Lion and the Unicorn*, a journal dedicated to serious discussion of children's literature, guest editor Wojcik-Andrews states:

> Children's films do not just reflect history but actively distort history in the name of ideology. (Wojcik-Andrews, 1996, p. v)

Of course, ideology has also been a focus of analysis in studies of children's literature (Hollindale, 1992). All the same, this is a noticeable assertion because it does not distinguish a particular film for this criticism but implies that this is the case for all children's films. In an introduction for a special edition about children's films, it also sets the scene for particular sorts of analyses, focusing almost entirely on representations relating to race (Neff, 1996) and gender (Wood, 1996). Wojcik-Andrews (1996) claims that children's films provide a convenient vehicle for driving home ruling-class ideas. Not only does this not allow that some children's films might not actively 'distort' history (or to put it another way that all accounts of history are constructed narratives) it also infers that this distortion is a highly deliberate and explicit act of socialisation. This claim leaves us with a caricature of the makers of children's films as deliberately setting out to distort history and oppress children. Walt Disney himself (Giroux, 1996) was an active anti-communist and a witness at the House Un-American Activities Committee (Giroux, 1999). However, Disney was also highly successful in identifying entertaining stories from children's cultural worlds to adapt in animated form.

Kline's (1998) description regarding children's culture taking shape within a broader cultural framework offers a more nuanced picture of the process in which stories are told through the medium of film to children. Furthermore, just as children do not always take up the ideas urged upon them by adults (Kline, 1998) nor do scriptwriters, directors, actors or editors adopt the position of an agent of explicit socialisation. Children's authors would certainly not be perceived in the same way and so it seems that simply by introducing the special focus on children's films, new questions arise that would be addressed differently if (British) books rather than (American) films were the focus. The questions Wojcik-Andrews (1996) applies to children's film are:

How do children's films function ideologically and pedagogically? What is a child viewer?

What role or function does the child's body play in children's films and adult society? (Wojcik-Andrews, 1996, p. vi)

These questions are those associated with Media and Cultural Studies, despite being identified in a Children's Literature journal. Buckingham (2003) demonstrates, in relation to the teaching of English, that different questions are applied to books from those applied to films and other media. Buckingham argues that the questions that emanate from Media Studies should also be applied to the print texts studied in English curriculum:

There is no reason in principle why English teachers should not address for example, the economic structure of the publishing industry, or the ways in which books are marketed and distributed to readers. Indeed, critics would argue that the neglect of these aspects in English teaching reflects an essentially individualistic approach to questions of cultural production and reception. (Buckingham, 2003, p. 95)

Equally, the questions that arise from the study of children's literature exploring definitions, pleasures and personal response (Nodelman, 1992) and changing aesthetic qualities (Nikolajeva, 1996) can be useful to the study of children's media and, in this case, children's films. Both sets of questions associated with individual response and critical cultural analysis can provide interesting insights into the meanings of text, whether in print or film form. Yet this is not common practice, especially in teaching about these texts in mainstream UK education (something I will discuss further in the next chapter). Rarely in academic research or film criticism are children's films taken seriously as narratives worthy of further study or accolade. The question of the evolution of a significant corpus of work is not often posed, despite the many useful links to be made between children's popular culture and the study of children's fiction (which again I discuss further in Chapter 3). Instead, the strong emphasis on ideology in children's films can be linked to a sense of unease or disquiet regarding the global commercial activities of the Hollywood film industry.

The appropriation of stories

A key aspect of the global domination accusation made of Disney is that of appropriating and changing existing stories. Stories have always been subject to change in the retelling, depending on the time and place and changing forms of expression. Fairy stories, for example, have been told and re-told, translated, subverted and adapted initially through an oral tradition, which Zipes (1997) describes as a process in which 'small groups of people interacted with a storyteller' (Zipes, 1997, p. 3). Later, stories were adapted into literary form and then later still into radio, film and television. As Zipes (1997) argues in relation to the adaptation of folk stories by the Brothers Grimm and Charles Perrault, stories are often appropriated to reflect dominant bourgeois values of the time, a tradition Disney follows rather than creates.

All the same, Disney's acquisition and transformation of stories, myths and legends, appropriating them into what has become the Disney 'family film', has been criticised both in terms of the cultural imperialist act of appropriating significant cultural stories, but also because of the way in which the films have come to be seen as the original version of the story:

The normative influences of Disney's animated fairy tales has been so enormous, that the Disney spirit – already once removed from the originals – tends to become the standard against which fairy tale films are created and received. (Haase, 1988, p. 196)

In *Living By the Word*, author Alice Walker describes her feelings about the appropriation of the Brer Rabbit stories. First, written up and published by Joel Chandler Harris, a white Atlantan who created Uncle Remus by 'walloping together' three or four of the Negro slaves whose stories he listened to as a child, and then adapted for film by Disney in *Song of the South* (Foster and Jackson, 1946). Walker recalls:

> I don't know how old I was when I saw this film – probably eight or nine – but I experienced it as vastly alienating. (Walker, 1988, p. 31)

As Miller and Rode, in 'The Movie You See the Movie You Don't' (1996) point out, *Song of the South* was objected to at the time because of its representation of slaves as essentially, 'happy campers'. It is clear that *Song of the South* (Foster and Jackson, 1946) in particular was serving a personal agenda of Walt Disney, to present a contented, enslaved workforce with a well-established work ethic who accept their position in the hierarchy. These stories of the cunning of Brer Rabbit had already been appropriated by a white man – Chandler Harris. Originally told by Africans forced into slavery, the oral versions of the stories were heavily laden with themes of resistance and ingenuity, featuring a traditional 'trickster' character from African folk stories (Neff, 1996). Walker continues:

> I believe that the worst part of being in an oppressed culture is that the oppressive culture – primarily because it controls the production and dispersal of images in the media – can so easily make us ashamed of ourselves. (Walker, 1988, p. 32)

The process of adaptation can be a painful and damaging one and the proximity between early versions of the story and the reader has a considerable impact on the reader's response to the text. For a child not familiar with the original stories, the Disney films might elicit a different response. For example, although I have never seen the film, I was introduced to the Brer Rabbit stories by Enid Blyton who adapted them in a series of books in the 1960s (Blyton also introduced me to Greek myths in the same way). Years after enjoying them in this form, I encountered this response by author Alice Walker. I was shocked to discover their source, as nothing about their origin was implied in the version I remember.

All the same, I had responded to Blyton's characterisations of the trickster Brer Rabbit with considerable pleasure. He was the little guy outsmarting the big guys; a figure Neff (1996) argues influences such Warner Brothers' *Looney Tunes* animated characters as Daffy Duck, Road Runner and Bugs Bunny (Avery, 1930–1969). Some aspects of the story then, such as the figure of the very smart rabbit, have gone on to have an influence on future stories. The flow of stories, their characters, plots and themes here could be seen as positive. The trickster character originating in African culture has found a place in American culture. However, concurrently highly problematic representations of race and gender are made opaque by the use of anthropomorphism.

Neff (1996) examines the character of King Louie from the Disney adaptation of *The Jungle Book* (Reitherman, 1967), describing him as a familiar incarnation of 'the unschooled Negro's attempts to assimilate white speech and culture' (Neff, 1996, p. 56). She points out that far from being absolutely unacceptable to audiences today, this film has been regularly re-released. Neff argues that children's films are sites of the great struggles for identity and often make invisible or commodify and appropriate aspects of marginalised culture 'which might be useful to the development of the American self' (Neff, 1996, p. 54):

> To the white audience, even the most exotic racial group must somehow be made recognisable – and to a certain extent acceptable under the rigid standards of membership in the American cultural continuum. But for the members of the marginalised group – and especially the children of ethnically diverse cultures – the face in the great mirror of the silver screen is strangely unfamiliar and deeply alienating. (Neff, 1996, p. 56)

That Disney films incorporate particular representations of class, gender and race is irrefutable. In his discussion of the early Disney animations based on fairy stories, Zipes (1995b) describes the films as, essentially, having the same plot, 'the disenfranchised or oppressed heroine *must* be rescued by a daring prince' (Zipes, 1995b, p. 111). Of course this is one aspect of the narratives that already existed in earlier fairy story versions (Propp, 1968); however, it is fair to say that Disney does nothing to shift the focus away from the conservative values expressed in some traditional texts. The films are also accused of adhering to rigid structures including, 'heterosexual happiness and marriage ... the ultimate goal of the story' (Zipes, 1995b, p. 111).

Zipes (1995a) argues that the characters of Disney films do not undergo change, good is good and evil is evil and 'only the good will inherit the earth' (Zipes, 1995b, p. 111). Again, this is an aspect that Propp (1968) identifies in his morphology of folk and fairy stories, that is to say that characters have their moral function and they retain this throughout the story. Zipes argues that in early Disney films it was only the uses of technology that were new and that an over-concentration on technology led to explorations of fairy stories which were 'unimaginative and heavily influenced by dated racist and sexist ideology' (Zipes, 1997).

In subsequent re-releases of the early canon of Disney animations, representations of women in particular seem dated. As Bell (1995) points out, the early fairy story heroines scarcely spoke, since their design was based on silent movie stars, moved regally like the ballet dancers whose movement they were modelled on and 'wished' to be rescued by a Prince. Later films, such as *The Little Mermaid* (Clements and Musker, 1989) and *Mulan* (Bancroft and Cook, 1998) reflect different influences visually and considerable changes in attitudes to women. One of Disney's most recent drawn animations *The Princess and the Frog* (Clements and Musker, 2009) attempts to address the many criticisms of racist ideology in their films. The characters are black and are voiced by black American actors. However, in line with Neff's argument (1966), in the posters the princess is shown in silhouette and this image reveals that, other than skin tone, she looks very similar to Disney's earlier incarnations of princesses.

All the same, it is fair to say that Disney is changing as a result of changes in society. Oprah Winfrey, a significant black American woman, was employed as a consultant on this film, which was made during the period leading up to the election of Barack Obama as the first black American president. Thus it can be argued that Disney are now more careful to be in line with recent middle-class values about race and racism, just as the Brothers Grimm were concerned about the values of their day. *Song of the South* (Foster and Jackson, 1946) is clearly a racist text, a product of a time in which such attitudes were tolerated and it is not considered appropriate now. Subsequent unfavourable public reactions to *Song of the South* (Foster and Jackson, 1946) resulted in the film never being released on video or DVD, again reflecting a degree of change in Disney's corporate attitudes, although Zipes (1995a) and Giroux (1999) would criticise films such as *The Lion King* (Allers and Minkoff, 1994) and *Aladdin* (Clements and Musker, 1992) (Giroux, 1999) for their depictions of race and gender.

Critiques of the Disney films play an important function in raising our awareness of the extent to which particular ideological stances are taken in cultural texts. They also highlight the extent to which some groups read cultural texts such as the Disney films by resisting the ideas and messages they find there (Tobin, 2000). Learning about the provenance of stories and tracing their influences on later texts is potentially a highly productive and significant way of looking at children's films. The example of Brer Rabbit demonstrates the way in which stories for children are changed and adapted to reflect the mores and values of the day, in this case a time of toleration of explicit racism. However, the provenance of the story and its adaptation to film according to the cultural conventions of society, impact on both film-maker and audience in complex ways and in the broader context of shifting global mediascapes.

It is thus important to remember that when children respond to stories, they may respond differently from the way adults expect and should be credited with considerable sensibility about ideologies in texts and how they relate to them. As James (1998) argues in relation to the way children eat sweets, children do not simply adopt the practices that adults urge them to, whether they are parents at home or film-makers working for global corporations. Tobin (2000) furthermore, proposes that children bring their own experiences to texts:

> We cannot know from analyzing the contents of a movie what it will mean to a particular group of children. (Tobin, 2000, p. 150)

Tobin (2000) demonstrates through his research that children do not simply adopt the ideological position as suggested to them in films. Citing Morley (1980), he argues that their responses are also greatly influenced by the discourses they have encountered in other areas of their lives:

> The meaning of the text will be constructed differently according to the discourses (knowledges, prejudices, resistances, etc) bought to bear on the text by the reader and the crucial factor in the encounter of audience / subject and text will be the range of discourses at the disposal of the audience. (Morley, 1980, p. 18)

Despite the many concerns raised about Disney, the Disney legacy also holds appeal for many children and adults:

> I dislike Disney's corporate wealth and power because it allows its products to monopolize and crowd out markets that might otherwise be occupied by others' products, but I have derived a lot of pleasure from Disney products, and in particular from the animated films. (Forgacs, 1992, p. 361)

Miller and Rode (1995) acknowledge the position of Disney as a significant cultural force which invites the 'kid in us' to recall our own favourite key moments from our own experiences of Disney. If we are to further understand children's films, including those produced by Disney, it is highly important to engage with children's affective responses to the films. *The Little Mermaid* is an example of an appropriation of a story. Disney takes the original Hans Christian Andersen story, which is about self-sacrifice and unrequited love, and turns it into a happy-ending love story with the ideal of heterosexual marriage as the ultimate happiness. Further Disney elements are added such as a musical structure and a sidekick comedy character (Zipes, 1995b).

However, like Tobin (2000) Richards (1995) argues that that the way in which audiences choose to act on media can be enlightening and unexpected:

> The Little Mermaid offers one version of the route to sexual maturity. Its romance is that of the heterosexual coupling in marriage and its moral lesson is that, in the achievement of romantic love, girls must preserve the grain of individual personality. (Richards, 1995, p. 147)

Richards suggests that his daughter and her friends are exploring ideas about sexuality in their responses to the text, which neither a feminist critique or Disney might have anticipated. This is not to say that children, like adults, necessarily construct one single reading of a film. It can mean different things at different times and different scenes from films can stand out as distinct from the meaning of the whole film. This usefully points to the need to examine carefully the ways in which children participate in the stories told by films. Young audiences may gravitate towards particular segments of film that are their favourites; they may rewind them again and again (Finch, 2008) and watch them avidly. It is these moments, that children select as their particular favourites, that they share with friends and interpret in their play, taking on the roles that excite them, which we need to focus on. Even where young audiences do engage with an overall meaning of a text, cultural factors also influence what they perceive to be the core meaning (Tobin, 2000).

Richards' (1995) daughter rejected the love scene, in *The Little Mermaid* saying 'I hate it when she does this' (Richards, 1995, p. 148). Young girls then might distance themselves from particular aspects of the film they are not prepared to engage with but clearly get a range of pleasures from the jubilant dance sequences. Children might choose to enjoy aspects of Disney; that does not mean they accept without question the moral meanings on offer, nor does it mean they take on the gender and sex roles represented without bringing to them their own characteristics and cultural experiences (Tobin, 2000). Hodge and Tripp (1986) demonstrate in their research focusing on children's understandings of television that adult readings of the whole meaning of the text are potentially distinct from those of children. Here the researchers were pointing to the fact that a level of maturity might be needed to recognise the intended 'moral lesson' of the film. However, they also point to an issue concerning research in this field, 'the danger being the tendency to impose our adult meanings on children' (Hodge and Tripp, 1986, p. 16).

Children may not be as interested in an overall meaning of a text, particularly where this is a didactic moral message. The extent to which they engage with and ask questions of children's films is of considerable relevance to gaining an understanding of their developing experiences of story (and is the subject of subsequent chapters). Furthermore, readers of texts are not entirely powerless in the flow between text-makers, texts and text-readers. As can be demonstrated in the example below, in the process of adapting stories there are occasions when shifts in contemporary attitudes, readers' responses and the director's gender and stance can lead to productive revisions in the way a story is told.

Adaptation: transformation

In her analysis of successive adaptations of Hodgson Burnett's *The Secret Garden* (1993), Gillispie (1996) presents the possibility that a film director can revisit a text and invest it with contemporary insights that were not possible at the time the novel was written. Originally published in 1911, the book has continued to be a best-seller, popular with female readers in particular and the basis of three filmed adaptations. Gillispie points out that feminist responses to *The Secret Garden* have identified a sense of loss for young women readers at the point at which the story abandons the central character, Mary Lennox, and takes on the story of Colin Craven, the invalid boy. As Gillispie demonstrates, Holland (1993) subtly addresses this issue in her filmed adaptation for Warner Brothers:

> By virtue of her time and gender, Holland [Director of the 1993 adaptation of the film] bequeaths a legacy of *The Secret Garden* that seems truer to the sense of the original novel. (Gillispie, 1996, p. 139)

Contrary to what Zipes (1995a) claims about Disney films, Gillispie demonstrates that it is possible for stories to be adapted, by commercial film studios, in ways that are 'true to the sense of the literary original' but also able to 'reflect contemporary mores' and utilise 'cinematic techniques' (Gillispie, 1996, p. 132). Furthermore, it could be argued that the process of adaptation has the potential to involve the film-maker in addressing readers' responses to the original text. In this case, the denouement acknowledges Mary's central importance to the restored health of Colin Craven and pays attention to her grief, her transformation and her reconciliation with her family. What I hope this example demonstrates is the way in which readers can engage with a story and love it but still reject the way it ends, in this case feeling rather betrayed. However, in the process of adaptation a film-maker can reclaim the text for some readers by reflecting shifting attitudes to what makes a good story, in this case that a girl's story is of equal interest to that of a boy's.

Zipes (1995a, 1995b) argues that American Hollywood films, particularly those of Disney, freeze the story, rendering it difficult for others to re-tell it. Moreover, he suggests that young people perceive the Disney version of fairy stories as the original source. Both in the process of film-making and in the reader's response there is a greater space for generating a range of meanings than Zipes acknowledges. For example, Zipes accuses Disney of turning complex fairy stories into simple 'happily ever after' stories. Disney does not shy away from sorrow, fear or even transgression in films, such as the death of the father, Mufasa in *The Lion King* (Allers and Minkoff, 1994). Yet Disney films do always have happy endings and indeed this has become an important aspect of both films for children and Hollywood films. However, Disney cannot claim to have begun this tradition. It is possible to argue that in narratives for children, a strongly reassuring closure has been a long tradition of stories. A happy ending is constituted by resolution, not only the love and marriage of fairy stories but also returning home safely or escaping from a bad place to a good. Even outside Hollywood there is a strong culturally-bound convention of a happy endings in children's films and other forms of children's fiction are similarly bound by this convention. Thus although clearly Disney has developed some strong conventions as identified by Zipes, they are equally influenced by historical traditions of children's storytelling. In recent years they have also been influenced by the emergence of new companies and new technologies which have expanded the production of films for children exponentially.

The new additions to the stable of commercial companies making films for families and children include: George Lucas, Don Bluth, Brad Bird, John Lasseter, Nick Park, Jeffrey Katzenberg, Stephen Spielberg and Walden Media. It must be acknowledged that these key figures in the children's film industry are all men and that furthermore most of the directors they employ are male. While there is a greater diversity of people producing films for children who are motivated by different experiences and ideas, the adult makers of films for children are, predominantly, remembering their boyhood or experiencing being fathers. Women and mothers are under-represented in the upper-echelons of film production for children.

Contemporary children's films can been seen to have a distinct range of conventions in relation to characters, plots and settings which become familiar to children; these films open up certain sorts of imaginative spaces, providing children with symbolic resources for play and text production. Kenway and Bullen (2001) and Grace and Tobin (1997) describe children's pleasure in the recognition of the familiar, but they also discuss pleasure in the transgression of 'adult' codes, which enable children to escape from the adult world.

Luke and Carrington (2002) describe the ways in which the child and childhood are constructed in the everyday and fantasy texts associated with the classroom. Carrington (2005a) argues that these texts 'are often silent on issues such as diversity, conflict and poverty' and do not represent 'worldly' postmodern childhoods (Carrington, 2005a, p. 21).

Children in the UK largely watch American films, some of which are close to Luke and Carrington's (2002) description of classroom texts. Others such as *The Simpsons*, represent children as 'worldly', engaging actively with the 'textual landscapes' they find themselves in (Carrington, 2005a, p. 20). In their use of both the familiar (fantasy stories and everyday stories) and the unfamiliar (intertexuality, ambiguity, parody) contemporary films make a range of demands on children as readers. Given the strong presence of transgression of textual and adult codes in children's films, it is possible to argue that the spaces created by children's films are open, complex and rich, rather than entirely closed and didactic.

Contemporary children's films, like children's literature, are markedly different from other films, particularly in terms of coherence. Coherence, or the way in which texts represent a consistent story world and plausible series of events with causality, is different in fantasy and everyday worlds. The coherence of a fantasy story may be markedly different from that of an everyday story but each must abide by rules established within the story world. Children's texts are often on the edge of coherence, so we might argue that in a coherent story a crocodile cannot just turn up in the front room and eat the baddie (or indeed the goodie), but actually this might well happen in a children's story. The rules of coherence can and are regularly broken. That is not to say that anything goes, so for example in films which depict other magical worlds, the internal logic of these worlds is quickly established; animals might talk, or children might fly, and boyfriends turn out to be vampires. However, within these story worlds there are internal rules of coherence which govern what might happen within a narrative. It would be interesting to see how children attempt to navigate the complex rules of coherence in their own stories and how compatible this notion of coherence is with school notions of a good story.

Children's films sometimes feature didactic themes or moral messages that are, if not central to the story throughout the film, dominant at the point of closure. In many films this is often a fairly straightforward message of good conquering evil. For example, in many superhero films it is the role of the protagonist superhero to save the world from domination by the antagonist, an evil baddie. This is not the only theme of children's films however, so at the end of each of the *Home Alone* films, the family is restored to each other, having learnt to appreciate each others' differences. In the *Shrek* films, the green ogre learns to accept himself and by doing so, accept the love and friendship of others. Zipes (1995b) argues that Disney children's films in particular, freeze the meaning of fairy stories. However, whilst moral messages are often key to the closure of children's films, as suggested it is important to recognise that children do not simply adopt these adult messages. Hodge and Tripp (1986) demonstrate that children's texts are complex and offer a range of meanings to children. Furthermore, as previously argued, children focus on aspects of films which they find most engaging rather than solely on the moral ending of the film (Richards, 1995).

In *Star Wars* (Lucas, 1977) it could be argued that pleasure is obtained because of the high-octane battle scenes in which a member of the audience can project themselves into a narrative pursuit to save the galaxy from domination by the dark side. However, *Star Wars*, also has a melodramatic storyline that reunites a brother and sister and reveals their father as the enemy (plot-spoiler) Darthvader. This storyline potentially offers audience members at least two very different narrative experiences.

Films for children should not therefore, be dismissed as entirely commercially driven, or as simple instruments of socialisation, or as ephemeral texts. Children currently attending primary school have grown up watching a much wider range of films, largely American films, for children and as a consequence it is critical to explore how these experiences contribute to their developing understandings of narrative, particularly in the light of the lack of UK film production for children.

Anxieties expressed about global industries dominating children's cultural lives are hardly surprising, especially in the case of children in the UK who rarely access UK children's film. Perhaps because of these anxieties, analysis of children's films focuses almost entirely on their ideological content. Questions are rarely raised about children's films as a corpus of work alongside children's books, children's television, children's comics and children's games which children read and experience as narratives.

In attempting to define children's films, useful questions arise about their conventions. The adopting of a child point of view, the movement from everyday to fantasy story worlds, the contested relationships between adults and children and the existence of transgressive elements are common in children's films and in wider children's culture. Children's books and children's films could be usefully studied alongside one another, recognising that they are not a homogeneous set of generic texts but are diverse, complex and of value. Although there is evidence that children's films, like other fictions, reflect didactically the norms and values of the day and that at times these include highly problematic, dated representations of gender and ethnicity, it is not adequate to dismiss them on this basis. Indeed, for this reason it is critically important to understand how children read, interpret and understand the children's films they encounter, and in particular how they draw on them in their own storytelling.

Marsh (2005) observes that mediascapes or globalised narratives (Appadurai, 1996) of children's popular culture permeate family life and are not simply adopted by children but are adapted into family practices. Marsh (2005) demonstrates ways in which children, siblings, parents and grandparents participate in play based on favourite films, which become a significant aspect of family narratives and children's identities. Marsh (2005) goes on to demonstrate that this process of permeation is not reflected in school, although children continue to experience films at home and in their social play. It is critical to understand why films and other forms of popular culture do not permeate school life in the way they do family life and to seek to understand the implications of this for children.

Children's films and popular culture are powerful and valuable aspects of children's shared culture, helping to shape and develop their experience and understanding of story:

> The style and narrative conventions adopted by modern writers for children develop less from earlier books than from the shared texts of television where new codes are made and learned as universally as in the medieval code of stained glass. (Spencer, 1982, p. 289)

I am interested in children's films in particular as a manifestation of children's culture. That is to say, children's engagements with and participation in children's films have a role to play in their emerging identities, particularly in relation to literacy. While recognising the significance of children's film, I have demonstrated that reading them simply as an instrument of socialisation is limiting. As a consequence, the next chapter draws on studies of the significance of popular culture, including children's films, in children's developing identity and literacy practices at home and at school.

3
Assets, Resources and Repertoires

We use narratives to formulate our identities and to share our culture. When we learn to read we do not only learn how to decode alphabetic text, we also learn stories and storytelling. Narrative, therefore, is a cultural aspect of literacy. Narratives are not only experienced through language, they are ubiquitous in other forms such as film, television, games, photographs, comics and music. Each of these forms of narrative incorporate common narrative characteristics such as characters, plot and settings, but they all also tell stories in distinct ways. Bordwell and Thompson (2003) define narrative in films as the cause and effect relationship between events so that a random selection of events could not be described as a narrative. They also define 'categorical films', 'rhetorical films' and 'abstract films' as films that do not present a series of events that have a cause and effect relationship and therefore cannot be described as narrative films. Chatman (1990) similarly distinguishes three text types as 'narrative', 'argumentation' and 'description', which again emphasises the potentially quite contrasting nature of a narrative film, an advert or a film montage.

Robinson (1997) suggests that these finite distinctions are not helpful and proposes the notion of degrees of narrativity on a continuum. This is a useful proposition since some texts, such as a still image, can have a high degree of narrativity. That is to say, when a series of elements such as characters (a young girl and a dog) and a setting (a stormy sea) are positioned in relation to each other, they may infer a story (the girl's dog is about to be swept out to sea). A more abstract painting involving a series of dots or blocks of colour may offer a lower degree of narrativity. Perhaps even more importantly, pictures or texts can be experienced as strongly or weakly narrative by the viewer. So an older person could look on a photo of themselves as a child on a beach and generate a series of stories about their early life, for another viewer the photo might connote little other than, 'here's a child on a beach in the 1940s'. The degree of narrativity is not inherent to the text or even the author then, but lies in the way a text is read by the audience.

We learn to read and respond to narratives in all these forms and as a result they become an aspect of our literate identities:

> I can't remember who took me to see 'Mandy'. It was such an intense experience that the cinema could have crumbled around me and I wouldn't have noticed. I was *in* that film, suffering alongside Mandy. (Wilson, 2007, p. 155)

In her autobiography, popular children's author Jacqueline Wilson describes her total immersion in the 1950s films featuring child star Mandy Miller. She became an avid fan of the young actress and described replaying favourite scenes again and again 'in her head'. The young Jacqueline also used the film melodramas to begin to create her own stories, playing with cut-out figures of Mandy and then reinventing a 'third Mandy'; an imaginary friend from whom she was 'inseparable for years' (Wilson, 2007, p. 156). Wilson's adult reflections reveal the way she drew on the films as a resource in her own emerging interest in storytelling, comparing the life of Mandy to her own. Her account illustrates the way children learn to suspend disbelief, to enter a fictional world and to bring with them aspects of their own experience which enable them to create meaning. When the film is over, Jacqueline's participation in it is only just beginning. While I am not claiming this as a universal experience for children, I use it to illustrate the connections between children's encounters with film narratives and their play, their identity formation and their orientation to literacy.

Narratives in some media are afforded more cultural value than others (Kress, 2003), so for example in school, print narratives are an aspect of the core curriculum whereas computer game narratives are not. Nonetheless, the valuable role of popular culture in children's lives is increasingly acknowledged, particularly in relation to their developing literacy and identity practices. Recent research has focused on popular culture at the forefront of technological innovation such as games (Gee, 2003; social networking sites (Davies and Merchant, 2009), or mobile phone use (Gillen et al., 2005). This research, situated in the New Literacies paradigm, looks closely at children's participation in a particular popular culture form as an aspect of their emerging literacy and reflects on the relationship between contemporary children's experiences of literacy at home and at school.

Film has also been impacted on by the development of new technologies, that have improved animation techniques and special effects. This has led to more challenging and ambitious fantasy stories being attempted, resulting in an increased industry confidence in audience appetite for films for children. Film is also often inextricably linked to other media such as games, websites and music as well as artefacts such as books, posters, toys and clothes. The characters, storylines and signature identity of children's films are at the heart of many children's experience of the 'narrative web'

(Marsh, 2005). Today children can also buy the book, CD, T-shirt, lunch-box or game of their favourite film, extending their engagement with it and signalling their affiliations to others.

Since Jacqueline Wilson went to the cinema in the 1950s therefore, there have been changes both culturally to the sorts of films now made for young audiences, and materially in the ways in which children can participate in children's films. Film may be an older medium, but like all forms of creative and communicative expression it is subject to renewal and renaissance. As well as increased innovation in production techniques, digital technological advances have impacted on film distribution and exhibition. For example, in the ensuing years, first video and then digital technology enabled children to watch these films at a time of their choice, at home, over again, rewinding and replaying favourite scenes.

Even more recently, the capacity for accessing content online and via mobile technology provides increasingly easier and wider access to films as well as to film production tools and this has provoked changes in viewing practices and increased opportunities for online responses, discussion and text production (Ito, 2006). For example, some children create mash-ups, tributes or fan-sites about their favourite films (Jenkins et al., 2009), thus sharing or distributing their responses in different ways. As a consequence, just as it is important to understand contemporary children's engagements with websites such as Flickr.com (Davies, 2009) or games such as *Club Penguin* (Marsh, 2010) in the light of current theories of literacy and identity, it is also important to research children's engagements with contemporary children's films.

Some popular children's films such as the *Star Wars* (Lucas, 1977) films or the *Harry Potter* series (Columbus, 2002) have significance for children, becoming what Bromley (1996) describes as almost universal, 'collective' texts. That is to say, some children's films become a shared text that forms the basis of play and social interaction. The popularity of these films cannot be entirely attributed to high budgets, high quality production values and marketing. Every week films with equally high budgets that are equally well-marketed fail to capture children's imaginations. Equally, some films are unexpectedly successful for example, *High School Musical* (Ortega, 2006), was first shown on television and did not get a theatrical release at the cinema. This television film became highly popular with children, especially girls, leading to additional spin-off films and the emergence of a hugely profitable brand. It is the popularity of these films and the accompanying branded toys and clothes that cause anxieties about the commercialisation of childhood. Yet it is not marketing alone that made these films successful. As I have previously argued, it is not adequate to dismiss children's adoption of certain texts over others, without examining that engagement further. Furthermore, it would be wrong to assume that all children have homogenous film preferences or read films in the same way.

It is my premise that popular children's films continue to be significant to children's lives and that, as such, they are an important early source of narrative. Furthermore, I would argue that children's films are at once similar to and distinct from other forms of narrative in both popular culture or literary print form and therefore contribute to children's understandings of narrative in particular ways. Given the important role of narrative in emerging literacy at home and at school, it is therefore useful to explore the particular contribution of children's films to children's understandings of narrative.

In this chapter I begin by demonstrating some of the ways that theories of identity and literacy have been utilised to further understand children's relationships with popular media, including film. I highlight the need to further examine the relationship between children's home experiences of film, and their encounters with film and film education at school. Although research exists that explores the role of film in education in relation to developing literacy (Bearne and Bazalgette, 2010) media literacy (Buckingham, 2003) and with a focus on school-based film production in particular (Burn and Durran, 2006), I identify a need for additional research to explore children's repertoires of experience of narrative (Robinson, 1997), including their experiences of popular children's films.

Popular culture and identity

Sarup (1998) has described identity as a construction, resulting from interaction between people, institutions and practices. This view calls into question the idea of a single cohesive identity, emphasising the importance of context and the existence of power relationships which contribute to identity formation. Mishler (1999) describes identity as relational and to do with attempts to align or distance ourselves from others, again implying that identity is particularly influenced by social contexts. Understanding identities as multiple or constructed has implications for research which addresses children and young people's relationships with popular culture.

Moje and McCarthey (2002) argue that theorising identities as complex, hybrid and contradictory helps us to understand the enactments of identity we encounter in schools. They propose that literacy practices are the tools through which we represent or perform particular identities. Marsh (2005) draws together a number of post-structuralist analyses that conceive of identity as a narrative process through which individuals construct a sense of self (Giddens, 1991). Marsh also stresses the importance of research which demonstrates the significance of context to children's identities (Connolly, 1998). This is not to say that identities are entirely ephemeral or superficial, but that they are reconstructed by individuals who draw on their own historical set of practices in response to particular contexts:

> In this theoretical framework, behaviour is to be viewed not as an outward indicator of an essentialist self but as a self-in-practice, a self

in the process of constructing identities located within socio-historical contexts. (Marsh, 2005, p. 30)

In the fields of Media and Cultural Studies, ideas about the relationships between children and popular culture, particularly media, have transformed from a simplistic effects paradigm, (Bandura, Ross and Ross, 1963). This prevails as a common sense notion today in which children are assumed to watch and imitate behaviour from media. However, a more recent body of work acknowledges that the relationship children have with media is more complex and that they are capable of agency and dynamic responses, (Hodge and Tripp, 1986; Buckingham, 1993; Tobin, 2000; Barker and Petley, 2001). Buckingham and Sefton-Green (1994) demonstrate the varying degrees of agency young people display in constructing and performing their identities and their relationships with popular culture:

> We have emphasised the diverse ways in which young people actively create and define their own social identities through their relationships both with their peer group and within their school. In the process we have adopted a view of subjectivity not as unitary and stable, but on the contrary as diverse and changeable. (Buckingham and Sefton-Green, 1994, p. 108)

They propose that popular culture offers a range of 'symbolic resources' through which young people can make sense of their lives (Buckingham and Sefton-Green, 1994, p. 108). They advocate a move towards enabling young people to 'reflect upon the relationship between the subjective and the social' (Buckingham and Sefton-Green, 1994). They argue that while this is a political process, it is not one which involves young people in 'relocating themselves' in ways adults deem appropriate. Through their case study of Pony Boy', they illustrate ways in which popular texts are resources which are drawn on by young people to work through their own identities in relation to others, in particular their peers. In this case, the science fiction and adventure film genres enjoyed by Pony Boy are also important to enabling the construction of imaginative spaces through which fantasy identities can be explored. Popular culture also offers much younger children resources for the playful exploration of identity.

The relationship between play, popular culture and text production is highly significant to children's emerging identities and literacy practices (Pahl, 2006). Popular culture texts for young children are closely bound to their play and they play, talk, dress up and dance characters from favourite films and television programmes (Marsh, 2005). Parents accommodate children's enthusiasms, creating spaces, buying them gifts or helping them make props that augment this play (Marsh, 2005). Marsh (2005) highlights the link between children's socio-dramatic play in relation to popular culture and the importance of play to children's language and literacy development. She argues that play becomes a ritual in which children take the opportunity to explore and understand schemas, for example common storylines in films or qualities of particular characters. Marsh demonstrates that play based on popular culture texts such as television programmes and films becomes an opportunity for identity exploration in which children place themselves as a character in the centre of the action.

Contemporary popular culture forms such as games also make visible children's enactment of characters within a narrative. Pahl (2005), for example, demonstrates that console games offer children the symbolic resources to explore multiple identities in an 'embodied' form. The child sees themselves represented or projected onto a screen and they control the movement and action of their on-screen self. Pahl demonstrates the ways children discuss themselves as avatars, players of games, and how they further immerse themselves in texts by performing and transforming the many different roles or characters from the games they play. Pahl also describes a video, created by a parent, in her study of two boys re-enacting but also adapting a sequence from a wrestling game:

> In this way, they [the children] demonstrate an awareness of performance and narrativised identities within that performance. (Pahl, 2005, p. 135)

Thus, children play and perform characters from games both online and offline, sometimes simultaneously.

Marsh (2005) emphasises the importance of family, self, peers and others in the development of children's identity and points out the role particular family members have in supporting children's identities in relation to media and popular culture.

Parents can be seen to encourage their child's collection of material objects that form part of a 'narrative web' in which that narrative can be experienced as dolls, comics, cards or bedding. Marsh uses the example of Winnie the Pooh, describing many different artefacts owned by one of the children in the study, demonstrating the role of toys and props to play. Marsh (2005) also describes a young boy playing with notions of gender identity by using his grandmother's shoes to perform being Cruella Deville from *101 Dalmatians* (Geronimi et al., 1961). This boy does not choose bought toys to play with but a pair of shoes, demonstrating children's inventive and resourceful responses to playing stories; a point I will return to later in the chapter.

Marsh describes the ways in which 'the literate identities of children, young people and adults have a significant impact on their orientation to literacy' (Marsh, 2005, p. 30). What is particularly relevant here is a distinction between the literate identities children develop in the early years at home and how these might be different from the literate identities they develop in school. Marsh describes this as a process through which 'literacy practices shape identities and identities shape literacy practices'

(Marsh, 2005, p. 31). Moje and McCarthey (2002) argue similarly, that identities help to shape our textual and literate practices but these practices can be differently valued in a particular context, which in turn can impact on the representation of identity.

Marsh (2005) suggests that it is possible to create a context in which school and home practices can meet and be explored and reflected upon by children who are then able to 'appropriate tasks' and 'transform their identities', a process also described by Dyson (1997, 2003). Marsh (2000) in her work focusing on the *Teletubbies*, argues compellingly that using popular culture texts in the classroom is key to engaging and motivating children in learning and assists with building bridges between home and school. Focusing on a nursery school, Kenner (2004, 2005) looked at a project which enabled parents to participate in the collection of popular culture materials from home, which were successfully used to stimulate individual student projects:

> Young children use the multimodal resources available to them to create texts which represent and further their 'interest' as an individual located in a particular sociocultural context. (Kenner, 2004, p. 6)

Kenner argues that if children's popular culture is not engaged with in school, children are in danger of living in a monocultural and monolingual curriculum – alienated from school.

The aspiration to provide a third space, in which literacy and identity practices, which emanate from distinct contexts and involve distinct sets of knowledge, can meet and be valued is explored by Moje et al. (2004). Although the creation of such a space is clearly key to the inclusion of children's diverse literacy experiences, at school children's playful practices in relation to films and other media are not so readily accommodated. Teachers feel uncomfortable with highly popular, commercial, mainstream media (Lambirth, 2004; Hilton, 1996) and children in the UK are most likely to encounter film at school as an end of term treat (Goodwyn, 2004). Meanwhile, the play and the social interaction continue in the playground.

Popular culture and literacy

Studies which set out to look at children's reading (Fry, 1990) find children keen to share their experiences of popular culture:

> What perhaps should have been mentioned at the beginning of this chapter is that Joanne much prefers films to books; I often felt she would have liked our conversations to be about the films she had seen, rather than the books she had read, and often she turns the talk towards that preference. (Fry, 1990, pp. 88–89)

In Fry's (1990) research, Joanne, like many of the other students, makes links between her experiences of narrative in the print form and in moving image form. Similarly, in tracing the influence of literature in children's writing Barrs and Cork (2001) find many instances of children drawing on experiences of popular children's films, especially Disney. And research that attempts to explore children's experiences of popular culture in relation to literacy regularly demonstrates that, alongside other popular culture forms, film is highly significant in children's lives, (Hilton, 1996; Dyson, 1997; Grace and Tobin, 1998; Kenner, 2005; Pahl, 2006).

The inclusion of popular culture in research about literacy reflects changes in the ways in which literacy has been researched and understood. Within the paradigm of New Literacy Research (Gee, 2003; Barton, 1994; Street, 1984; Brice Heath, 1983), a body of work has emerged that explores the relationship between popular culture and children and young people's literacy practices. Research into early years education in particular has produced a growing consensus that popular culture has an important role to play in children's learning (Levy, 2009; Kenner and Kress, 2003; Marsh and Millard, 2000; Pahl, 2006). This work draws on wider understandings of literacy as a social practice:

> Literacy is primarily something people do; it is an activity, located in the space between thought and text. Literacy does not reside in people's heads as a set of skills to be learned, and it does not just reside on paper, captured as texts to be analysed. Like all human activity, literacy is essentially social, and it is located in the interaction between people. (Barton and Hamilton, 1998, p. 3)

New literacy also acknowledges the role of home culture (Dyson, 1997, 2003) and those experiences outside school which influence children's lives. Children come to school with diverse experiences of media and storytelling and this knowledge has a value that needs to be recognised, (Marsh, 2000; Hilton, 1996; Dyson, 1997). Home language, narratives and culture offer enrichment to the classroom (Brice Heath, 1983). Kress (2000) describes the inventive and resourceful ways in which children use 'whatever is to hand' in their play and in their language use and eventually in their writing. What is to hand can be a physical item or something remembered from a film, book or previous experience. Children improvise, so fingers become guns, sticks become light sabres or horses, and jumpers become goalposts, Pahl (2005) describes the impact of children's popular culture on children's writing:

> I will argue that children's popular culture, in particular, the plethora of objects, artefacts, moving images, narratives and games that 'make up' popular culture, together with cultural objects and long-term narratives

in the home, offer children complex semiotic affordances which they draw upon in text making. (Pahl, 2005, p. 126)

Spencer (1988) argues that if we want to see what children have learned from the texts they have encountered, we have to look at their writing. She goes on to say that, given encouragement, children 'draw on the whole of their culture' in their writing (Spencer, 1988, p. 3). In the literature about the relationship between reading and learning to write there is evidence that in school, given the choice, children will readily attempt to draw on popular culture to create new stories:

> In the context of the widely used 'writing process' pedagogy, children are given free choice over their story writing topics allowing James Bond, Pokémon, Spice Girls, and Beanie Babies to enter the classroom. (Willett, 2001)

Furthermore, as Barrs (2001) argues, children develop intuitive theories of narrative based on their previous experiences that they use in their storytelling. The following example is given by Barrs (2004) from a research account in which a six year old girl begins her story:

> The circus was coming, and the animals had babies. But one animal did not have a baby. She looked high and low for a baby to suit her. But no, she could not find one. (Barrs et al., 1990, p. 83)

Barrs et al. (1990) emphasise the way the child has used rhythm in her writing drawing on her experiences of books. However, for anyone who has seen the Disney film *Dumbo* (Sharpsteen, 1941) this extract immediately conjures the image of Mrs Elephant on the circus train, waiting for her baby to come. In imagining this scene I am bringing to the child's text my own experiences and it is possible that *Dumbo* is not an influence on the writer at all. However, Barrs' et al. (1990) analysis of many stories written by children demonstrates the influence of both film and literature on children's writing and the need for those who teach children to write, to be able to tune into the wide range of experiences they might draw on.

As Kress (2000) argues, when children draw on their own experiences of narrative in creating stories, and as they gain in confidence as storytellers, they begin to transform them, creating their own meaning. So here, the six-year-old combines perhaps fables about animals and ideas from a popular film narrative. In the final sentence, however, she takes the story in her own direction. The mother couldn't find a baby to suit her. This demonstrates a development or progression in storytelling from the borrowings of ideas and imitations to transformation. It is highly important to try to understand this process in relation to the way children might draw on film in their storytelling.

Mackey (2002) critiques what she terms as a deficit model, which regards popular culture as replacing the more valuable activity of reading books, suggesting a shift towards regarding children as having assets. That is to say, acknowledging that children's experiences of popular media contribute to their understanding of narrative. Robinson (1997) demonstrates the ways in which children draw on both previous life and textual experiences to engage with text and are able to utilise different areas of knowledge according to the modality of the text. Thus, if the text is a fairy story they use their knowledge of fairy stories more than their experiences of everyday life to make meaning:

> As they read narratives in print and television, these children are actively engaged in resolving a dialectic tension between their existing knowledge and expectations and the new information they are taking from the new text and the particular reading situation. (Robinson, 1997, p. 178)

Robinson goes on to argue that, across media, familiarity plays a crucial role in determining the confidence and competence with which the children in her study approached their interpretation of texts, implying that familiarity might be an important convention in texts for children. Clearly, as Robinson (1997) argues, children do not segregate their knowledge of narrative into film or printed word categories but experience narrative holistically. However, in school they are often required to draw on their experiences from one medium and express it in another, and this presents a number of challenges.

Historically, children's use of film in their creative writing has been a cause for concern for teachers and education policy-makers as expressed in this comment from the Newsom report, *Half Our Future*:

> Occasionally free composition produces a shapeless mess in which the memory of many televised Westerns often seems to be still riding the range of the pupil's memory. (CACE, 1963)

Interestingly, it is recognised here that it is in children's free composition that references to popular culture, in this case televised Westerns, appear. Free writing implies writing that children exercise more control over. Their choices reflect aspects of stories they like and want to imitate. The presence of Westerns in children's writing is described here as unconscious, passive and therefore a negatively perceived aspect of children's writing. It is as if, in the classroom, children need to be shielded from or prevented from using the pervasive influence of Westerns. However, children are today perceived to have more agency over the texts they enjoy and the pleasures they take from them. Hodge and Tripp (1986) demonstrated that when children infer meaning from a television animation series, this is an active process of meaning negotiation. Furthermore, since the cultural value of film and television Westerns is better-established, perhaps now our question should not be whether Westerns (or any other film genre) ought to be allowed to ride the range in children's writing, but how we can help children to successfully transform their ideas from one medium to another.

Millard (1997) expresses a common concern about children's and especially boys' writing responding to the report above:

> The reference in the report [above] will strike a chord with today's teachers, equally familiar with contemporary versions of boys' narratives, that read like storyboard treatments of favourite video and television narratives, all dialogue and no narrative description. (Millard, 1997, p. 40)

Again, there is an inference that where children are using film or television narrative it is problematic and does not lead them to achieving successful writing because they copy ideas, use dialogue too much and do not use enough narrative description. However, questions arise both about what constitutes a good story and what is considered good story-writing in school. As Willett (2001) demonstrates, ideas about what makes a good story in school are ingrained in contemporary pedagogical practices. Drawing on Graves's (1983) work on 'writing process', as well as the more recent focus on teaching genres, Willett makes explicit some underlying rules about teaching children's writing and what children's stories should be based on. That is to say, children's experiences of popular culture are often not seen as appropriate choices in story composition, particularly in the current context.

In recent years, UK teachers have increasingly experienced new policies, strategies, initiatives and testing regimes, aiming to effect changes in the skills of the workforce.

> Governments seek to accomplish their educational goals through imposed national curriculum strategies that emphasize central regulation, high stakes testing and over determined pathways to accreditation. (Millard, 2006, p. 210)

Literacy has been a particular target of these new curriculum strategies and testing regimes, leading to the domination of particular pedagogies (Hilton, 2001). These changes have implications for the ways in which children encounter story in school. The UK National Literacy Strategy (NLS) commenced its focus on writing in the year 2000 with a strong emphasis on teaching grammar and spelling, word and sentence level objectives separated from their context, leading to 'reduced time spent on written composition', (Hilton, 2001, p. 5). In conjunction with the practice in schools to teach to the Year 6 SATs tests, this leads to what Frater (2000) describes as an 'anxious literalism' in the teaching of writing. Hilton describes activities such as filling in worksheets, writing in missing words and learning to spot adjectives and verbs. She goes on to highlight research (Bloor, 1979) which demonstrates that these activities, while not without value, are unlikely to improve children's ability to write or to enhance their performance in national tests:

> In other words it does not matter how able the children are at spotting adjectives or adding connectives to prescribed sentences. They will not perform well in any national assessments or indeed in the larger arenas of culture, if they cannot write clearly, imaginatively and logically for themselves. (Hilton, 2001, p. 5)

Hilton is particularly critical of the practice of shared or guided writing, which she argues is based on a misappropriation of research by Hillocks (1995) about the writing processes. Hilton demonstrates that potentially useful ideas about shared writing are distorted in *Grammar for Writing* (DfEE, 2000), a training manual for teaching writing, distributed to schools and newly qualified teachers. In this document, the practice of teaching separate sentence- and word-level objectives is espoused, leading to objective-led teaching. This is accompanied by a prescribed teacher-led guided writing process which continues to be a dominant pedagogic practice in primary literacy teaching. This involves the teacher working with a whole class leading an out-loud process of writing which could involve rehearsing sentences before writing them down, using specific objectives from the text, sentence or word level work or discussing and explaining why one linguistic decision might be better than another. Hilton (2001) argues that this, far from allowing children to gain an understanding of the drafting and editing processes of writing, as was encouraged by Hillocks (1995), limited children's opportunity to undertake independent writing and to 'explore their independent writer's voice' (Hilton, 2001, p. 6).

Hilton (2001) also expresses concern at the amount of time spent on shared writing, leading to almost constant teacher-led activities. Not only are recommended writing activities frequently teacher-led, when children undertake individual tasks they are regularly based on the immediate retelling of a story. Very limited time is available in the curriculum for independent or free writing, which is clearly an important part of enabling children to explore and experiment with the ideas, pleasures and understandings of story they may have encountered in a whole range of texts (Hilton, 2001). In recent years, the curriculum and imposed pedagogic practices have focused attention away from the notion of film and popular culture as part of a repertoire of experiences of narrative and as a consequence away from identifying what help children might need to draw on their knowledge of film narratives in their writing and, importantly, vice versa. It is imperative to return to an examination of these questions.

In their study of the way children express their knowledge of computer narratives in their story-writing, Bearne and Wolstencroft (2006) discuss the challenge teachers face in acknowledging what children know about texts from popular culture and what is valued in the curriculum:

> Children's cultural capital in terms of text knowledge may not always square with the kinds of literacy curriculum on offer in schools. (Bearne and Wolstencroft, 2006, p. 72)

However, it is not only the content, such as characters and plots, of popular culture texts that do not square with the literacy curriculum. Although children assimilate aspects of their experiences of popular culture texts into their literacy practices at home and at school (Pahl, 2005; Kenner, 2005), and experience narrative texts holistically (Robinson, 1997), it is important to acknowledge that popular culture texts are often also media texts. It is therefore, not common for children to make texts in the form in which they experience them. For example, children might draw superhero characters they admire and invent new ones, but they have limited opportunities to create films incorporating these characters. Given the central role of writing in the literacy curriculum, in school it is not surprising that children try to incorporate their ideas from popular culture media texts into written narratives. This important process of adaptation and transformation warrants further research.

Mackey (2004) and Bearne and Wolstencroft (2006), explore the relationship between children's playing of online and computer games and their writing. This serves as a useful potential comparison with research focusing on children's use of film in their writing. They emphasise the importance of the social context of games and their strong association with play. They describe play as important to learning and as having a certain grammar following 'procedures, patterns and rules' (Bearne and Wolstencroft, 2006, p. 73). They attempted to look at how children's writing 'combines the imaginative, performative and regulated aspects of play drawn from their experience of computer games texts' (Bearne and Wolstencroft, 2006, p. 73). In the study the children aged 8 and 9 could make distinctions between the pleasures of being involved in stories in books and those in games. The children were asked to turn the story of Red Riding Hood into a game using paper-based resources (rather than games design software).

The children in the study demonstrated their knowledge of both the traditional tale and the conventions of a computer game. Their games retained the overall narrative required for good game play but also drew on the structuring device of levels of accomplishment, collection of objects or back-story clips. Children's games showed different levels of complexity in the choices offered within the game and the consequences of actions. Their use of language changed, for example they used imperative verb commands such as 'collect', 'get' and 'avoid'. This perhaps demonstrates the importance of the modal affordances of different texts.

When children attempt to draw on a fairy story to create a game they use both traditional narrative and game structure as resources, but the mode of the final outcome determines the extent to which they can use their knowledge of games. A story based on a game would substantially shift this process of text production. In Bearne and Wolstencroft's study the children were creating games, in paper-based versions, which allowed them to express their knowledge of the conventions, structure and language of games in their own narratives. It is therefore useful to explore how children draw differently on multimodal resources in their text production and the extent to which the medium (written, drawn, filmed, acted) impacts on their ability to do so.

Kress (2003) developed the concept of 'multimodality' to recognise that texts, such as web sites, films, television and radio have affordances specific to their form and that engagement with them involves broader literacy practices than the reading and writing of traditional printed text. In his own work Kress concentrates considerably on print, such as magazines and adverts, and focuses on layout, font and use of colour. The moving image tells stories through visual, aural and spatial conventions and elements that are significantly different from oral or print storytelling traditions. It is critical then to take these differences into account when researching the relationship between film and literacy. Parker (2006) suggests it is film's distinctiveness, its difference from print texts, that offers students the opportunity to develop understanding of communicative features 'criterial' to particular sorts of texts. It is important, therefore, to reflect on children's understandings of narrative in different media, in this case film, and how these understandings are valued in the classroom.

Film in the curriculum and the classroom

Throughout its history, film has struggled to find its place within education, regularly having to renegotiate the changing models of English and Literacy teaching. In particular, advocates of film education continue to have to argue for its role in relation to literacy:

> The education, information and entertainment industries are becoming ever more dependent upon the communicative power of the moving image, whether delivered through cinemas, broadcast, video or online. The existence of an informed citizenry – essential to the democratic process- is increasingly sustained through the moving image media. This unique and vital language must surely, therefore become part of basic literacy at the start of the third millennium. (BFI, 1999, p. 7)

Rationales for the inclusion of film in the school curriculum have emphasised the relationship with wider literacy, drawing on an analogy between language and film language. It is useful to look at where media and moving image texts were historically listed as curriculum content within the UK National Curriculum for English at Key Stage 3 and 4. Under 'Reading – Non-fiction and Non-literary texts' it was recommended that students should be taught:

- how meaning is conveyed in texts that include print, images and sometimes sounds
- how choice of form, layout and presentation contribute to effect [for example, font, caption, illustration in printed text, sequencing, framing, soundtrack in moving image text]
- how the nature and purpose of media products influence content and meaning [for example, selection of stories for a front page or news broadcast]
- how audiences and readers choose and respond to media (DfES, 1999)

Film is included here alongside adverts, newspapers and magazines rather than alongside narrative texts. Study of these texts is not, therefore, intended to enable students to appreciate 'author's craft' or access stories from 'literary heritage' or 'other cultures', although these criteria are suggested in relation to print narratives. The questions asked of media texts are focused on gaining an understanding of how texts are constructed and how they exert influence on audiences (DfES, 1999). The conceptualisation of the study of media texts as a means for children to learn to distance themselves from popular culture draws on discourses of critical literacy.

This 'critical literacy' approach to popular culture is advocated by Alvermann, Moon and Hagood (1999), who emphasise the need to teach children to critically analyse texts and to recognise influential ideologies which they may then decide to question. This is problematic in its conception of popular culture as 'other' than representational forms such as literature or music. Arguably, there is an implication that we approach popular culture texts with a different set of questions from those with which we approach a poem or a novel:

> [Children] need to be shown by teachers some different ways of critically examining the assumptions underlying the various popular culture texts that they encounter. (Alvermann, Moon and Hagood, 1999, p. 60)

Would we ask children to critically examine the 'assumptions' underlying a poem in the same way? It was evident in the previous chapter that in a wide variety of distinct academic fields, including Cultural, Media and Film studies, as well as studies of children's literature, media texts for children generate distinct sets of discourses relating to anxieties about changing childhoods. Buckingham (2003) argues that the critical literacy questions that we apply to media texts can usefully be applied to literary texts. For example, he suggests introducing students to questions about who the book publisher is and how the book is marketed. These questions are clearly useful across a range of texts but tend to be applied more to media than to print texts. Equally, it might be argued that the sets of questions usually applied to literary texts might be useful to the study of media (a point I will return to).

Despite an expansion in Media Studies courses in secondary schools, in primary schools the relationship between popular culture and literacy has been acknowledged in a context of caution and concern, for example Hilton, in her 1996 edited book, *Potent Fictions* highlights in the title 'the challenge of popular culture'. This ambivalent attitude towards popular culture can be heard in the work of Whitely (1996) who focuses on Disney films and popular television series such as The Power Rangers (Saban, 1993 – 1996):

> It is important here, clearly, not only that classrooms do what they have always struggled to do – to provide a serious context within which children can advance in a whole range of knowledges – but that there should be space for developing a critical awareness of ways in which these knowledges relate to their more playful counterparts and revisions in the more visceral world of entertainment. (Whitley, 1996, p. 62)

Whitley's use of the word 'visceral' in relation to entertainment implies an underlying concern about the value of these texts, despite an acknowledgement that they can be usefully studied in schools. While acknowledging the pleasures children take in engagement in popular culture texts, teachers clearly have anxieties about some of the more transgressive elements these texts contain.

Media Effects research (Bandura et al., 1963), as well as contemporary discourses about popular culture texts, positions children as recipients of harmful effects of popular media, particularly in relation to violence, sexualisation and commercialisation. Mackey and Robinson (2003) critique research that has focused on children's popular culture to claim that watching television in particular leaves children with a language deficit:

> Such an approach misapprehends the intertextual and cross-media understandings that young children develop from their earliest months. (Mackey and Robinson, 2003, p. 126)

Furthermore as demonstrated by Kendeou et al. (2008) and Van den Broek (2001) children develop comprehension skills from their engagements with moving image texts, which help them in their reading of print texts.

All the same, teachers may see themselves as having a role to play in protecting children from harmful media:

> Furthermore, with its emphasis on the negative effects of television and other forms of popular culture, communication research leaves educators

confused about what media effects have to do with classroom practice. Most have responded to the theory base provided by media effects studies by extending their gate keeping role to include the monitoring of television, the Internet, and other sources of information – or to banning popular culture as much as possible from the classroom. (Tyner, 1998, p. 58)

Lambirth (2004) illustrates the way in which a group of primary school teachers did not incorporate popular culture within the existing literacy framework. Lambirth found that in the context of a creative writing project the teachers did not value and were wary of popular culture texts. Although they talked with nostalgia of moving image texts they watched as children, they were often disgusted by the popular culture texts of today. Some questioned the quality and some blamed it for lack of attainment in children.

Highly popular texts are often the subject of censure and concern from teachers and parents (Arthur, 2005). In her description of the context in which UK literacy teachers work, Millard (2006) uses Foucault's (1977) analogy of the panopticon design of prison, used in the nineteenth century, to illustrate the way in which teachers in Western societies currently 'experience their professional lives as under constant surveillance' (Millard, 2006, p. 221). In her analysis it is the policies and strategies which lead to prescribed curriculum and testing that become a means of social control. The panopticon prison was designed to save money in such a way that prisoners would feel observed even when they were not being observed – the watchers become the watched. Teachers are watched but they also watch – they practice self-regulation and this potentially impacts on them, ruling out anything which falls outside the prescribed curriculum. This also impacts on their relationships with the children, potentially limiting the opportunities for them to draw on their home knowledge of popular culture and film in school.

Studies of trainee teachers (Marsh, 2006) and established, confident teachers (Millard, 2006), highlight some further barriers to drawing on popular culture in teaching literacy. The factors described in Marsh (2006) influencing teacher's use of popular culture include teacher attitudes, the curriculum, teacher confidence, and teachers' own experiences, a lack of guidance in this area and a feeling of being constantly observed. Not all of these factors may be as important for a confident and well-established teacher, but it is possible to hypothesise that teachers' attitudes to texts, their own experiences of school, the curriculum and other contextual factors within the school would influence the way in which popular culture might be valued, or not, in the classroom. Recent research (Robinson and Mackey, 2006; Buckingham, Burn, Parry and Powell, 2010) demonstrates that there is a smaller gap between children's and teachers' popular media preferences and practices than has been previously assumed, demonstrating that it is perhaps the contextual issues of curriculum and pedagogic practices that result in both children and teachers leaving their funds of knowledge (Moll et al., 1992) of popular culture outside the classroom door.

Perhaps as a consequence of concerns about popular culture, film education advocates have attempted to make a special case for film in relation to the teaching of literacy; this too has become problematic. In the context of perennial debates about raising children's literacy attainment, national standardised testing and school league tables, considerable emphasis has been placed on the potential for the study of film to enhance children's school and print-based literacy learning. During the period in which the National Literacy Strategy and the Literacy Hour were introduced in UK primary schools both the BFI (British Film Institute) and Film Education produced education packs that linked work on film to specified National Curriculum criteria. This led to films being used instrumentally to teach specific print literacy criteria. Parker (1999a, 2006) examined the extent to which film production and film adaptation activities provided children with further opportunities to recognise the structural similarities and differences between books and films. Parker explored the use of a 'grammar' common to film and written language which might enable film education to act as a parallel or scaffold to learning to write. He also raised some suggestions about the particular affordance of film, which he describes as its 'explicitness', as a helpful scaffolding tool in teaching literacy:

> How can the explicitness of moving-image media be used to improve conventional print literacy? Can explicitness be used to reveal some of the seemingly hidden elements of literacy? And can moving image media demonstrate through its own shortcomings some of the qualities peculiar to the art of writing? (Parker, 2006, p. 157)

Reid (2003) draws on short film to describe ways in which children can be encouraged to infer meaning in both print and moving image form. This research raises some very interesting questions about the ways in which children move from one media to another, as readers and creators of narrative texts, an issue I will return to. However, the film texts used were either short films or adaptations of children's literature. Teaching adaption is useful but runs the risk of privileging the written version over the moving image form. Short films with their ambiguity, non-linear structures and elliptic endings are often outside the experience of young children. Of course, I would advocate widening children's experience of film and acknowledge that showing new texts can extend children's analytical tools, rendering the familiar (film) unfamiliar. However, if space is not also made for popular film, then film education can potentially subjugate children's own experiences of films and unhelpfully reify film in relation to other popular media. Parker (2006) acknowledges the need to move away from a perception of literacy centering on print and the need to recognise and value children's engagements with other media.

Despite the unsatisfactory way in which the word literacy is, 'irrevocably related to language' Burn and Durran (2007) argue that the term media literacy is useful, 'drawing our attention to important connections between print literacy and the way people engage with media' (Burn and Durran, 2007, p. 3). Burn and Durran (2007) argue that far from being a simple process of communicative competence or the ability to decode and encode language, literacy is cultural and social. Furthermore they demonstrate, through analysis of young people's engagements with the *Harry Potter* (Rowling, 1997) series, that literacy is cultural, critical and, through transformation, creative. According to their cultural-semiotic model, developing media literacy incorporates lived experiences, critical exploration and response, as well as semiotic analysis of popular culture. They highlight the need for the cultural (the personal, social) and creative (response, transformation and production) to be included alongside critical approaches to media texts. This model for the study of media texts draws attention not only to the critical literacy questions raised in media education discourses but also those traditionally applied to print texts.

Much of the work discussed by Burn and Durran (2007) takes place in the context of specialist media education courses or projects. It remains critical, therefore, to argue for the development of media literacy through media education in core subjects in mainstream schools across the curriculum and age ranges. Watson (1990) proposes that film should be studied as part of a wider 'narrative arts' curriculum which places film in its proper context alongside other narrative forms. Whether in the context of specific study of media or that of English or other subjects, I propose that many teachers are interested in film education. This is demonstrated by the popularity of the BFI short film and education packs and also by teachers' registration with Film Education, now defunct, which organised National Schools Film Week and offered education packs for contemporary film releases. However, to overcome the barriers outlined by Marsh (2006), teachers need the support of policy-makers and those who devise curriculums and pedagogy to extend their interest into core classroom practice (Barratt, 1998) and to enable them to create spaces in which film is not just an expedient tool for the enhancement of motivation or the teaching of decontextualised literacy criteria but is present as an aspect of children's lived experience. *Look Again* (Bazalgette, 2003), a DfES funded teaching guide to using film and television for three- to eleven-year-olds, advocates the use of moving image in primary schools based on five key arguments, reflecting this shift of orientation:

The necessity for active learning
The power of linking home and school

Deepening understanding of texts
Creativity
Understanding of culture and society (Bazalgette, 2003, p. 3)

Clearly, where curriculum restraints and teacher anxieties about popular film and media are surmounted, children benefit from opportunities of sharing their home experiences of film. Grace and Tobin (1998) demonstrate that young children benefit from undertaking film production because it offers them the opportunity to explore their 'informal, unofficial and everyday interests' (Grace and Tobin, 1998, p. 43) Burn and Durran (2007) demonstrate that creating a space for production in which students can bring their home experiences to the media classroom enables them to articulate and make explicit their understandings of media language, while also sharing their personal responses.

Despite claims of an increased participatory culture associated with creative digital and online production (Jenkins, 2009), there is evidence that film production, beyond 'filming family and friends', is not a widespread practice (Buckingham, Burn, Parry and Powell, 2010) and that home film productions often remain unedited, unfinished and unpublished (Buckingham et al., 2012). In focusing on film, then, it is important to acknowledge that there is a disjuncture between home film viewing and home film production. Furthermore, film production in schools is not as widespread as the writing of stories. Kress (1995) uses an analogy, the concept of design, to describe an English curriculum that enables engagement with and creation of diverse cultural texts, inviting recognition of the need to teach children and young people to create representations of themselves and the world through ever-evolving representational forms:

> The means for making representations which we provide for children and for adults, are the means which enable them to be fully human and fully social. (Kress, 1995, p. 75)

Burn and Durran (2006) recommend that schools provide this interstitial space between home and school to enable children to move beyond intuitive understandings of texts towards an explicit understanding of 'media technologies, the grammars they use and the contexts in which they are deployed' (Burn and Durran, 2006, p. 275).

Media education as a form of protectionism obscures the potential to acknowledge what Williams (1989) describes as the distinct importance of narrative to our culture. One consequence of the dominance of the critical media approach in education is a lack of recognition of moving image as providing opportunities for both pleasure and personal growth, identified as important aspects of English (Protherough, 1983). The social, and cultural relationships children develop with films need to be valued as part of their experience of narrative through which they learn to experience the stories of others. The strong affective engagements children have with texts, including popular culture texts, need to be recognised as instrumental to their learning about narrative:

> Cognition, that is to say learning and knowing in human beings, has become recognised as an active process closely organised around affect. We learn because we are emotional beings, and what we learn and how we learn is closely related to how and what we desire, fear, sense, feel. (Hilton, 1996, p. 5)

While the teaching of media and popular culture in schools has emphasised critical analysis and deconstruction rather than personal response, the teaching of reading of print texts is associated with encouraging a lifelong habit of reading for pleasure.

There remains a need, then, to enable children to draw on their experiences of children's films to make explicit their understandings of both narrative and the particular affordances of film. Furthermore, there is a need to value children as developing readers of film (and other popular culture forms); reading for pleasure while accruing experiences of narrative.

In this chapter I have demonstrated that children engage with a 'narrative web' of popular culture texts and artefacts which enrich their literacy and identity practices. By the time children go to school they have already built up a range of 'symbolic resources' they use to enable play and participation. Children's films are often at the heart of the 'narrative webs' children encounter. Material artefacts such as toys, costumes, games and cards extend opportunities for exploration of a particular narrative. There is the pleasure of using toys, props and costumes to try out new identities (Marsh, 2005) and there is further satisfaction linked to marking yourself out as belonging to a group which likes a particular film, programme or character. Both experiences potentially form an aspect of children's early literate identities and in particular their participation in stories.

While children's films clearly provide children with cultural resources for play (Marsh, 2005) and text production (Barrs, 2004; Pahl, 2006), it is clear that at school, this presents a number of challenges. Children's writing based on popular culture discords with what is considered appropriate in school. In the current context of imposed pedagogy, external scrutiny and self-regulation, the role of popular culture in children's life remains largely unexplored in the literacy classroom. Important questions about the process of adaptation of stories into different media have been overlooked. Barrs (2004) argues that it is useful to trace the influence of children's experiences of texts on their writing as this elucidates how we might enhance the teaching of writing. I propose that it might be equally useful to trace the influences of children's experiences of film in their storytelling and in particular in their film productions.

4
Movies Teach Movies

Spencer (1998) argues that children learn to read texts from the texts they read. Hilton (1996) develops this argument in relation to media texts, proposing that media 'texts themselves could thus "teach" the learner to unlock further ones' (Hilton, 1996, p. 8). Robinson's (1997) notion of a repertoire of narrative experiences extends this idea further, recognising that children's understandings of narrative are drawn from all their experiences including oral, print, film and media sources (Robinson, 1997, p. 178). Protherough (1983) argues in relation to books that, 'Reading abilities and habits are formed primarily through encounters with fiction', (Protherough, 1983, p. 174). Children also learn about how to read and enjoy films by watching and engaging with them. The complex and sophisticated meta-language of film is regularly made sense of and enjoyed by children, who develop implicit knowledge of the way films are constructed; movies teach movies. This has become the central argument of this research, opening up questions about what and how children learn about narrative through their engagements with children's films. To address this question, it is first critical to consider the different processes involved in reading film and print narratives.

Active

The process of reading books and films involves readers in becoming 'active meaning makers' who draw on their own resources, including knowledge of particular genres, to make predictions, (Marsh and Millard, 2000, p. 146). Marsh and Millard (2000) observe a number of similarities between the process of reading films and books involving the development of 'social, cognitive and emotional skills', as well as the 'orchestration of a range of skills – either phonic, graphic, syntactic and semantic (print) or aural, visual and semantic (televisual)' (Marsh and Millard, 2000, p. 146).

By contrast, Iser (1980) identifies what he sees as differences between the reading of print and moving image texts. He describes the participatory nature of the process of reading and argues that a literary text offers the reader the opportunity to work things out for her/himself. Furthermore, he argues that this 'active and creative' process is key to pleasure in reading (Iser, 1980, p. 51). Iser describes the aspects of a text that a reader must participate in as the 'unwritten' element. He acknowledges the role of the reader in this process of 'filling in the gaps' and that this enables the reader, and what the reader brings to the text, to influence the effect of the text. Iser (1980) claims that what marks out a literary text is not the fulfilment of predictable expectations which make the author's construction overt and disappointing to the reader:

> The fact that completely different readers can be differently affected by the reality of a particular text is ample evidence of the degree to which literary texts transform reading into a creative process that is far above mere perception of what is written. (Iser, 1980, p. 54)

Similarly, Chatman (1989) argues that the audience of narrative texts is able to generate multiple meanings from what might be left out, rather than what is explicitly said and that offering the reader greater opportunity to interpret and anticipate is what adds value to a narrative. Regardless of notions of value in children's fiction both in film and print, there are many distinct uses of gaps which children have to learn to make sense of. Furthermore, even when watching a predictable and formulaic film (which might nonetheless be pleasurable) the reader is involved in filling gaps or making inferences (Marsh and Millard, 2000).

Iser (1980) proposes that film is, by its nature, more closed, more fixed, leaving less space for audiences' responses. Chatman (1989) argues that in a film you cannot simply say a man walked into a room, because the man has to be visually represented so this results in film being less open to reading or interpretation. Similarly, Iser (1980) argues that film requires a less active reading from the audience because a film would show a mountain, whereas a written story would leave the reader to imagine the mountain. However, film has a set of symbolic resources through which it reveals ideas about setting or character which require active reading. For example, in relation to the character: the acting, shot type, lighting, use of sound and music, setting or landscape and costume all potentially suggest complex ideas about the man or the mountain.

In attempting to draw out the differences between reading print and moving image texts, Marsh and Millard (2000) argue that the internal world of the character is more accessible to the audience in print texts than in film. However, again the internal world of the character can be represented visually and aurally in film, differently from the way print text uses narration, but with no less sophistication. Voice or focalisation (Genette, 1980) that is to say, from whose point of view we see and hear events, is created differently in film and print texts. For example, in the print stories of His

Dark Materials (Pullman, 1995) we read dialogue between the main character Lyra and her daemon (her soul), in the film we see the reactions of the
daemon, indicating Lyra's thoughts and feelings. The reader of any text is
thus involved in making a complex series of inferences based on the symbolic resources available to the storyteller, this depends to a great extent on
the media through which the story is told. The reader must learn to read the
meta-language of the medium. Clearly film involves some similar and different reading processes from print narratives which are worth considering
further. The perception of the reader as active stems from reader response
theory, and it is useful to reflect on this provenance in our consideration of
the affective engagements children have with films.

Affective or aesthetic

The role of the reader has long been discussed in relation to literature, as
illustrated in Eco's (1994) analogy of reading as taking a walk in woods created by the author; the reader choosing the paths of narrative they wish to
follow. However, just as print narratives set paths like small, shiny pebbles
for us to follow, so moving image narratives also offer cues (Bordwell, 1985).
Our role as a reader is in noticing the cues and acting on them depending
on our previous experiences. Rosenblatt (1970 – first published in 1938)
scrutinised the way in which a reader emotionally engages with a literary
text. She attempted to establish how best to teach literature to ensure that
individuals are not simply expected to offer reactions which imitate 'given'
critical or teacherly opinion about a piece of art but are expressions of their
own personal response:

> Yet ultimately, any literary work gains its significance from the way in
> which the minds and emotions of particular readers respond to the verbal
> stimuli offered by the text. (Rosenblatt, 1970, p. 28)

This represented a shift in thinking about teaching literature away from the
text and onto the reader. Rosenblatt argued that the reader brings 'common' experiences to a text based on their social and cultural lives but that
the nature of these 'experiences', 'images', 'memories' and 'associations'
(Rosenblatt, 1970, p. 32) will be peculiar to the individual and will influence
their response to a text. She divided the reading process into two distinct
experiences shaped by the planned outcome for the reading. 'Efferent'
reading, reading to 'take away' meaning from reports or instructions, and
'aesthetic' reading, to 'sense or perceive' or to 'experience' a text. Rosenblatt
was disheartened by efferent reading of literature, that is to say, teaching a
poem because it illustrated a particular feature of language or use of a poetic
device. She argued for an environment where aesthetic reading is nurtured.
In doing so, she made important claims for literature as having a central

role in the development of young people. Focusing particularly on empathy, Rosenblatt described the experience of reading as one in which:

> We participate in imaginary situations, we look on characters living through crises, we explore ourselves and the world about us, through the medium of literature. (Rosenblatt, 1970, p. 37)

I propose that literature is not alone in enabling us to enter the lives of others, to identify with their situation and to follow their story with interest and anticipation. Film, a narrative medium, also, if differently, invites us to participate in rich, imaginative experiences. Experiences of life and of other texts shape and develop our experiences of film. It is important to recognise that early experiences of film and moving image might be as influential on developing an understanding of story as early experiences of literature are, and that these experiences help us develop as readers of books and films and of other narrative forms. Although early reader response theory emphasises the role of the individual reader, the reading process is demonstrably social (Fish, 1980).

Social

Marsh and Millard (2000) extend the comparison between readers of books and films, noting that both involve the 'formation of interpretive communities', (Marsh and Millard, 2000, p. 146). In the case of children's films it may well be that both at home and at school an 'interpretive community' (Fish, 1980) exists in which readings of films are explored and contested. Robinson (1997) emphasised the role of a community in enabling children to create collective interpretations, arguing against the distinction between private reading of books and group viewing of television.

Robinson's research suggests that children respond to texts drawing on a 'fluid network of social interactions' which might draw on their individual responses to a text but these in turn contribute to group discussions and responses. Bromley (1996) makes extensive use of her own classroom practice to describe examples in which children effectively and enthusiastically use popular films in their role play and social interactions. Bromley describes children drawing on films as part of a 'collective memory', engaging in talk about films because the talk was a familiar discourse that they were able to position themselves within (Bromley, 1996, p. 76).

Mackey (2002) uses the term 'play' in relation to children's engagement with text rather than the verb 'to read'. She argues that children play rather than simply read texts and that the notion of play can be useful in helping us to 'understand how we respond to texts in many media' (Mackey, 2002, p. 182). Within this notion of playing texts Mackey includes the ability to step inside and outside the diegetic world of the text, to imagine or suspend disbelief. She also describes performing, and engaging with rules and interpretation as playing. When children 'play the text' their engagements are often social and the boundaries of the text are fluid. Children actively, read and play in the imaginative spaces provided by film as individuals but also socially. Both reader and text also draw on a wider cultural context.

Cultural

Films involve children in making inferences that relate to the use of culturally shared frames of reference or schemas. Some characters in some stories are highly familiar and predictable to the audience and can be denoted very simply. Children can base detailed inferences on a comparatively simple sign, that is to say a king denoted by an image of a man wearing a crown. Children learn to recognise character types through previous experience of texts so that they are able to quickly identify heroes and villains, for example, from a still or moving image and can make predictions about them based on knowledge of superhero stories. These conventions, once learnt, form the basis of an understanding shared with the director or author which Barker (1989) describes as a cultural contract entered into both by the storyteller and the audience. He demonstrates the ways in which readers become familiar with the particular narrative structure and conventions of a comic strip in which, for example, a hotel is haunted and a new character each week must stay over – almost all are scared away but the pleasure is in how the haunting unfolds. The pleasure of reading the comic strip is not so much in wondering what will happen next but in how the creators of the comic use ever-increasing inventiveness to complete the narrative structure.

This notion of schemas or cultural contracts perhaps implies a uniformity or underlying patterns or structures in children's stories, rendering them predictable and formulaic. Similarly, structuralist theorist Propp (1968) described characters in folk tales as functional, interchangeable and highly predictable. However, that is not to say that characters always remain simple, flat or functional, nor that rules cannot be broken. However, these shared ideas are a form of storytelling short-hand which enable quick access to the narrative. What is more, children learn this short-hand from the texts they encounter and each new text adds to a child's repertoire of narrative experiences. Initially, as Robinson (1997) points out, this familiarity enables engagement with stories, but still involves recognition of conventions, prediction and anticipation. So children quickly learn the function of a king in stories and might expect him to have three daughters or sons and they might also expect that he has a character flaw; perhaps he is foolish or greedy. They base these ideas on kings in previous stories and the storyteller can choose whether or not to fulfil expectations or subvert them. Furthermore, the storyteller can add complexity and detail to the king to make him more interesting. In film they might use music, costume, lighting, or shot types to add this detail all of which involve the reader in making inferences and predictions. To return to Iser's (1980) description of an active process of reading, children learn to read films by bringing to them their own previous experiences of texts (Robinson, 1997) and filling in the gaps. In film they are not reading between the lines of the language but reading the different visual, aural and spatial modes of film, that is to say, the kinekonic mode (Burn and Parker, 2003). It is important to understand how children read the kinekonic mode of film alongside their individual, social and cultural reading processes.

Semiotic

Marsh and Millard (2000) situate children's engagements with film in relation to reader response theory but call for teachers to also pay attention to the semiotic affordances of multimodal texts. Semiotics, the study of signs, encourages a recognition of the existence of elements of texts which connote meaning. Meaning is dependent on the way the sign is constituted, its context and the experiences of the reader. So, for example, a close up of a character's face has come to be a familiar sign, enabling the reader to infer meaning about the emotional state of the character. Although we actively read signs on a daily basis this process is often implicit and intuitive:

> Meaning is not 'transmitted' to us – we actively create it according to a complex interplay of codes and conventions of which we are normally unaware. (Chandler, 2004, p. 12)

Burn and Parker (2003) critique the Cultural Studies approach for contributing accounts of the social and cultural uses of moving images by young people, without 'a theory of signification to complement these accounts' (Burn and Parker, 2003, p. 156). Parker (2006), and Burn and Parker (2003) suggest the need for a 'grammar' of film comparable to the grammar underlying language. Marsh and Millard (2000) express caution at the suggestion of a grammar of film comparable to that of a grammar of language first on the grounds that grammatical models are contested, and second on the basis of the complexity of any given unit of meaning, so for example, a close up may infer meaning quite differently in different contexts. Also as Buckingham points out:

> Whether or not this adds up to a 'grammar' remains to be seen; and even if it does, there are bound to be further questions about how that grammar should be taught. (Buckingham, 2003, p. 185)

The focus on a grammar of film also shifts attention onto the text and away from the reader or audience. However, as the authors acknowledge in discussing an A' Level student's response to the film, *Hannibal* responding to film is a cultural and social activity for which a theory of the grammar of film can only contribute a partial account. The student's responses differed in his two distinct social situations, with his friends and with his teachers:

> This is a complex, hybrid production of language and gesture to remake narrative images and structures, to evaluate, and to establish different degrees of social proximity, indicating different interpretative communities and his relation to them. (Burn and Parker, 2003, p. 74)

The semiotic-cultural model of media education suggested in subsequent work by Burn and Durran (2007) seeks to enable children to make explicit the grammar or language of media while recognising that signs have shared cultural significance. In relation to film in particular, Burn and Parker (2003) propose that we acknowledge the multimodal nature of film by attention to the kinekonic mode which includes aspects such as music and gestures, which Metz's (1974) earlier use of the term 'cinematic' did not. Reid (2009) outlines the need for attention to the meaning created by the distinct modes of:

> Speech, writing, pictures and moving pictures, music, and the dramatic modes of performance and gesture and the 'mise en scene' of theatre design. (Reid, 2009)

Burn and Parker (2003) also describe the spatial and temporal modes, particularly in relation to editing and the structure and sequencing of film. They describe the 'combinatorial affordances' of the modes which children begin to recognise when they edit films for the first time.

Films are constructions of the world which draw on shared stories, as well as shared symbolic systems which makers of films are experienced in and children are learning about in a variety of contexts. We need to examine both the shared stories (the characters, events, themes and structures) and the symbolic systems (visual, aural, spatial signs) or kinekonic mode (Burn and Parker, 2003) from which children's films are constructed to be able to further understand children's responses to them.

Reading plot and structure in film

It is worth looking at the similar and different ways film and print texts construct narrative in greater detail to further understand the process of reading films. Here I focus on one aspect of narrative, that of plot and structure, which is explicitly taught in schools and is therefore particularly pertinent. In primary schools in the UK the teaching of written stories is influenced by Todorov's (1968) theory of a circular narrative structure of equilibrium, disruption and equilibrium restored. This idea is often referred to by teachers as a character having a problem to be solved or as a 'story mountain' (to be climbed). It is intended to help children learn to shape stories, to explain cause and effect and to conceive of satisfying endings. This desire to find universal patterns or structures underlying narratives is common to early structuralist theorists. It is useful to reflect on these early studies and subsequent changes in narrative theory, which also reflect changes in the mode of expression.

Early narrative theorists focused on popular forms such as folk tales to identify patterns and structures. Propp produced a morphology of the folktale which was originally published in 1928 but not translated into English until 1958. Propp (1968) explains his use of the term 'morphology' as a description of the tale according to its component parts and the relationship of the component parts to the whole. He proposes that analyses of fairy tales by theme or form are problematic and identifies thirty-one functions of fairy tales which relate to the action. These functions are described in detail and include, for example, 'the hero is pursued' or 'the hero is rescued from pursuit'. He identifies the plot elements of 'a search', 'a pursuit' and 'a task' as well as the conventional closure of fairytales 'the marriage and ascension to the throne of the hero' (Propp, 1968, pp. 24–65). Propp describes the characters as variable but interchangeable elements in fairy tales, but argues that the functions remain the same. Propp's objective, to establish a universal pattern to the structure of fairy tales, greatly influenced film theorists who have tried to apply Propp's morphology of fairy tales to films.

Bordwell (1988) critiques both Propp's work and the appropriation of his work in the context of film theory. He argues that attempts to understand films by literally applying Propp's thirty-one action-functions to film plots are a misappropriation of his ideas. Bordwell (1988) acknowledges that Propp did not suggest that his functions could be applied outside of the fairy tale form. While Propp claimed to identify the universal elements of the fairy tale and was keen to explore the cross-cultural similarities in folklore, he also acknowledged diversity:

This explains the two-fold quality of a tale: its amazing multiformity, picturesqueness and color, and on the other hand, its no less striking uniformity, its repetition. (Propp, 1968, p. 21)

Bordwell suggests that a milder version of this application: 'a morphological analysis of a corpus by reducing its narrative patterns to a list of abstractions' (Bordwell, 1988, p. 17 footnote 5), as potentially enabling the identification of common narrative events in a genre or sub-genre of films. So, for example, Porter-Abbott (2002) identifies master plots, that is to say recurrent storylines such as the Cinderella, rags to riches, storyline which reflect particular cultural concerns. Although limited, then, both Propp's functions and Porter-Abbot's master plots are potentially useful tools in recognising common events in children's films. In children's films key narrative events such as the hero setting off on a journey or the passing into another land via a magical portal, or the restoration of the main character to her/his home, are familiar conventional events which establish audience expectations. These events are cued in particular ways, which are culturally shared by the film-maker and the audience. It is therefore useful to explore the extent to which children draw on these narrative characteristics of children's film in their own texts.

Bordwell's (1985) work on the structure of narrative films, like reader response theory, focuses on the spectator or reader, rather than solely on the text and offers some useful tools for developing an understanding of the relationship between the text and the audience. Bordwell (1985) uses the Russian Formalist terms 'fabula' and 'syuzhet' to distinguish between the actual events of the film and the order in which they are unveiled to the audience. These distinctions are particularly pertinent for the study of film, especially film genres in which the relationship between the text and the audience is bound by strong conventions and traditions in which audiences have particular expectations of the events of films for example, in the detective genre or the musical. Children's films, including the many sub-genres of children's films, are bound by conventions which potentially shape audience expectations of what can happen. This distinction can help us to understand the way in which texts are told and, as Bordwell points out, enable us to perceive the way in which certain aspects of the story are obscured (or 'retarded', to use Bordwell's term) to create anticipation, suspense or tension:

> Narration is the process whereby the film's syuzhet and style interact in the course of cuing and channelling the spectator's construction of the fabula. (Bordwell, 1985, p. 49)

Examination of the fabula and syuzhet or story and discourse (Chatman, 1989; Genette, 1980) of children's films might usefully shed light on the spatial qualities of children's storytelling. That is to say, it will be useful to consider the way children draw on film and other media to help them relate the events they decide on in particular ways. For example, do children tell the events in their stories in chronological order or do they use flashback or forward. It would also be interesting to consider their use of kinekonic cues, which might set up audience expectations of later events.

Iser (1980) describes the units of meaning of literary texts as being built up of sequenced sentences which relate to each other. He emphasises that whatever the purpose of the sentence, it indicates or creates an expectation of what is to come later in the text. Equally, sentences are seen as able to help us to reflect on earlier moments in the text in a process of anticipation and retrospection. Spatially, films use a series of shots, sequences and scenes as the units which build meaning, and establish a similar pattern of anticipation and retrospection. In terms of the audience's perception of a film, rules are established which rely on another process of gap-filling. So it is crucial that we have knowledge that when a scene is introduced, usually through a cut to a wide angle of a new establishing shot, that we also understand that this will represent a shift in time and place.

The spatial and temporal organisation of a text, for example, the passage of time, the movement from one scene to the next, the way events are linked and causality implied, all require active reading. In written texts language is used to express these qualities as well as changes in paragraphs and movements to the next chapter. In film, continuity editing is used to fulfil the same function but there are some complex differences. Continuity editing, which is the dominant editing style for narrative films, works much more like the prosaic 'and then' or 'meanwhile' or 'sometime ago' than montage editing (the juxtaposition of contrasting shots). The aim of continuity editing is to add coherence, link events, and show the temporal relationship between events – to create a continuous story.

There are conventions of continuity editing which children learn to read implicitly. So when a character leaves the room, a shot of a slamming door behind them might signal their exit. When the next shot shows the character jumping into a car we know that in between they have perhaps climbed down the stairs or walked along the street to arrive at the car. We do not see this action but we do infer it. The film-makers signal what we should notice through their shot composition and in the style of editing which dictates, unless clearly signalled otherwise, that the character leaving the room and the character in the car are the same person. In this case we might especially notice that the door slams and the character jumps. We do not spend very much time at all, if any, filling the gap represented by the question: What did they do between exiting the building and getting in the car?

It is clear that as well as making meaning from words and from visual or aural signs, children develop skills as readers of film by gaining an implicit understanding of editing conventions. It is important therefore, to consider the extent to which children draw on their intuitive knowledge of editing conventions in their own film productions. In my use of this example of how plot and structure is constructed in print and film narratives I attempt to demonstrate the need for a multifaceted approach to understanding children as readers of multimodal texts. Just as plot and structure are constructed differently in different modes, so too are characters, settings and point of view, for example. These differences (and similarities) are understood and read by children in their everyday encounters with narrative. It is useful, however, to consider the extent to which children are able to draw on this intuitive knowledge in their reading and production of texts in different media. It is particularly important to examine this question in relation to children's films.

Children attempt to draw on all their cultural resources to help them to tell stories (Spencer, 1988). Children use what they know but also make connections to help them with ideas they are less familiar with (Kress, 2000). Engagement with narratives involves not simply a literal reading, or reading between the lines but reading beyond the lines (Dale, 1946; Kress, 2000; Burn and Durran, 2007). Through play children extend and potentially transform their experiences and understandings of narratives. These experiences contribute to children's emerging, holistic understandings of narrative, forming a narrative repertoire.

The notion that children learn about films by watching them can be usefully examined in further detail. When children watch and enjoy films they develop skills of decoding the language of film, making inferences from the semiotic affordances of the multimodal text. Films are not, however, isolated from other forms of narrative and they share many characteristics of narratives in other forms. For example, they incorporate characters and settings and follow plots. Children learn about how films work by watching them as well as gaining experiences of elements of narrative that are common across media. However, children's films, with their particular conventions, also shape these experiences in particular ways. In seeking to understand the role of children's film in children's developing repertoires of narrative then, it is critical to attempt to explore both aspects: film language as well as the common narrative characteristics of children's films. This is the focus of subsequent chapters. However, before presenting these chapters I share details of the rationale for my fieldwork, which has particular relevance to film education in many other contexts.

5
Researching Film with Children

When devising an approach to my fieldwork, my main concern was to work ethically and meaningfully with children to explore the questions outlined in my literature review. Hart (1992) observes that in research, children are commonly subjects of formal, language-orientated methods:

> Unfortunately most social science research with children is still of the distant adult controlled type: questionnaires and structured interviews which barely scrape the surface of what children are able to tell. (Hart, 1992, p. 14)

Such research is met, by some children, with a resounding 'culture of silence' (Reason, 1994, p. 328). Gauntlett (2005) argues that relying solely on formal methods of data collection, based on analysis of spoken and written language, can restrict participation. Furthermore, research which enables children with particular verbal and written language skills to dominate can obscure the experiences of others. In the emerging literature about participatory approaches to research with children there are many calls for diverse, flexible and culturally appropriate methods which overcome the 'I don't know syndrome', which acts as a barrier to research (Malone, 1999, p. 18). Furthermore, as Hart argues:

> One must identify situations which will maximise a child's opportunities to demonstrate her competence. Similarly, one should also use alternative techniques for enabling different children's voices to be heard. (Hart, 1992, p. 31)

Research that attempts to understand the relationships between children, media and popular culture has been criticised for its perceptions of children as vulnerable and in need of protection (Barker and Petley, 2001; Gauntlett, 2005) as opposed to being capable of actively negotiating their own engagements with popular culture (Hodge and Tripp, 1986). I was concerned, therefore, to ensure that my methodology was compatible with recent increased awareness of the capability of children to engage with research (Christensen and James, 2000) and the need to draw on methods incorporating different modes of expression rather than relying only on what the children could articulate in written or verbal responses. In this chapter I outline the rationale for the participatory, visual and collaborative approach adopted in my fieldwork. I also introduce the school, class and children who were involved in the research and the activities I undertook with them. Finally, I describe my approach to the analysis and interpretation of my data.

Participatory approaches with children

In his work with children, Hart (1992) draws on a participatory action research (PAR) methodology (Foote Whyte, 1991), emphasising the need for research and action to be linked. PAR is carried out by and with marginalised people, often in the most economically poor contexts, and the researcher demonstrates a commitment to those people and to ensuring they have control of the analysis (Fals-Borda and Rahman, 1991). The research begins with a concrete problem identified by the participants themselves and proceeds to investigate the underlying causes of the problem so that the participants can, themselves, address these causes.

Reason (1994) proposes that PAR should create and develop knowledge which is useful to a particular group of people but should also act as a means of empowerment. PAR developed as a response to Freire's (1970) idea of 'conscientisation' or consciousness-raising. Freire demonstrated the way in which authoritarian education contributes to the oppression of the poor, and condemned the social sciences as contributing to economic and cultural domination of one culture over another. Drawing on his observations of children's responses to the education system Freire (1970) observes:

> Children increasingly view parent and teacher authoritarianism as inimical to their own freedom. For this very reason, they increasingly oppose forms of action which minimize their expressiveness and hinder their self-affirmation. (Freire, 1970, p. 134)

Freire's work calls for a curriculum appropriate to the cultural and economic context of the community and pedagogies of continual shared investigation. In developing my own research, I was keen to ensure that I had identified a focus that would be relevant and significant to children, and to involve children in pedagogies which enabled shared, mutually beneficial, learning.

Within the diverse field of 'Childhood Studies' (James and Prout, 1990) the relationship between children and research has been explored in the light of changing perspectives about children's rights. Morrow and Richards (1996) argue that the ability to recognise children's competences should become a methodological technique in itself (Morrow and Richards, 1996, p. 100). O'Kane and Thomas (1999) suggest that through participatory approaches, many of the challenges of working with children in research are overcome. Whilst Christensen and James (2000) argue that children do not require special methods as distinct from adults and urge that in research an 'adult / child distinction' should not be assumed (Christensen and James, 2000, p. 2). However, they go on to describe the need to adopt practices which resonate with children's own concerns and routines.

Tandon (1989) critiques non-participatory research for being absolut-ist, inappropriately searching for one truth, and purist, for attempting to achieve objectivity. For example, when a distance is maintained between the subject and researcher to be rigorous, the power remains with the researcher. Furthermore, Tandon (1989) suggests that the dominant research paradigm is rationalist in its focus on objectivity and thinking as the only means of knowing, at the expense of feeling and acting. Contemporary qualitative research methods actively engage with feeling and action through narrative approaches (Goodson et al., 2010; Clough, 2002; Polkingthorne, 1995) and life history (Goodson and Sikes, 2001) as well as visual approaches (Banks, 2001; Pink, 2001; Prosser, 1998; Rose, 2001). However, in research with chil-dren a power imbalance between researcher and researched is potentially, although not always, heightened through practices such as:

- Devising research questions without reference to the needs and interests of the research group
- Using only dominant methods such as interviews, questionnaires or focus groups which rely heavily on written and spoken language and assist in confirming the higher status of the researcher
- Not involving participants in the analysis or dissemination of findings.

This power imbalance is, to some extent, ubiquitous, particularly in relation to working with children whose lives are shaped by adults in positions of authority in almost every context (Mayall, 2000). However, paying attention to this imbalance, and attempting to decrease it, has potentially positive implications for the research which might then begin to move beyond scraping the surface, facing the silent treatment or only reflecting a partial range of experiences.

Visual and collaborative methodologies

I drew on participatory approaches to working with children to minimise the power relationship between adult and child and to enable each child to access the research in a manner appropriate to her / his own needs and interests. While I acknowledge that my approach should not be described as fully participative, I did attempt to draw on participatory research practices to varying degrees at different stages of my research so that the children had different levels of choice in terms of the extent of their engagement and the mode of expression for their responses. Methods associated with participatory approaches include visual approaches (Blackburn et al., 1998) and activity that draws on the culture of the particular community, for example songs, drama, drawing and painting.

In both qualitative and participative educational research there is an increased recognition that language, written and verbal, are not the only forms of expression for the purposes of collecting and disseminating data. Blackburn et al. (1998) argues that 'visually, more diversity and complexity are expressed than can be put into words' (Blackburn et al., 1998, p. 8). Eisner (1993) proposes that educational researchers engage with the arts whose different 'modes of representation' make a wider range of meanings available:

> Artistic approaches to research are less concerned with the discovery of truth than with the creation of meaning. What art seeks is not the discovery of the laws of nature about which true statements or explanations can be given, but rather the creation of images that people will find meaningful and from which their fallible and tentative views of the world can be altered, reflected or made more secure. (Eisner, 1993, p. 9)

Eisner suggests that the arts should be used in the display or dissemination of research findings as 'artistically crafted works' that can make 'aspects of the world vivid and generate a sense of empathy' (Eisner, 1993, p. 10). My main concern, however, was to ensure that a range of possible modes of expression were available to the children during the fieldwork stage. Gauntlett and Holzwarth (2006) use creative and visual research methods to enable participants to 'make things' such as sculpture, three-dimensional models, photographs or films, which helps them to focus on his research interest and to generate theories and observations themselves.

It is not the case that children can only respond to visual or participatory methods (Christensen and James, 2000), but this level of creativity and reflexivity potentially enhances opportunities for engagement in the research process. Eisner's (1993) theory that research involving the production of a work of art can enable us to represent, or make public, 'consciousness' is congruent with Freire's (1970) notion of developing consciousness-raising through education. I chose to focus on film production as a useful means of eliciting responses about concepts that are abstract, elusive and complex such as popular culture, narrative and identity. This was also an attempt to enable the children to make their intuitive knowledge about media and popular culture explicit. I anticipated that, although the children might have limited experience of the theories and ideas which surround concepts such as narrative, they would have rich personal experiences which they might be able to share through film and for which the spoken or written word might not be the most appropriate form of expression, at least as the sole form.

Using the medium which is also the focus of the study to research and share insights provides opportunities for a fully reflexive process. Niesyto, Buckingham and Fisherkeller (2003) argue in their work on children's video productions in research into youth culture, that 'the method of research should follow the object of research' (Niesyto, Buckingham and Fisherkeller, 2003, p. 1). They emphasise that verbally based methods such as narrative interviews, group discussions or written field notes 'only provide limited access to the emotional and symbolic aspects of children's experience, and to media-related models of expression' (Niesyto, Buckingham and Fisherkeller, 2003, p. 1). Gauntlett (2005) also highlights the benefits of working in the medium, which is the subject of research:

> By operating on the visual plane, these visual/creative methods mirror the visual nature of much contemporary media – so that there is a match between the research process which operates (or at least begins) on the visual plane, and the research area – people's relationship with contemporary culture – which also operates (or at least begins) on the visual plane. (Gauntlett, 2005, p. 144)

Having identified film as a potential mode of expression in the collection of data, I looked for previous examples of uses of film in educational research to determine what the potential challenges, barriers and benefits might be.

Multimodal research

There has been an increased interest in using film or video to record interviews of classroom activity to capture multimodal communication. Film has been used as a tool for research to record interviews and enable researchers to see body language or contextual data. Software such as Transana has been devised to ensure that film can be coded and analysed as effectively as transcripts of speech. As Flewitt (2006) points out in her study of children's interactions in the early years classroom:

> Rather than focusing on a single mode, such as spoken or written language, using video to collect data reveals the multimodal dynamism of classroom interaction, giving new insights into how children and adults coordinate different modes as they negotiate and jointly construct meanings in different social settings. (Flewitt, 2006, p. 4)

Kress et al. (2005) use a multimodal approach to their research into urban English classrooms, collecting data relating to body language, background noise, pauses, and the classroom environment using video recordings:

> A multimodal approach is one where attention is given to all the cultur-
> ally shaped resources that are available for making meaning: image, for
> instance or gesture, or the layout – whether of the wall display, or the
> furniture of classrooms- and of course writing and speech as talk. (Kress
> et al., 2005, p. 2)

There are challenges to the use of video to record the multimodal communication of the classroom. As pointed out by Kress et al. (2005), it is important to supplement video recordings with opportunities for discussion of
what is recorded, through researcher observation and follow-up interviews
to capture the 'rationale behind specific events that occurred' (Kress et al.,
2005, p. 9). As rich as this use of film is, it does not draw on the potential
of 'film as an inherently narrative medium' to communicate (Ruby, 1980,
p. 143). I decided to use film-making both to interview the children and to
record activity, and a video camera was in the room and used to capture the
children engaged in activity or talk during most of the sessions. However,
more importantly, the children undertook narrative film production which
I anticipated would stimulate talk and also provide an insight into the
children's implicit understandings of narrative.

Intuitive or trained?

Some visual researchers (Cavin, 1994; Young and Barrett, 2001) have given
cameras to children as part of an ethnographic approach and have not worried
about their aesthetic qualities of the photographs the children have taken.
They perceive the resulting photographs as an opportunity to explore how
children intuitively frame the world. I was unsure about whether this was
an appropriate stance in my research. I felt that I would not expect children
to write without teaching them some foundation skills first. I had also frequently observed children's ability to take photos improve dramatically with
appropriate guidance, without the child's chosen subject of the photograph
being obscured. Having had experience of film and photography production
projects with children, I felt that some training was essential to ensure children
acquired a level of competence in film production. If film production was to
fulfil its potential to prompt thinking and elicit responses which were richer
than could be expressed verbally or in writing, I felt the children would need
to gain confidence through production experiences. Of course, this shifts and
influences their choices in relation to the style of shot, for example, but this is
a necessary and valuable part of their involvement.

Rather than drawing on children's intuitive photos or films, I decided
to offer training in film and photography production so the children's

reflective process and representation of their experience was enhanced by their developing skills. Pink (2001) argues that no text, visual or otherwise, is produced in isolation from forms and conventions of existing texts. The form is also influenced by the purpose and the cultural context of those involved in production, so that in the case of producing media with children, they draw on their knowledge of popular forms. I therefore ensured that the training and production opportunities offered referred to the conventions of popular culture that children were familiar with.

Pink (2001) highlights various issues that arise when ethnographers attempt to collaborate with 'informants' to produce photographs or video. Firstly, she argues that to be described as collaborative, visual material should combine the intentions of the researcher and the informant and should 'represent the outcomes of their negotiations' (Pink, 2001, p. 48). Although I certainly collaborated with the children, the texts they produced were not negotiated outcomes in this way. The children were trained and they collaborated with each other. I enabled and mentored them, but the texts they produced were, in the same way as their school-based written stories, a result of their own process of decision-making. I attempted to stand back from shaping in any way the stories the children told and how they told them. Where I did advise them on uses of the camera, microphone and editing, this became useful in the process of analysis. For example, I was able to reflect on decisions the children made as a result of negotiation and collaboration with me, but also on the decisions they made where they had strong ideas they wished to pursue that were outside the advice, training or ideas that I might have suggested.

In an anthropological research project working with African immigrant workers in Spain, researchers Cerezo, Martinez and Ranera (1996) found that the workers did not like the filmed images of themselves, comparing themselves unfavourably to what they watched on television at home. I have also experienced children becoming dissatisfied with the lack of professional standards in their work which they felt made them 'look bad'. As a facilitator, it was therefore important to ensure the children worked within genres that were achievable in the time frame and would compare favourably to children's media experiences. For example, in the production tasks I devised I avoided the need for expensive special effects or costumes. Film-making as a method became a key aspect of my research which enhanced the children's participation in addressing my research questions. However, using filmed representations of children as data raises some ethical concerns which must be addressed carefully.

Situated ethics

There are ethical concerns that are specific to using film as a research tool with children and still more in using film for dissemination. As Flewitt

(2006) argues, 'informed consent' is integral to good ethical practice, but in the process of making film with children she recommends:

> Rather than following a detailed, preconceived code of conduct imposed upon participants by the researcher, 'provisional consent' assumes an ethical stance that evolves out of researcher/participant relationships, where ethical dilemmas are resolved as they emerge in the field, in their local and specific contexts, on a minute-by-minute basis. (Flewitt, 2006, p. 4)

I found that the children were extremely enthusiastic about making their films and appearing in them and as a result they wanted their names in big letters on everything and were not keen on the idea of becoming anonymous in the research, until I pointed out they could chose their own pseudonym. The children's own names appeared on their films, as they requested, but have been changed in the data chapters to the pseudonyms they chose.

The school

My research took place in a one form entry, voluntary aided, Church of England, primary school close to a city centre in the North of England and with 197 three- to eleven-year-olds on roll. The school serves a local community; the majority of children do not travel far to school. Ofsted (2007) describes the number of pupils eligible for free school meals as slightly above average. Ofsted also observes that the numbers of children from backgrounds other than white British are higher than usual and that a small but increasing proportion of the children speak English as an additional language. The school is also described as having a higher than average number of students with special educational needs or disabilities. I approached this school because in the past the head teacher had demonstrated an interest in children's engagements with film and had involved pupils in screenings of films and practical workshops I had set up.

I was confident that because of the interest of the head teacher I would be able to gain some support for the activities and also that the school community would also potentially be interested in the research findings. Since I was undertaking a small-scale, qualitative piece of research which was not attempting to establish statistically demonstrable generalisations, I felt that in deciding on the school, it would be more important to opt for a context where the work was welcomed and valued rather than one that could be shown to be representative of a wider group of schools.

The head teacher elicited the involvement of the Year 5 class teacher and I was therefore extremely fortunate to have the support of a well-organised and positive class teacher. She enabled me to make my presentations to the class, helped me distribute consent information, discussed group selection and also took an interest in the activities I had planned.

In practical terms this meant that I was allocated a time (one or two days a week for over a year) and space (a small room often used for learning support and music tuition) in which to work. I was also given access to the classroom to observe, teach and set tasks for the whole class and to make copies of children's existing narrative work. I was able to observe playground play and could access areas of the school during the film-making process that the children had decided would be appropriate settings.

The children

I elected to work with primary-aged children and in consultation with the head teacher opted for a Year 5 class, children aged 9 and 10 who would have recent, even immediate, experiences of engaging with children's film. Having presented my project to the whole class of Year 5 children, I asked them to volunteer for participation using a very brief questionnaire. Of the class of thirty children, twenty-four volunteered. It was my aim to identify a group with a diverse range of experiences of film, and a mix of gender, ethnicity and social experiences. I was not attempting to achieve a representative sample but a group of children from which it might be possible to establish telling cases. I decided that six was the maximum number for the group both to enable an in-depth look at their responses to the research, and to enable them to interact socially, that is to say interact with each other and not just with me.

In Media Studies research, as Gauntlett and Holzwarth (2006) point out, groups are often identified by their interest in a particular media form such as a popular television programme, *Nationwide* (Morley, 1980) and *EastEnders* (Buckingham, 1987) in ways which negate their wider interests in media, their identity and other social and economic factors about themselves. It is clearly important to Gauntlett and Holzwarth (2006), as it is to myself, to recognise that these are groups constructed by research and are not homogenous or 'other' and that, above all, they are able to contribute more extensively to the research process. I therefore avoided grouping the children because they watched the most children's films or were fans of particular films, but opted to try to identify six children with distinct experiences.

Of the children who volunteered to participate, some were ruled out because of participation in another project. Others were ruled in because of their strong interest in film, which was reflected in the volunteer questionnaire they completed. Others were ruled in because the class teacher or head teacher felt that they would benefit from the opportunity to take part in a film-related project. Overall the group was composed of three girls and three boys and the gender balance was explicitly aimed for.

Table 5.1 Activities related to gaining 'assigned but informed consent'

Assigned but informed consent	Activity	Response
The children understand the intentions of the project	• A presentation about the project was made to the children which described the aims and the sorts of activities involved and asked the children to consider if they would like to participate • If they wanted to participate they could signal this in a brief questionnaire about favourite films and film memories • I used a power point presentation and answer sheets for this activity • Benefits and challenges to participation were pointed out in, hopefully, accessible terms	24 of a class of 30 volunteered to participate.
The children know who made decisions concerning their involvement and why	The children were told about the reasons for their selection and the school selection and the need for a diverse group. They were given the opportunity to raise questions about this and share their response to being selected	The children's status in the school as the 'film group' was a positive identifier that was distinct from usual school distinctions based on achievement or behaviour.
The children have a meaningful rather than decorative role	I drew on visual and collaborative research methods to ensure that the children could access the research activities and participate in them to a degree which they had some control over.	The children participated in the different research activities in distinct ways according to their own interests and skills.
The children volunteer for the project after the project was made clear to them (Hart, 1992, p. 14)	• Following selection the children and their parents were asked to complete a consent form which described the project plans and intentions, again in an accessible form, and gave contact details for myself and the university so they had clear lines of communication through which to raise concerns • I sent a further consent request to parents of children involved in the film production activity	All consent forms were completed and returned and communication with some parents developed.

Assigned but informed consent

I opted to ask for the children's consent for what Hart (1992) describes as 'assigned but informed' participation. In Table 5.1, I take Hart's description of the qualities that characterise 'assigned but informed' participation of children, and describe how I attempted to ensure this level of participation in my research.

The activities

My research was not focused on how children read, understand or respond to particular films but sought to understand how children made sense of all their experiences of narrative, and specifically the role of film within that. I hoped to gain an understanding of the ways in which children drew on their experiences of narrative when creating stories of their own. Hart proposes that key to overcoming barriers to participation is to involve children in decision-making processes:

> The important principal again is one of choice: programmes should be designed which maximise the opportunity for any child to choose to participate at the highest level of their ability. (Hart, 1992, p. 1)

In my research I found that offering choice in relation to mode of expression was highly important to the children's participation. It became clear that to enable the children to express their ideas and experiences I would need to build in choices in terms of both content and media as well as group composition in each of the activities I undertook. In Table 5.2 below I outline the question, the activity and the sorts of data I anticipated being able to draw from each of the activities.

The activities took place over the course of an academic year. Since some of the creative and collaborative activities I undertook were not conventional research methods, I have provided a description of each one below, incorporating a brief rationale and a reflection on the advantages and disadvantages of each.

'Free-writing' – stories

Having collected the children's literacy work from a six month period, I found that there had been no opportunity for the children to undertake what could be described as a 'free-writing' task. That is to say, the content and form of the children's work was largely dictated by the task set by the teacher and modelled according to shared writing practice. As a consequence, I asked the teacher if the children could be asked to undertake a free-writing task, which also encouraged them to draw on their knowledge of film. The teacher and I jointly planned a drama activity through which children could devise

Table 5.2   Research questions / activities

Question	Research activity / data	To identify and explore:
In what ways do children participate in and engage with children's film?	Initial questionnaire Individual filmed interviews Sketch books / diaries Photo audit (at home and school) Classroom observations Playground observations	Favourite films. Recent film experiences. Film memories. The way film is engaged with at home and at school. Film-related play.
What do children learn about narrative from children's films in the classroom?	Collection of class literacy activity (6 months) 'Free-writing' – stories Oral storytelling	Understandings of character, setting, plot and structure, Traces of influence of popular culture including children's film.
How do children draw on children's film when creating their own moving image narratives?	Paper animation Drawn/Plasticine characters Live action film production	Understandings of character, setting, plot and structure. Traces of influence of popular culture including children's film. Examples of (explicit and intuitive) uses of film language / the kinekonic mode to create meaning. Children moving from one mode of expression to another.

characters and plots based on popular culture. They were then given the chance to write their own story, which could be adapted for film.

The whole class were asked to undertake this activity because the teacher was keen to see what they would write about. Although I focus entirely on the research group's written stories, there was a great deal of data generated by the whole class which implied that popular culture was indeed a rich source of ideas for stories that popular culture was not emerging in their regular classroom work. The advantage of this activity was that I was able to compare the children's free writing with their school-based literacy work, and also see how they were attempting to handle the movement from one media, film, to another media, writing.

Oral storytelling

Much of the emphasis of work on narrative in school took a written form. I decided to include an oral storytelling activity in the fieldwork to encourage the children to draw on all their cultural resources for storytelling without anxieties about successful or unsuccessful writing. The whole group sat in a line and played a game whereby one would be given one (incomplete) story sentence to start off and then they would tell a piece of the story and pass it on to the next person in line. I did not give starters which were specifically film-orientated, in fact they were everyday, nor did I explicitly say to the children to draw on their knowledge of popular culture, although by this time the children were very aware of my interest in children's film. The advantages of this activity was the space it created for children's storytelling, which drew on their home knowledge of film and popular culture in extremely interesting ways. Some children dominated these stories and limited the participation of others, although interestingly this was a reversal of the classroom dynamic. That is to say, the children who dominated this activity were usually less vocal in tasks such as preparing for shared writing activity.

Photo audit (at home and school)

As I have argued, I believe it is critical to equip children with skills in film production in a research context where film production is an aspect of method. As part of this approach, I worked with the children in groups providing them with still cameras with which to compose shots, such as close-up, long-shot, medium-shot, high-angle, and low-angle, around school. I asked them to focus on anything they could find in school that related to film. I followed up this activity by asking the children to complete the same task at home with disposable cameras. This enabled me to provide the children with some training which would hopefully help them in their film production task, but also with a photographic audit of where film appeared at home and at school. These images provided a useful discussion point and gave me access to the role of children's films in their lives. Although all the children in the research group took part in the school-based photo audit, none of the boys in the research group returned their cameras.

Paper animation

The first specifically film-based activity I undertook with the research group was a simple paper animation activity. I grouped the children into pairs to work on a story with two characters and three settings. I asked each of the pairs to create two characters on paper and showed them how to give them moving joints, if they wanted to. I also showed them how to turn these characters easily into moveable figures, like puppets, using pencils and sticky tape. As they developed the characters on paper, I then set them the task of thinking of ideas for stories and backgrounds or settings, which they created on large pieces of paper. They then devised the stories rather as if

they were playing puppet shows and finally they filmed each other presenting back their story. Again, although I did not explicitly ask the children
to draw on popular culture influences, they were aware of my interest in
children's films and the medium was animation.

I set this task up recognising the positive impact creative constraints can
have on learning. Burn and Durran (2007) demonstrate in their animation
activities with young people the way in which 'purposeful, practical, aesthetic and imaginative constraints' can 'fuel learning, rather than inhibit
it' (Burn and Durran, 2007, p. 40). Many of the constraints of production
activity are inherent in the medium and, as a consequence, production
work potentially enriches learning about the affordances of the medium.
Imaginative constraints can also act as a helpful starting point, and practical constraints can ensure the task is achievable within the given time and
resources. The point at which children push at the boundaries or question
these constraints becomes a point of interest. For Burn and Durran (2007)
for example, the children they worked with completely upturned the imaginative constraint of the given theme of aviation, choosing to devise an
alien invasion with many popular culture influences instead. It is possible
to infer that the form had an impact on the choice of content, that is to
say that the choice of animation as the mode of expression might not have
encouraged the children to undertake a serious historical study of aviation.
The tensions between the task and the constraints inherent to it presented
useful challenges to the children, which they addressed in interesting ways.

The main aim of this activity was to observe what, given 'free' choice and
with no written element, the children would come up with in relation to
characters, settings and plot, using drawing as a medium with the added
possibility of movement and sound. I was also keen, however, to begin to
use video cameras with the children to gain an understanding of their creation of meaning through shot composition. Burn and Durran (2007) argue
that children can infer meaning from shot composition as viewers, but do
not necessarily intuitively or explicitly understand the role of shot composition in early attempts at film-making. They point out the importance of
story-boarding and production work to increase understanding so I included
this task early on in the research process. For this activity, which is not
animation but is close to it, the children needed to be proficient at holding
still close-ups and the puppeteers had to work carefully to be out of shot.
This was not easy (working without a tripod at this point) and the more
involved in playing the story the children became, the more the position
of the camera was forgotten. It was this level of involvement in playing the
story, exhibited by the children in their approach to the task therefore, that
became the focus of my analysis.

As Burn and Durran's (2007) work demonstrates, a more sophisticated
approach to animation production would enable far more in-depth exploration of the affordances of the medium. However, even this simple and

accessible activity can emulate some of the processes through which children come to understand how film is constructed. Furthermore, the speed at which this activity can be undertaken and completed and its ephemeral nature create a particular sort of space for production that enables knowledge of popular culture and narrative to be played with and parodied. Furthermore, in the short time available, this was an effective way to explore engagements with animated film, without getting too caught up in learning the skills involved in animation production.

Drawn and Plasticine superhero characters

In this activity I wanted to explore the children's ideas about character in two different animated forms, that is to say drawn and Plasticine model. I was keen for the children to have an opportunity to do at least one creative activity individually, rather than as group work, which is a feature of all the other research activity. I asked the children to make up a new superhero character for an animated film or television programme. I suggested that they considered whether there were lots of story ideas that could go with their character but I did not ask them to generate these storylines. I opted for superheroes because they are such a strong feature of children's cultural texts and there were recent film adaptations of superhero characters such as Spiderman (Raimi, 2002) and The X- Men (Singer, 2000), which the boys had referred to. Children have also often been observed appropriating superheroes in their literacy work (Dyson, 1997; Marsh and Millard, 2000) and I was interested to see the extent to which children aged 9 and 10 continued to be engaged by this genre. The live action film production had already commenced at this point (see below) and it was clear the children had opted for everyday or real stories so I hoped this, albeit very short activity, would give me a fuller picture of the children's experiences of character from this genre.

In this activity I had effectively removed the collaborative element and asked the children to produce characters individually. Interestingly, this lack of dialogue had two strong impacts. The first was to reduce dramatically the sorts of social interaction described above. This in turn limited the extent to which initial ideas were developed. This is important in terms of pedagogy and, as argued by Parker (2006), would imply that just as films and popular culture texts are experienced and participated in socially the production of these texts is also greatly enriched by being a group process.

Live action film production

When creating their films the children were involved in a range of activities including:

• Devising, Scripting, Filming, Editing, Screening

The idea of making a film was by far the most motivating aspect of the project for the children. Just having the equipment in school; a video camera, tripod, laptop and clapboard slate, created a buzz so that the children became a focus of attention of other children and staff. They were extremely excited by the idea from the beginning and all their earliest questions related to what sort of film it would be, how long and whether it would be animation or live action. They were also keen to know who the film was for, who was going to see it. This was so important to them that I agreed to see if I could organise for the film to be screened at a local film festival as well as at school.

Many of the answers to their questions were decided by neccessity rather than by any particular creative or research orientated focus. I set the task that the film would feature two or three main characters because all the children wanted to be in their film. I set further criteria such as live action, short film and based in school to be confident that we could complete the task in the limited time we had and with almost no budget. The children were keen to work in gender groups and I felt that this was compatible with the aims of the research, so two groups were established – boys and girls. The children were invited to come up with their own idea for a story for their film. They took very different approaches to this, although it became clear that the inherent constraints of the medium of live action film had an impact on their choices.

Screening

In terms of the stages of research, the dissemination process traditionally excludes participants, identified as it is with the reputation of the researcher and their institution. I was keen to enable the children to share their films with a wide audience and so were they. We were able to arrange for the films to be shown at a children's film festival I had set up and still had connections with. Parents, peers and film-makers were invited to attend and the children were able to show their films, watch some other international short films and receive certificates and prizes at the event. In this context I was not disseminating the findings of the project, although we did generate some local media interest in the subject matter chosen by the children in their films. However, the children were able to share their films and experience of making them and this was echoed when they ran a similar event to the whole school.

Watching their films with an audience usefully heightened their awareness of how effective they had been in their storytelling. This emphasised to me the need to undertake parallel activities at the stage of dissemination, including sharing the children's films in this social context rather than only at academic conferences.

In the event, the visibility of the research also impacted on perceptions of the children in school. I became aware of the children, parents, teachers and other school staff, retelling stories that emerged from the research:

> One often saw a bit of experience becoming an event to be told, being told and being retold until it took shape as a narrative, one that might become a narrative told by others. (Hymes, 1996, p. 118)

The activities that took place during the research offered opportunities to some of the children to formulate stories of experiences which they were keen to share. As a result they shared aspects of their identity, which had perhaps been less visible in school previously, but which the school staff valued and were increasingly interested in.

Analysis: narrative approaches

Throughout my fieldwork I explored what children understood about narrative by enabling reflection on previous experiences of narrative, engagement with new narratives and opportunities to create narratives in different forms. Having collected a considerable amount of data in oral, visual, film and written form I had to devise an approach to analysis that would enable me to explore the meanings expressed in the different media and make comparisons in terms of my research questions. I therefore took the decision to divide up the data into three categories:

- Children's film, identity and literacy
- Written and oral narrative
- Film narratives.

I made the decision to compare home and school contexts where possible, since differences had begun to emerge, demonstrating context to be highly significant. The categories helped me to divide the data as follows, although of course in the process of reflection and analysis they were not entirely distinct:

Children's film, identity and literacy

- Initial questionnaire
- Individual filmed interviews
- Sketch books/diaries
- Photo audit (at home and school)
- Classroom observations
- Collection of class literacy activity (six months)
- Playground observations.

Written and oral narratives (at school and as part of the research)

- Written stories
- Oral stories.

Film narratives

- Paper animation activity – filmed.
- Drawn/Plasticine model production
- Live action film production.

Each of the research activities required distinct approaches to analysis which I describe below.

Broad themes I identified to look for and make comparisons about related to:

- The extent to which film and other popular culture forms were significant to them (at home and school) in their talk, play and text production
- the children's own reflections on their literacy identities and in particular what they perceived to be the ingredients of a 'good' story.

Having identified many different individual expressions relating to the above, I then took the decision not to express these as a set of anonymous data relating to the group as a whole but as a set of storied accounts of the individual children. Although I compared the children's experiences I attempted to keep my storied accounts of their experiences 'intact' Riessmann, (2008) 'theorising from the case rather than from component themes across cases' (Riessmann, 2008, p. 43). That is to say, I organise the children's experiences in conventional narrative structure with a temporal framework. Each child's identity is presented distinctly, with aspects of their particular practices drawn on to deepen understanding of their experiences of narrative. Although I see the data as evidence of the children representing or constructing themselves in particular ways, I accept these constructions as evidence of how they want to be perceived and treat this as useful data.

Analysis of written and oral narratives

The focus of this analysis was to address my core question of what the children knew and understood about narrative and what they could express in different forms. As a result I drew on narrative theory, film theory and cultural studies frameworks to assist me in identifying what the children were able to express in written, oral, film and photographic form. In my initial plans for the research I had anticipated focusing largely on narrative structure, drawing on the work of Propp (1968); Todorov (1968) and Bordwell and Thompson (2003), whose ideas are influential on how narrative is taught in schools. However, as I widened my focus to respond to what I saw as key aspects of the children's engagements with narrative, I also began to look more widely for theoretical explanations for what I was finding in the children's texts, so I drew on additional narrative theorists such as Genette (1980) and Chatman (1990) and further research relating to children's responses to film production activity (Grace and Tobin, 1998). It also proved to be extremely useful to compare what understandings of narrative children were able to express in different forms and highly important to consider the multimodal affordances the form offered the children (Kress, 2003).

In my original plans I had not anticipated analysing the children's written stories. However, as these were such a central aspect of the school experience of literacy, I shifted my focus to incorporate writing. This also led to me looking to theory (Hilton, 2001; Barrs, 2001), which increased my understanding of children's development as narrative writers. Unlike the first data chapter in which I story accounts of the children's identities in relation to film, I group the analysis for story production into traditional characteristics of print narratives, as reflected in the meta-language of narrative the children drew on. So I organise the analysis of each section into consideration of what the children were expressing in relation to character, setting, plot and structure. At times, the distinct affordances of film make this division unwieldy but it was all the same useful in highlighting some of the differences in relation to specific children's texts.

Having made some preliminary analysis of the children's texts and drawn some conclusions, in the subsequent year I continued to visit the school, offering an out-of-school film club. This enabled me to continue a dialogue with the children involved and in particular provided an opportunity to discuss with them some of my interpretations and check these against their recollections of events and dialogue. Although clearly this is not including children in data analysis, I felt it addressed some of the issues raised when children are entirely excluded from this stage of the research. That is to say, the children were given an opportunity to feedback to me regarding the way I planned to represent them in my thesis. Although I think there are very interesting opportunities to involve children in research analysis, I did not feel this was the appropriate course of action in this case.

The children's engagement with the research could be described as running parallel to my own. Each participant had distinct aspirations for what they would learn by taking part. For the children, the research was largely perceived as an opportunity to make narratives in other forms, and in particular to engage in film production. In participatory educational research, therefore, the process throughout can be considered as one in which the participants are all engaged equally, if differently, in a collaborative enquiry.

Analysis of film production activities

Grace and Tobin (1998) note the importance of not idealising children's productions. Burn (2007) identifies an issue with research undertaken by advocates and pioneers of film production in education and suggest that they tend to be celebratory. As a consequence I have attempted below to make explicit my approach to analysis, which enabled me to reflect critically about what the children were able to express in different media forms.

Paper animation

In my analysis I focus both on the texts the children produced and the process of production. I reflect on the characters, settings and plots the children devise, but I also consider the children's use of sound and visual design – aspects of the kinekonic mode. In this example I do not look at the shots used or lighting, for example, because the children were using the camera for the first time and composed shots while getting familiar with the process of film-making. Furthermore, each child filmed another group's story so that the camera work was not an aspect of the decision-making process for the storytellers. To interpret the children's markedly playful and transgressive response to this activity, I draw on the work of Grace and Tobin (1998) and Mackey (2002).

Live action films

To analyse the children's films I have taken the approach of Burn and Parker (2003) and adapted it to the different context of this activity. Burn and Parker (2003) use kiniekonic mode rather the cinematic (Metz, 1974) to include all the affordances of film. In their analysis they focus on those aspects of the kinekonic mode that their students have made significant choices about in their final edit, an approach I have utilised by including discussion of the process of production. They include in their analysis a consideration of how both the pre-planned and improvised elements of their students' focus on skateboard film shape the kinds of representation they create. In my analysis I focus on the children's uses of the distinct modes of film and 'combinational affordances' (Burn and Parker, 2003, p. 16) of the kinekonic mode to articulate (represent) ideas about narrative. Thus, I include in my analysis considerations of the planned, improvised and performed elements of the children's films including uses of sound, music, shots, light, costume, gesture, performance. I relate these elements to the elements of narrative – character, setting and plot – to make comparisons between the choices the children made in print, drawn and oral form.

When it came to filming their scripts, I had planned to let each group film their own story so that I could observe the groups' decision-making process about their own idea. I remain convinced that this would have given me some useful insights into the way the children made decisions about shots and angles, but since they decided to act in their own films, we had to reorganise so that the girls in the group took turns to film the boys' story and the boys took turns to film the girls' story. To try to ensure that each group kept creative control of their film, they had produced storyboards and when shots were set up they were invited to take a directorial role.

The storyboards the children produced were not particularly successful in terms of helping them make decisions about shots, although I had undertaken some camera work teaching with them. My aim was to try to equip the children with some understanding of camera shots and then to observe them put these ideas into practice. When they created their storyboards, these were mostly helpful in ensuring they had organised their films into a number of scenes. The storyboards did not help them to consider the best position for the camera and most of the sketches they drew were of the characters in mid- or long-shot, something Burn and Durran (2007) also observed when young people make films. Decisions about the type of shot and angle to use were therefore made at the point of filming. Some of these decisions were made hurriedly and in a quite arbitrary manner and this shows in their final films, but many of them were carefully considered and it is these that I analyse further. I did not intervene in the process of filming but if the children asked my opinion, I tried to show a range of options available to them, to help them make up their mind what sort of shot to use. I took the same approach to enabling them to select sound, music, costume, titles, and the like.

To analyse and interpret the children's story productions in oral and written form (Chapter 7) and film form (Chapter 8), it is critical to understand the children's identities. I therefore present a storied account of each child's identity in the subsequent chapter.

6
Film Identities in Practice

In the early stages of my fieldwork, I arrived at my research school at playtime, to meet the class teacher. I walked past the nursery children out in the playground. 'You're Darth Sidius! You're Darth Sidius!' said one boy to another who was lying on the ground with his arms raised into a triangle, holding his imaginary light sabre in an accurate re-enactment of a Jedi warrior character in *Star Wars Episode II: Attack of the Clones*, (Lucas, 2002). I made a mental note to add this to my research journal at the time, and this moment has since increased in significance because of the many times I encountered similar play. These children were four-years-old, the film upon which their play was based was shown in cinemas two years before their birth. This playful engagement demonstrates that film is far from ephemeral (Robinson, 1997) but is a source of narrative, providing symbolic resources (Buckingham and Sefton-Green, 1994), in this case an iconic gesture, for play as well as identity negotiation (Marsh, 2005).

In the previous chapters I presented research which demonstrates that children's films, like other popular media, provides children with some of the resources with which they can play and perform identities and explore and develop literacies. Furthermore, I have argued that narrative is a cultural aspect of literacy and that many children's earliest encounters with narrative are in the form of popular children's films. In the two subsequent chapters, I explore the particular contribution of children's films to children's repertoires of narrative as expressed in different contexts and different media. The focus of this initial data chapter however, is to explore the ways children participate in and engage with children's films and the impact of this engagement on their identities and their orientation to literacy.

I therefore attempt to describe the identities of the six children who participated in the research and their associated memories and experiences of watching film and playing film-based games at home and at school. As described in Chapter 4, the interviews were edited into six video vignettes and in the following written accounts I draw on this video data but also map these experiences against data about the children's experiences of film at home and school that were expressed in the course of the research including, for example, the photo audit and a number of research conversations.

Connor

When I first visited Year 5, I presented them with information about my area of interest, my own background, what the research would consist of and how to get involved if they would like to. The presentation title was 'Children and Film' and I showed some images and clips from films to illustrate my main points. Throughout this process I asked the children in the class to raise questions if they had any. The whole presentation took much longer than I had anticipated and this was as a result of the highly enthusiastic response I received. Many of the children asked interesting questions, but one hand went up more than any other. Within the first few minutes of the presentation I had learnt Connor's name and had tried to respond to his ideas. For example he commented:

> I think all children's films have a message, Miss, a moral at the end. Do you?

Later he responded to a clip from the opening scene of the film, *Mirrormask* (McKean, 2005), by saying:

> Well I think that girl is going to be the main character, the one we see in the first shot and the rest of the film will be about her problem and how she solves that problem.

I had asked the class what they thought might happen next. The film is unusual; a British film with a long opening sequence animated with grotesque illustrations. I chose it to illustrate that the research might not only involve looking at popular children's films so that this did not come as a surprise later in the process. Connor was able to apply his knowledge of children's films to a new and unfamiliar text, that is to say, that often the main character is shown in close up in the earliest moments of the film, and that she has a problem and that the film will conclude by solving the problem. He was applying the version of Todorov's (1968) theory of narrative structure he had encountered in school to help him make sense of a new film. What is more, it was clear that he was externalising ideas he had been thinking about for a while.

Initially, I was quite overwhelmed by Connor's enthusiasm. I had agreed with the teacher and head teacher that we would select the final six from those who said they would like to be part of the group on the basis of their opportunity to benefit from the project and, in terms of the research, to attempt to explore some distinct experiences. I was concerned that while

I might have wanted to work with Connor, because of his interest and enthusiasm and his perceptive comments, I did not want to choose someone who would dominate the group too much or someone who perhaps always got chosen for everything. When I discussed these concerns with the class teacher her response came as a surprise. She pointed out that Connor, while being a popular member of the class, had never responded like that to a group discussion activity before and that the subject of film had clearly been the prompt for his reaction.

Pompe (1992a) demonstrates how the inclusion of popular culture in school can lead to a shift in the hierarchies of learners, that is to say which children are perceived as successful and which are not. Here Connor's usual classroom identity shifted and his expertise in film was highlighted. Furthermore he was able to demonstrate complex and sophisticated understandings of an unfamiliar text; a text which left the rest of the class uneasy. As a result, the teacher encouraged me to work with Connor as she felt that he had demonstrated that film was a special area of expertise for him and this would be a great opportunity for him to explore this interest further. It became evident that for Connor to enact an identity in relation to learning that was both motivated and curious and to be able to demonstrate his 'funds of knowledge' (Moll et al., 1992) about stories, he needed to be invited to draw on his particular love and rich repertoire of films.

Connor saw his interest in film as something which defined him and used the word 'always' in an interesting way:

I've always wished that I could have my own film when I'm older.

Here 'always' implies a longevity of interest about watching, creating or owning a film. Film, for Connor, was not background wallpaper, something he could take or leave or something to pass the time. Film was extremely important and part of the structure of his life. He described it as part of a routine; playing sport after school, watching television, having his tea and then at night, after bath time but before bedtime watching films. In a fleeting discussion he named two films he had recently watched, *Wedding Crashers* (Dobkin, 2005) and *Cool Runnings* (Turtletaub, 1993) both of which were screened on television in the week prior to the interview. Neither film is specifically a children's film, nor are they popular contemporary films. Connor does not therefore only watch recently released children's films; he also watches older films targeted at more mature 'tween' audiences (Willett, 2005a).

Connor, the only boy in the group with access to television channels in his room, described regularly making decisions about what he watched. He commented on a number of occasions that he did not just watch something if it was on. He did not flick channels; he noticed if there was a film on he wanted to watch and then set aside time to watch it. He also described choosing films from his own collection, ensuring he had built up enough time since he last saw it so that when he watched it again it was not boring. If we substituted books for films in this description we would have a picture of an engaged and selective reader, who sought out new experiences and occasionally returned to old favourites.

Connor was highly popular both with adults in school and his peers. He had high social status to the extent that he was not afraid to express his interest in dance, even performing in assembly and persuading other boys to join in. He candidly talked in interviews about himself; he saw himself as being 'mixed race' and having two families and a gran who let him use her mobile phone to make films. In terms of his peers he appeared to lead taste rather than follow and would always be the first to see a certain film. His love of film was matched with his love of street dance and he drew on these two interests throughout the project, as can be seen in his film preferences.

Connor talked sometimes about being able to see stories in his head. He came to see me at break time one day in the early stages of the project and told me he had 'a dream of a film last night':

C: It was about these two boys, brothers, and they had a real dad who was a yoga master. Anyway it was one of the boy's birthdays. They weren't twins. A big storm blew up and the two boys were separated. The father died. Then it was about seven years later and the two brothers were bought back together again.
B: How do you know it was a film and not just an ordinary dream?
C: It just was.
[He looked at me as if to say, 'can't you *see* it' and I began to think I was participating in a film pitch.]
B: Well, it's a cracking idea for a film!

He described having lots of ideas for films and not being able to work out why real filmmakers do not make films similar to his ideas. Within his idea he encapsulated a great deal of knowledge of film and not just children's film. He knew that films have to have key characters who have relationships with each other. He recognised the importance of dramatic moments, which are sometimes connected to extreme weather, the storm, or significant life events, a birthday. He also knew films have to have a dramatic event early in the narrative, the disruption of order; the dad's death and the brothers' separation. Finally, he showed he understood the conventional requirement for resolution, the reuniting of the two brothers. As he told me his idea, he visualised it in scenes including flashback and flash forward, which signals his understanding of the particular way film can move swiftly through time. Connor's creative ideas for film demonstrated complex understanding of the underlying structures of narrative and the particular ways films tell stories.

Going to the cinema was also a special experience for Connor. He described memorable visits to see new releases and described himself as not patient enough to wait for some films to be released on DVD (by which, like some of the others in the group, he usually means obtaining a pirate copy). Some films, he said, he has to see at the cinema on the big screen because; 'you can just tell they're going to be good'. It could be anticipated that Connor might be on the trajectory to becoming what the UK Film Council describe as an 'avid' (UKFC, 2007).

> Avids' identities are bound up in film. It is who they are: a constant that frames and informs their perception of themselves and the wider world. (UKFC, 2007, p. 3)

Very young 'avids' in this report are described as often developing a strong liking of film to form bonds with parents or older siblings and as an escape from home life, supported by the availability of films on television or DVD and memorable cinema experiences. This description resonates with the picture that had emerged of Connor's relationship with film.

It would be reasonable to assume that Connor's love of stories in the moving image form would assist him in accessing the literacy curriculum. However, Connor's orientation towards school literacy was highly negative and appeared detached from his sense of himself in relation to his love of films. He regularly said he was not good at writing and occasionally expressed frustration about the stories he had in his head that he thought should be turned into films. He was less motivated by getting his ideas down on paper because he became disappointed with the way his writing failed to match up with his multimodal imaginings. Evidently, Connor's avid engagement in film enabled him to infer meaning and respond to texts in complex ways, but this asset did not positively impact on his school literacy identity.

Connor related incidents from his life with a high degree of performance, re-enacting key moments such as his first visit to see (Lasseter, 1995), which was an important memory he shared with his mum of eating popcorn like a robot because he was so involved in watching the film. The 'Toy Story' films became highly significant, favourite films, to Connor:

> I used to always play *Toy Story* with my friends. I used to go and get my green pyjamas on and they were actually Buzz Lightyear pyjamas and once when I were little, I weren't very clever, I stood at the top of the stairs, I closed my eyes and went, To infinity and beyond' and I jumped off the stairs and cracked my head. [Laughter] I was only little though and I really liked Buzz Lightyear. I were about three.

Later he said, 'I'll always like *Toy Story*. I know that because it's a good film'. Liking *Toy Story* has become an aspect of his 'ongoing' identity (Giddens,

1991, p. 54). He used the word 'always' again here in a nostalgic manner, acknowledging that he had moved on in his taste but also that the film had a particular status both as a favourite film and as a source of a story about him as a child that he had shared with his mum.

Connor's taste in film changed over time. He reflected on his early child-hood, saying that he loved *Toy Story* but that now he liked real films. At the time of the first interview he used the example *High School Musical* (Ortega, 2006) which he said had real people in and was about dancing, but by the second phase in the project when the group were devising ideas for their own film he rejected *High School Musical* for films such as *Save the Last Dance* (Carter, 2001) and *Step Up* (Fletcher, 2006), which he perceived as more mature, not as babyish, while still about real people, difficult situations and dance. According to Rosenblatt's (1970) definition Connor 'experienced' films, entering the lives of others and identifying and empathising with their situation. He sought out 'everyday' (Luke and Carrington, 2002) films which incorporated not only his love of dance, but also reflected his own circumstances and significantly found space to represent the poverty, con-flict and diversity, absent from many classroom texts (Carrington, 2005a).

Connor's response to *Home Alone 2* (Columbus, 1992) is particularly of interest in the light of Kincheloe's (1998) critique referred to in Chapter 2:

> Well *Home Alone 2* it's like, it's not that good at the first bits but when the boy like plays tricks it's really good how they could actually think of tricks like that. It's like, like un-normal tricks. It's like normal tricks would be like to put a bucket on top of a door, so when you walk though the door [gestures to explain trick]. But instead he like puts flame things on't door and when they open [gestures to show trick] and he uses loads of string. It's like they burn their heads off and stuff like that.

Here Connor had similar expectations to those explored by Barker (1989) in relation to the formulaic conventions of comics, forming a cultural contract between storyteller and reader. Connor was aware of the formula of the *Home Alone* films, having watched the first in the series. That is to say, a boy is left behind by his parents and has to fend off two evil robbers, by himself, before being reunited with his family. Just like the regular comic audience, Connor did not have high expectations of the narrative; it is 'a given' that the story will follow a particular pattern, but the pleasure Connor had in the *Home Alone* films was in *how* the character, Kevin, trapped, tricked and outwitted the baddie robbers. These tricks cannot be 'lame' like a 'bucket on the door trick', they have to be clever and complex; this is the contract between maker and audience.

Appreciating how 'they', the film-makers, come up with these tricks is also part of the pleasure of the film for Connor and the issue of the child being abandoned by his parents is not even mentioned. As Hodge and Tripp

(1986) demonstrate, children do not only respond to the moral or adult meaning of a text; they take pleasure in other aspects of the text, in this case the empowerment, ingenuity and transgression of the child, albeit temporary. Connor identified with the central (male) child character, but what he recalled most vividly was the process of wondering what the makers of the text, 'they', were going to do next. As a reader of films then, Connor was able to immerse himself in the text, but he also steps quickly inside and outside the diegetic world of the text (Mackey, 2002) often positioning himself as an insider, alongside the makers of the *Home Alone* films. Being a reader of film then, involves different processes in different contexts, including thinking like a maker of films.

Connor was the only child in the group who had tried out film-making before, at home. He had used his gran's phone to create a film because he was bored. He described the making process here:

> I've made that. It's not exactly a film. I've made up a voice. I've got a couple of teddies. I got her phone and I put it on video and what I did so it didn't see my hand: I kept pressing the pause button and then I moved it into a different place and pressed play [means record] and then spoke a bit and then moved it again.

Here Connor described using a stop motion animation technique, voice over and editing in camera, displaying considerable intrinsic motivation. He has tried to teach himself filmmaking to entertain himself. Motivated by 'having nothing else to do' and his own interest in film, Connor chose to try to make a film. Just as other children in the group described reading and then writing stories, Connor described watching films, dreaming films and imagining ideas for films in his head. Engagements with texts, in this case film, have close links to the urge to produce texts. Being a storyteller is a strong aspect of Connor's identity but his stories are moving image stories. It is important to contemplate that although language clearly has an important role to play in expressing narratives (Robinson, 1997), for some children the moving image has become at least as important.

Abbey

Abbey approached me after the first classroom presentation to tell me how much she would like to take part in the project. She talked about liking realistic films and as this was quite distinct from other interest expressed by the class, I was intrigued. Abbey described herself as 'helpful, funny and caring' and commented:

> Really I just like to be involved in things.

This was certainly evident and Abbey was desperate not to miss any of the research activity and was always the last to leave. Abbey described herself as a book lover mentioning for example, the Enid Blyton and Louisa M. Alcott series. She said she enjoyed writing stories and preferred to write, more than type, but also stated that she loved making and watching films. Although it transpired she had not in fact ever made films before, she clearly was enthused by the idea. She also mentioned participating in other activities including Guides and playing a musical instrument at school and church. She did not have a television although she could watch DVDs; she did have a Gameboy but said her brother used it more than she did and she suggested that she would like an MP3 player, with things *she* likes on it. She perceived herself as successful at school but thought that other people saw her as a 'nerdy chatterbox'.

Throughout the research process Abbey expressed herself thoughtfully and carefully, which at first I interpreted as confidence in her ideas. She was prepared to 'hold the floor' and take a good deal of time to explain what she meant to the rest of the class. This was not always popular and it took me a good while to work out what was going on when Abbey talked to an audience outside her trusted friendship group. Abbey's identity was influenced by her family's religious identity but this was not something she emphasised. In fact, she had developed strategies to avoid being given any particular label linked to her background. Abbey's overt construction of self appeared to illustrate Giddens' (1991) suggestion that self-identity is formed through the narratives that we attempt to construct about ourselves and share with others. However, Abbey was not constantly playing a role, she did not exhibit multiple identities, she managed to develop what Kenner (2005) calls a hybrid identity which drew on her distinct experiences at home, in the classroom and in social situations at school.

> The individuals' biography, if she is to maintain regular interaction with others in the day-to-day world, cannot be wholly fictive. It must integrate events which occur in the external world, and sort them into the ongoing 'story' about the self. (Giddens, 1991, p. 54)

Like all the children in the group, Abbey presented her identity in a way that enabled her to access social groups. For Abbey particularly though, this was a more overt and conscious process in which she perceived her own differences from others and tried to assimilate. Abbey seemed to spend such a long time explaining her ideas because she was also considering, even worrying about, how they would sound to her peers and teacher. I came across this strategy in the first interview. I noticed that she talked about watching *Stormbreaker* (Sax, 2006) the filmed adaptation of an Anthony Horowitz, Alex Rider novel. Quickly, she reverted to discussing the books. I think this was because she thought I would be more interested in what she had to say if she was talking about films, but that her own responses stemmed from her readings of the books.

Abbey had had her fair share of teasing and intolerance in school and had learnt to reveal only so much about herself to others. However, when Abbey was among her trusted friends, and two of these were also in the research group, she was much more spontaneous and less concerned with what others might think. In fact, at times, unfettered by the censure she often received from other classmates, her enthusiasm carried her away and it became harder for others to 'get a word in!'

Of the children in the group, Abbey had watched the fewest films. Initially, she could not think of a film she had recently watched when first interviewed:

> I don't think I've watched any this month actually although I might be watching one later because it's my brother's birthday today and he's got, he's just got *Toy Story* and *Superman* from mum and dad.

Films were not the significant element to her that they were to Connor or others in the group. She said for example:

> We are not the first family to go and see a film.

She laughed at this, as if to say, 'Well in fact we're usually the last'. She went on however, to describe an incident when her family missed out on seeing *The Incredibles* (Bird, 2004) and saw *National Treasure* (Turtletaub, 2004) instead, which turned out to be a film she preferred and helped her develop her interest in mysteries. It is significant here that although Abbey watched far fewer films than the others and did not watch as wide a variety of films, the films that her peers watched, were known to her and she was keen to be involved in related play and discussion of them:

> Well quite often, there's something like, there's a new film out and say if they've watched it they tell me a bit about what it's about. I decide if I like it or not.

Abbey talked about this process in the context of a discussion of playing games such as *Star Wars*. She described playing these games with her brothers, she has three, and at school. When talking about playing *Star Wars*, it would seem as if she was basing her knowledge of the film on her friends' accounts.

> I remember, we used, we quite like watching *Star Wars* em and we quite often played, em tried to remember what the film was about and sort of act it out. And sometimes it ends up quite funny sometimes because we

forget what it says and we make up something different and it just goes ...
it just goes completely wrong. [laughter]

Abbey described the films as serious and said that she thought the 'actors
in it never tell a joke at all'. This might imply that Abbey did not respond
to the humour in the *Star Wars* films and takes as her primary reading the
more serious elements of the story. It might also imply that Abbey, again,
did not repeatedly watch films so she was basing her play, her response and
her reading of the film on a single viewing or possibly from second-hand
accounts. This did not stop her from playing the story of *Star Wars* with her
siblings and also sometimes in school. As Buckingham (1993) demonstrates,
giving an appearance of knowledge of popular culture texts is critical to
maintaining social standing in school.

Abbey explained early on that her parents were not too keen on films and
that they sometimes only let her and her brother watch half a film. She was
the oldest of four, and this led to her watching texts for younger children
than those in the group who have older siblings. However, this was hardly
a case of restricted viewing. Abbey described her parents as selecting films
for her that they have seen already. She suggested that they know what she
would like and that 'usually they are right'. Abbey had been to see *National
Treasure*, a recent cinema release, and *The Incredibles* on DVD. She was the
only one of the group who did not have a DVD player in her room but she
watched films occasionally and at the cinema as a very special treat. Her
first cinema experience was as part of a school visit to see *Piglet's Big Movie*
(Glebas, 2003) and this was an important memory for her. Initially, when
she discussed her memories of this trip I was concerned that she was again
anticipating what she thought I wanted her to say. I mentioned liking sad
films and enjoying a good cry when I presented to the whole class, Abbey
also described her emotional responses in her questionnaire:

> I went to see *Piglet's Big Movie* in 2002/3. I went with school which meant
> I didn't have anything to eat, but no one told me that usually you do
> have food. I loved it! I cried because parts were sad.

In her interview she described in detail the moment that made her cry. She
suggested that the film was about friendship and that the scene that made
her sad was a moment when the character Piglet felt left out:

> I think I like it because it's sad. I don't know why. I just like sad films.

She also recalled that it was her first cinema visit and that this was not the
case for the rest of the class. She recalled this visit much more vividly than
any of the other children, suggesting that it was indeed a significant first
experience. Her comment that she did not know 'you were supposed to have

food in the cinema, nobody told me' suggests that this first experience was significant in other ways too. She was learning what you do when you go to the cinema and she noticed and remembered her difference from others because her peers already seemed to know the rules. As a reader of films Abbey had fewer experiences than the others to draw on but she clearly demonstrated the ability to identify and empathise with characters and had begun to develop a particular orientation to certain sorts of films.

Eight Below (Marshall, 2006) was another film seen with the school that Abbey described as based on a true-life story. The moments she remembered are those of extreme difficulty and hardship for the protagonist, ending with the abandonment of the sled dogs (Matilda also remembered this scene vividly):

> My favourite film was *Eight Below*. I liked it because it was sad and had animals as some of the main characters. Now I still think it's one of my favourite films!

It is striking that Abbey did not refer to subsequent viewings of this film; she recollected from her initial viewing. However, the film appears to have made an impression on her preference for real life rather than fantasy films with fairies or talking animals. She suggested that there are a lot of realistic films for children but then could not think of any. She then changed her mind, commenting:

> I think most children's films are fantasy actually. In fact *Eight Below* is the only one I can think of at the moment.

This reflects a number of things, firstly that Abbey had not seen a vast number of films, but all the same she knew she liked live action drama. She perhaps also liked the more realistic elements of films such as the *Harry Potter* series. Although she pointed out that these films have magical fantasy elements to them, she particularly referred to Harry's situation with a family who don't love him and the issues that arise in the stories about friendships. It is, perhaps, also important to acknowledge that there is not a plethora of realistic films, as Abbey defines them, available in Britain. A realistic drama is more likely to be found on television and as a consequence Abbey sought to satisfy her enthusiasm for the more 'real' aspects of texts where she could and sometimes those realistic elements could be found in animated Disney films or fantasy and adventure stories. As she pointed out in her interview 'sometimes animation can be real', by which I think she meant the stories present the point of view of a child which she can relate to.

Abbey's sharp recollection of her emotional response to Piglet's situation in *Piglet's Big Movie* where she recalled thinking 'oh no they're leaving him out' suggests that she had begun to develop empathy with characters in texts and had an expectation that films will invite her to emotionally engage with a character and that this is an important part of the pleasure of the text. Abbey recalled that it was only her who cried at the film and this could be because it was her also her first cinema trip and as such quite a momentous occasion for her. But it could also reflect her emotional response to the text:

> Well I loved it because it's [pause] mainly about friendship? And it's just a really nice film.

Abbey said this second sentence in the present tense, not distancing herself from it, as if she had grown out of it. Like Connor with *Toy Story* she stays loyal to the film as if it represents an important experience for her. However, like all the girls, Abbey distanced herself from overtly 'girlier' films, texts and artefacts. At one point she told me about a girl at church who was obsessed with being a princess, who always wore a princess outfit. She was dismissive of this and described how in her own play, based on fairy stories, she was more likely to be the 'king's servant[!]' and that she would only have wanted to be a princess when she was younger, aged 5. Unlike Connor, who stated he had to be Buzz in any game he played, Abbey did not claim one particular character that she played but many, and most often taking up an adult role.

Abbey's photos of home do not display the same number of film and popular culture artefacts as Eve's and Matilda's do. Most of the objects she photographed were clothes, bedding, bags, books and soft toys many featuring popular characters from television series for very young children. The toys she photographed were also those of her younger siblings. However, the jewellery box she photographed, that was her own, was *Winnie the Pooh* themed, again reflecting her immersion in the younger fictional choices of her siblings (the images of Winnie the Pooh in Abbey's house are all from the Walt Disney franchise version of the character). She photographed fewer DVDs and Game Boy games and they are not positioned on a shelf or in a drawer, they are taken as single images. Abbey photographed one of the books from the *Horrible Histories'* (Deary and Hepplewhite, 1993) series, which demonstrates her judgement that popular books published in series are commercial brands and as such are perhaps considered more closely aligned to popular culture artefacts.

Two other items of clothing were displayed: a *Star Wars* T-shirt and a *Harry Potter* sock. Abbey talked about both of the films occasionally, although not in any depth. She did refer to playing the films and can certainly adopt the *Star Wars* action postures. However, she did not demonstrate the intimate knowledge of the films that the others had, nor did she position herself as a fan in the way Matilda and Eve do. For example, she did not have a poster display or a shelf dedicated to her own enthusiasms, but all the same these texts are visible in the weft and weave (Pahl, 2002) of the family's existence; in their clothes, in their school bags and in the covers they sleep under.

One of Abbey's photos, above all the others stands out. It is of her brother in a Spiderman outfit. When she saw the pictures she laughed, recalling how hard it was to get her brothers to do what she wanted them to, once the Spiderman outfit was on. In fact, as soon as he had the costume on her brother became Spiderman complete with web shooting wrists and the posed foot ready to spring into action. He displays engagement with what Reid (2009) describes as the gestures of film from Spiderman without having the intimate knowledge of the films that comes from repeat viewings.

Some films, such as the *Star Wars* or *Spiderman* (Raimi, 2002) films acquire status as almost universally shared experiences. Bromley (1996) describes children's film-related play based on Disney's *Aladdin* (Clements and Musker, 1992) as drawing on a 'collective memory' which children of varying degrees of expertise can access. Abbey and her siblings found various ways to learn about films from their peers and then join in, however Abbey was never an expert in a popular film or film genre. This contrasts with Abbey's school literate identity where she was perceived by staff to be a very high achiever and by her peers as being very clever.

Abbey was not saturated in children's film and popular culture. She was an enthusiast but she had seen fewer moving image texts than her peers and owned far fewer related artefacts. Despite this Abbey had memories of film that were significant to her and contributed to her identity as a reader of particular sorts of 'real', dramatic and adventure stories. Abbey was also able to access the game-playing and talk about significant films she had not experienced directly through the existence of an 'interpretative community' (Fish, 1980) who shared their knowledge and experience and enabled her to join in. Children's readings of children's films are social, offering useful resources for group play. Some films such as *Star Wars* become highly significant shared and collective memories so that individual children will develop a whole range of strategies to ensure they are able to (in Abbey's words) 'be involved'.

Liam

Liam was selected to take part in the group because in his questionnaire he referred to being able to talk with his friends about films in school and this struck me as interesting:

> My favourite film is *The Simpsons Movie*. Me and my friends talk about what happens. I like it because it is funny.

Liam told me he was good at 'chillin' and the only thing he was good at, at school was Maths. From the outset Liam responded very differently according to context. In his first interview he talked in his own accent and he was not afraid to show enthusiasm. In small group work Liam often displayed a different identity, speaking in an American gangsta accent complete with hand gestures and with an attitude that was meant to imply he was not interested. He said he believed people at school thought he was a gangsta and used words like 'chillin', 'fit', 'homies' 'sic'. Often he allowed himself to be drawn in and did get involved in the activities on offer, but if he felt he was being observed by his peers he was careful to show that he thought it was all boring.

During one interview Liam told me he wanted to run a strip club and be a 'pimp' for the 'laydeez' when he grew up, asking me if I knew what he meant. Clearly Liam was trying to shock me, but at the same time he was alerting me to that fact that he felt there was a big distance between my life and his. In one drawing activity he described how he quite likes *Horrid Henry* (Unwin, 2006) on television because he's naughty, but he went on to say:

> He couldn't dream of half the stuff I do.

Again he was emphasising the gap between children's lives as seen on popular children's television and his own life, echoing Luke and Carrington's (2002) observation about the absence of representations of some children's lives within classroom or, in this case, children's television texts. Unsurprisingly, he looked to adult programmes and said he liked 'dramatic stuff on television like *EastEnders*'. Liam at the end of Year 5 was displaying a very different persona from the one I encountered in the first interview. Here he presented a cosier picture of watching films at home:

> Well, I sometimes, mostly I watch films at home because it's free and at least you get to lay on the sofa and stuff with your family.

Liam shared enthusiasm for the music and popular culture tastes of his older brother, especially rap music and magazines that he 'can't remember the titles of'. In his first interview though his taste in film was much closer to his peers:

> I like funny films that make people laugh. Stuff like *Alvin and the Chipmunks* – the chipmunks are squeaky and dodgy and funny.

He described his mum surprising him with a new DVD from time-to-time. He said that because he is the baby of the family he gets special treats. For example his mum bought him the latest Pokémon deck, Pokémon Pearl, when it first came out. Having something like a DVD or Pokémon deck or football cards when they first come out was seen as real treat and reward; a signifier of status by all of the group, although sometimes they also see this as 'being spoilt' or 'having everything'. Liam was not often the first to have things, though. Mum also played an important role in cinema visits, organising family trips 'five or six times a year' or enabling him to go with friends. Liam presented these visits as special occasions:

> Well I think of the food cos when you get to the cinema you have food and you get to see a film you haven't seen before so it's kind of exciting.

Although Liam did not appear to drive cinema visits in the way Connor did, he was enthusiastic about going to the cinema and especially about going with friends. The rest of the group described going to the cinema with family, unless it was a birthday visit or a school trip. Liam did not necessarily always decide on the films that he wanted to see at the cinema, but he could be said to know what he liked and more particularly what he disliked. So, when he went along to the cinema with friends the group chose *Alvin and the Chipmunks* (Hill, 2007) over *Enchanted* (Lima, 2007) because the boys did not want to see *Enchanted*. Liam did not give his reasons for this choice, he just smiled as he spoke knowing that I would understand that *Enchanted* is distinctly a girls' film and so not really an option. Film preferences for Liam were distinctly social, indicating family, friendship and gender allegiances.

Liam described stories he liked as:

> Like some stories like action stories films stuff that are like don't really happen but it's like quite good and make believe and stuff like that.

Here, Liam demonstrated his full awareness that when watching his favourite films, such as superhero films, he is entering into a fictional world. He suggested that although he knows they are made up and not realistic that was what he liked about them. Film also generated social activity for Liam, enabling him to enter into talk with his friends. He talked about this again with reference to *The Simpsons Movie* (Silverman, 2007) in the first interview where I sought clarification of his written questionnaire response:

L: So we talk about what happens ...
B: Well that, so that's really important then. So if you hadn't seen *The Simpsons* [pause]
L: Then we wouldn't be able to talk about it ... what happens
B: [Speaks over] you wouldn't be able to talk about it ... So what ... so, would you say that *The Simpsons* was particularly true of that ... you needed to see? ...
L: See it to talk about it [Nods and smiles]
B: OK so what sorts of things did you talk about?
L: We talk about what happens in it and start laughing and memories of when we went to see it.
B: Can you think of any now?
L: It's like when Homer [begins to laugh] gets this pig and he's walking it on't wall, he's like on't roof and he's going 'Spiderpig, Spiderpig' [does actions and sings] and it's funny.

B: And do you think it helps because you've all seen Spiderman as well ... there's sort of that ...

L: yeah ... yeah, it takes the mick.

Like Abbey, Liam recognised the social value of having seen films but it is not just social status that motivates him to talk about his film experiences. He clearly derived pleasure in re-living funny moments of particular films, retelling them and explaining the joke.

Early on Liam said he liked to play imaginative games based on films. He talked about doing this both with friends in the park and at school on non-football days. The three main films he played were *Harry Potter* where he liked to play Harry and be a goodie, *Star Wars* which is a game he played with a particular friend where they were both wookies in their own version of the story as well as a more generic army action story:

L: Sometimes we pretend we are fighting each other with guns and magic

B: So it's army games

L: Yes army games and magic and stuff like that

B: Or more magic?

A: Yeah magic

Liam explained that in this game different ideas are drawn on and mixed up and that although the children draw on films they don't always follow them rigidly. Liam described how sometimes when they played they moved away from the storyline of the film and 'go wherever our imagination runs'. This seemed to be evident in relation to characters in particular. So Liam described making up new characters in *Star Wars* games. This was a tactic which allowed the play to move beyond re-enacting the story and resolved tensions over who was going to be a main character. It was also clear from group work that Liam rarely got to be the role he wanted to be, so he was very keen to use this strategy.

At other times Liam would say that he did not play games, but that he 'hung out with his homies causing mayhem'. This was towards the end of Year 5 and could reflect changes in Liam's after-school activities, being given more freedom to play out. Although markedly different from his earlier descriptions of play, it was potentially just as much about re-enacting fantasy – a world that he would like to be connected to. It was also a world that he perceived through his relationship with his brother and his shared interest in niche music, 50 Cent, an American rapper, and related films and television programmes. Connolly finds that children's identities are 'contingent and context specific' (Connolly, 1998, p. 190) and clearly, Liam had a foot in a number of distinct social and cultural spheres, one of which he was able to share with his peers and one which he felt distinguished him from them and from school.

Liam is not black but was beginning to signal his affiliation with aspects of black culture. He was trying out or practising a version of self which was almost entirely based on his experiences of popular culture. He did not do this in class and his peers, who teased him about it, limited the extent to which he did this socially. It is, however, important to acknowledge the way Liam made use of aspects of culture, through language and role playing, to explore his identity at a time of transition. He was approaching year 6 and his siblings were in secondary school. He looked beyond what he saw as the younger experiences of his past, to films such as *30 Days of Night* (Slade, 2007) an 18-certificate horror film that he had recently watched. However there are some universal texts such as *The Simpsons*, *Spiderman* and *Star Wars* which occupy space on the border between childhood and adulthood, which he felt safe and able to share his pleasure in.

Eve

Eve, on first impression, was quiet, successful at school and, while not one of the 'popular' girls in the class, and very respected by her own group of friends. She had confidence and maturity so that sometimes during the research I over-looked the idea that she was just as keen to have fun and should not always have to be the sensible one. It was clear on a number of occasions that Eve found her 'sensible' identity limiting. However, this was a role she occupied in most of her time in school. Eve's participation in the project became a chance to slip out of this identity from time-to-time with interesting consequences.

Eve described watching one or two films per week at home, usually over the weekend, and television most nights. She said she went to the cinema about once every two months. Like most of the group Eve could play DVDs and videos in her room but not television channels. Eve highlighted the influence of her family on her viewing carefully. Her younger sister regularly persuaded her to watch things that she finds a bit babyish such as *Bee Movie* (Hickner and Smith, 2007). Her parents, especially mum, clearly took great care over film choices, looking at film programmes collected at previous cinema visits and recommending films for Eve to consider. Eve also talked about a neighbour who was a close family friend who sometimes recommends films or theatre for her to go and see.

For Eve, like Liam, going to the cinema is an occasional treat:

> If there's something good on and we, and then – it's a sort of special occasion or if we haven't been for a very long time – we might go and see something at the cinema.

Here Eve identified three reasons why her family might opt to go to the cinema to watch a film and implied that sometimes it might be all three reasons at once. She pointed out that her parents are just as likely to want to go and see these films as herself. Children's films can be very closely linked to special family events such as birthdays and are significant aspects family life.

Eve also talked about funny or comedy films as an important genre that would stimulate a cinema visit. All the children expressed a preference for funny films at some stage throughout the research process, demonstrating another often overlooked aspect of children's films, that is to say their humour. By 'something good' Eve was often referring to big budget, well-promoted main-stream films adapted from popular fiction series such as *The Golden Compass* (Weitz, 2007) and *Harry Potter and the Chamber of Secrets* (Columbus, 2002). Her *film-viewing* seemed to be carefully connected to her reading:

> My favourite film is *Harry Potter and the Chamber of Secrets*. I've seen it at the cinema and I've got the ones that are out and I'm reading them.

Both Eve and Matilda described how they are reading the *Harry Potter* books before watching the film adaptations although this requires patience and care so that no one gives away the story to them. This indicates quite intricate group interactions and negotiations to maximise pleasure from both book and film. Although Eve is considered average in terms of school-based literacy, she has an extremely positive view of both reading books and watching films for pleasure and has developed tastes and preferences, some which she felt linked her to others and some which marked her out as distinct.

Eve openly discussed playing games based on stories, books, and films as well as television programmes such as *Doctor Who* (Davies, 2005) and *Primeval* (Hodges and Haines, 2007–2011), two particular favourites of hers. She described how she used to play games when she was little based on animals, but that now she plays slightly older games and she emphasised which trusted friends play these games with her:

> I've got this group which I'm in, we're playing this game where we're these creatures and then we're sort of magical and we have sort of powers and we save the world [smile].

Eve displayed her knowledge of the narrative structure of a fantasy adventure film which incorporates all the things she liked. She liked animals, magic and fantasy and she understood that the plot of fantasy is usually driven by the need for there to be good characters vanquishing bad characters to stop them from destroying the world. Eve described watching film and television at the weekends, playing them at school the following week:

> When we watch TV or read a book we just tell them and we sort of just play on that storyline.

Here Eve identified herself as someone who gained knowledge of particular texts which she then shared with her friends, particularly those who did not encounter as many different texts as she did, like Abbey. This gave her some status in the group and she was seen as a valued contributor to the group's imaginative games.

In the context of both engaging with texts and playing the texts, groupings were carefully managed to ensure that those involved shared the same pleasures. Outside this group it was clear there were children who would laugh at their tastes and games. Groups, aligned through their interest in popular media, existed within a constellation of groups, some of which had higher or lower status. Some of these groups, like Connor's street dance group and Eve's animal games group, were quite firmly formed and exclusive. Other groups were more fluid and inclusive and these were often based on collective texts such as *Harry Potter* and *Star Wars*.

There is a photograph taken by Eve that demonstrates well the range of her interests and enthusiasms in relation to media texts. She had positioned posters of *Doctor Who* (Davies, 2005), *Harry Potter* (Columbus, 2002), *Pokémon* (Yuyama, 1998) and *High School Musical* (Ortega, 2006) alongside some posters of animals. She commented in an early interview about a time when she and her friends were really mad about animals. Indeed the other girls in the group regularly said that she was mad about animals but Eve was quite keen to distance herself from this aspect of her identity, which she felt she had grown out of.

Eve's photos also suggest her tendency to collect, so we have sets of books including those collected from cereal packet offers and noticeably here Eve has complete sets. Eve also chose to present books and DVDs together, for example the *Horrid Henry* (Unwin, 2006) series. Both Eve and Matilda showed figures of film characters in their photos and there is evidence of the process of positioning them for each shot, encouraging them to be playful and to pose.

Eve's collections were extensive and demonstrate why she was such an important resource to others in her friendship group. Popular culture, including children's films, clearly provides resources for playful performance of identity. In the social contexts of school (in the playground), knowledge of popular culture texts also acts as cultural capital, enabling participation in talk and play. As can be seen in Eve's case, (but also Liam and Connor's) her changing popular culture collections reflected her deliberate shifts in identity towards what she saw as more grown-up choices.

It is important to note that Eve, like Liam and Connor, having watched so many children's films, was also keen to watch films she had not encountered before and in her case these are films her mum signalled as those which she might like because she was older and more mature than her sister. These are films such as *It's a Wonderful Life* (Capra, 1946) and *Miracle on 34th Street* (Seaton, 1947) which she described as favourites, although she does not talk about them during the group research process. Much later when the group watched a clip from *Great Expectations* (Lean, 1946) it was interesting to see Eve's enjoyment of the film and her greater preparedness to engage with an older, black and white style of film-making.

Aaron

Aaron was well-liked at school and was able to access the school curriculum more successfully than the other two boys in the research group, who often said he was the best at writing and asked him to write down anything related to their film. Aaron was considered by his teacher to be of average ability in relation to literacy and it was clear that writing in particular was not a favourite activity. Aaron and Connor were very good friends. Although I did not know this at the point of selection, it was highly useful to see how their interest in film and involvement in the research was heightened by being able to work with each other as trusted friends (this was also true of the girls). Aaron shared Connor's interest in street dance and had begun to take classes out of school. He was also influenced by Connor's taste in film. Connor often got the DVD first and then Aaron might, if he thought it sounded like his sort of film, watch it himself. This led them to have conversations about films outside the more universal texts of the group so they both independently refer to the film *Ghost Rider* (Johnson, 2007). However, where Connor's experience of film-watching is almost entirely individual, for Aaron it is most often a shared experience.

Aaron watched films as part of his relationship with his dad and brother at weekends:

> I always go to the cinema with my dad to watch movies and I've seen at least seventy or something like that because I go to that Cineworld one and I get these passes and I see as much movies as I can.

He was conscious that he had watched a lot of films but often he could not name one in particular that he really liked from recent viewings. Going to the cinema had become much less of a special occasion than it was for all the other children in the group and was almost casual:

> We don't buy all the food – all we do is just get the cinema tickets and just watch things.

This is also the case with watching at home, which was almost a daily activity like a bedtime story:

> Every night well nearly every night before we go to bed we have, we watch a movie and then we go to sleep.

Aaron also talked about 'culling' his collection occasionally so that he no longer had films that he had watched so many times they had become boring. He didn't have the same degree of complexity to his selection process as Connor and it appears that there are certain films he would repeatedly watch because they are favourites:

> *Spiderman 1, 2* and *3*. They're good cos you do not know what is next and I get into it still now.

Aaron described a number of times when he felt scared watching films but said that he watched them because he wanted to know what would happen next. He showed me how he covered his eyes with his fingers but peeped out at the screen. He also told me about his younger brother's taste for horror films, which he did not share and a time when his mum tapped on the window when he was watching the film, *Scream* (Craven, 1996) with his brother. As Aaron retells the story, he recalls the combination of fear, excitement and humour, but he is firm in his dislike of horror films. His enjoyment of action films was quite different:

A: They're exciting, and they've got, I like to erm see them all shouting – [laughs and looks to see if I approve] they're funny.
B: So you like all the shouting and the what else, go on ...?
A: The chu chu [gestures and makes sound as if using a machine gun] them shooting each other .... I sometimes laugh because when they're shooting each other and they die and it's funny ...
B: It's actually quite funny ...?
A: It's like, if there's an army tank, they'll blow a missile and people sort of jump backflips over things [shows how the people spiral in the air].

Throughout this dialogue, which took place early in the research process, Aaron checked my reactions, only admitting his humour at the spiralling bodies when he was sure I would not be offended. He clearly recognised that some people do not like or approve of violence in films. Interestingly, Aaron enjoyed action violence and at a great distance, in a certain context he could find it funny, whereas, in another genre (horror) he found violence frightening. Clearly, he deploys different readings of texts, depending on their modality in a similar way to the children Robinson (1997) observed. However, this reading strategy is inflected by his preferences for one genre over another. Robinson (1997) argues for the use of familiar texts in developing children's reading, highlighting the important ways in which children's tastes influence their reading. Since genres such as action films, do not have easy equivalence in the classroom, it would therefore be difficult for Aaron to draw on these familiar, preferred texts.

  Other than his dislike of horror, Aaron enjoyed many of the same films as his brother because they are very close in age. He described the least conflict with his sibling by comparison with Abbey and Eve, for example. He marked himself as someone who liked action films, but was just as keen to define himself by what he did not like, horror. Like Eve then he sees himself as someone with tastes in common and distinct from his siblings and peers. Aaron's friendship with Connor often involved the swapping and sharing of films, although for the most part this was Connor suggesting titles to Aaron. One of the films they both watched around the time of the first interview was *Ghost Rider*, a vigilante/biker storyline with a 12a cinema certificate but a 15 DVD rating. The film had an impact on Aaron that it didn't have on Connor. He told me:

> He's like quite nasty because – like if they've done something wrong he don't send to jail – he kills them.

Here he was talking about the hero or anti-hero of the story and clearly this is a first encounter with a text that moves beyond the expected conventions of films for children. In films for children goodies send people to jail, they rarely kill them and, if they do, it is following much provocation and is a central moral dilemma the main character has to solve. Perhaps this film was Aaron's first encounter with an anti-hero, a flawed character who none-the-less we are asked to side with. Although usually he enjoyed high octane action sequences with big body counts, Aaron was less confident with this film because he could distinguish between the comic book style, superhero-action-film-death, to prevent the baddie destroying the world, and death that is given out as a punishment by the main protagonist. The moral distinction made him uneasy with the film. Connor, however, had encountered far more films where the narrative tension is built on a more complex notion of morality than the polarised good and bad of many children's films; the shades of grey in more ambiguous texts. Children's film narrative shape children's expectations of characters and events in stories and, in certain contexts, when they encounter these rules being broken for the first time, texts provoke strong reactions.

Like the other boys, when Aaron played *Spiderman* he wanted to be the main character and he positioned himself as a fan:

> I'm a big fan of *Spiderman* so I used to play that.

However, like Liam, he did not always get to be the main character and for this reason he had to be resourceful. He described a character he made up when playing *Star Wars* called Yoshi who is small like Yoda but has 'better moves'. During the interview I read this as part of the game negotiation because more than one person wanted to be Yoda. Indeed, who you get to be in a group-game that relates to films, appeared to be an interesting indicator of social status. However, I also found many instances where the children adapted the characters from films so that they could fulfil their own pleasures and fantasies in the play. These character changes were highly connected to identity and this was intricately connected to their own film enthusiasms. So Aaron here chose to play *Star Wars* and opted to be Yoshi because he liked to play this sort of character. He adds to the character, giving him better fighting moves so that although he is a funny character, he is now also able to take part in important and serious battles. Creating these changes was also a way for Aaron to display his expertise in the world of *Star Wars*. He made a character that he was confident could exist in the fictional world and be taken seriously by other children playing the game.

Matilda

Matilda was very keen to be part of the project and approached me after the first workshop to tell me about the *Harry Potter* corner she had at home. As can be seen in the photograph, her corner was displayed carefully, with images of the actor Daniel Radcliffe in role as Harry Potter. The images she had chosen were in the style of some of the more sophisticated graphic design for the films with creams and golds and ancient looking calligraphy rather than the more child-like black and purple designs featured on some of the Warner Bros. branding for the films.

Matilda had also chosen to separate these posters and photographs from any of the other material in her room. This contrasts with Eve's poster wall that was, although very neat and carefully spaced, a mixture of all her different interests (Figure 6.1).

Figure 6.1 Eve's bedroom wall

Her display was an opportunity to signal to friends and family that she had what she saw as a special bond with the film and the characters. She describes her strong emotional link to (plot spoiler) Harry's loss of his godfather in book 5. She listed her favourite characters as Harry, 'obviously', then Ron because he's funny and then Hermione. She took some time to justify why she did not like Hermione first, as if I would expect her to like the main female character. Matilda put Hermione third because Hermione is bossy, even though Matilda went on to acknowledge that Hermione is smart. Interestingly, Abbey also said she took the role of Voldemort's sister rather than play at being Hermione. Furthermore, in her discussion of *Ben 10* (Rouleau et al., 2005–Current) although she said she agreed to take the character of Gwen with her brother and cousins she actually thought Gwen was rather sensible; a 'tell off girl' who was not someone she would like to be. In this description Matilda astutely observes a character type often used in films and programmes with a male lead who needs to be kept in check. In both *Ben 10* and *Harry Potter* Matilda did not find the female characters she would like to be when playing games.

Matilda was an enthusiastic film and television viewer and had watched all the recent children's film releases such as *Ice Age* (Wedge, 2002) and *Shrek* (Adamson and Jensen, 2001). She also asked me if I could recommend some adventure films she could watch and she watched a variety of films I bought in for her throughout the project, returning them and feeding back her thoughts about them. In all the research activities Matilda displayed a high degree of independence from the rest of the group and from her peers. By which I mean she chose what she wanted to contribute because it interested her rather than because it was what her friends were doing. At one point when the group had decided to make what they described as realistic films, she explained how she would go along with them but that really she would have preferred some element of fantasy, 'Fantasy is my middle name', she declared. This is also revealed in her enjoyment of the fantasy elements of the *Harry Potter* books and films:

> There's magic about it so there's stuff that's not true like a griffin and unicorns and magic and a three-headed dog.

Like Connor, Matilda openly displayed her enthusiasm for films in her interview, for example, she laughed, inviting me to participate, while explaining how funny it is that Hagrid called a three-headed dog Fluffy:

> He called the dog Fluffy. He's a three-headed dog and he called it Fluffy!

Matilda loves art and described herself as having lots of imagination and throughout the research she drew pictures, diagrams and graphics extensively to express her ideas and sometimes just to create new characters for fun. For example, she drew a diagram showing that her friends like her because she is funny and she likes drawing. She enjoyed talking about some of the imaginative games she plays both on her own, and with others. The games she plays on her own are intricate and sophisticated and based on her own invented animated characters. They take place during car journeys, for example, but are highly distinctive stories/games that link to her interest in animals. Matilda asked me not to explain the full story to the rest of the group, she said, 'but don't tell anyone' and this echoed a point Connor made about still playing with his *Toy Story* toys. Both children had strong pleasure in playing imaginative games but were aware that not all of their peers shared this pleasure and that some said that they have 'grown out' of this sort of playing.

Matilda is the eldest of four children and also had very close links with her two cousins so is always surrounded by other children. She was very keen to emphasise that her dad is Australian and she was interested in Australian culture. Mum helped her decide which films to watch and had allowed her to watch an over 12 film *Harry Potter* which she told me about as if it was of great significance that the rules had been negotiated so that she, was allowed to watch a particular favourite.

In her photos she, like Abbey, highlighted the toys and objects of her younger siblings. She carefully photographed their school bags that depict a wide range of contemporary films, DVDs as well as of books. Another photo shows Matilda doing her homework with a branded drinking bottle nearby taken by her younger brother. There are also Nintendo DS games and towards the end of the project Matilda listed playing with her DS as one of three favourite activities with watching television and reading. Two other films that are chosen for display are *Ghostbusters* (Reitman, 1984) and *The Italian Job* (Collinson, 1969) and Matilda was the only one of the group to show films she said were favourites of her parents.

In her first interview Matilda claimed to be a tomboy, explaining that she preferred boy films and programmes. In one picture she also placed a toy Mr Incredible next to a toy Spiderman. Again Matilda is keen to display that she is not a 'girlie' girl and that she enjoys action films and superheroes. Children's films often offer up a particular character for children to bond with, but very often the main character is male. The girls do not choose to be this main boy character but neither do they like the female characters enough to choose to be them. They all reject Hermione in *Harry Potter* , for example. In play all the children adapt and transform characters from favourite films but this has particular implications for the girls. Matilda resisted and rejected the female roles available to her in film and television texts.

The story of *Ben 10* , who transforms into aliens with special powers, is shown on Cartoon Network and at the time of the fieldwork this was the only one series which Matilda and her brother had watched 'endlessly'. Matilda described her first viewing of the programme when mum was in hospital having her younger sister. She watched it and thought how much her brother would like it. She told me this story to illustrate that she discovered *Ben 10* and shared it with her brother, not the other way around. She also described watching as the boys played *Pokémon* and although she does not say it, there was a hint that she might have liked to join in.

In her talk and play Matilda drew on many ideas from films and television, which she blurred together, and had developed some strong individual tastes for fantasy and for action-orientated stories where the characters might have magical powers or superhero-type qualities. As Matilda talked about the texts she became immersed in them, remembering many details of the stories and recalling her emotional reaction to certain scenes. Like Connor she has a rich repertoire of moving image texts to draw on, and like Abbey and Eve in her play she does not allow herself to be limited by the gender roles offered in the texts she encounters.

Children have home experiences of media and storytelling and these experiences are central to their developing literacy in the early years, (Marsh, 2003, 2004). Film can clearly be seen to contribute to this home experience or what Robinson (1997) describes as developing 'repertoires' of textual experiences which children draw on in their talk, in their play, in their encounters with new texts and their production of new stories. Even the participant in the group who had the least experience of film, Abbey, had recent knowledge of contemporary film releases, had everyday objects and artefacts from contemporary films in every area of the home, played games based on film ideas and had developed a distinct preferences for adventure films, featuring animals. The children's engagements with film clearly impacted on their practice and performance of identity and literacy.

Even in these brief accounts of the children's individual engagements with film it is possible to observe them reading film, actively, socially and culturally and this is further demonstrated when the data is combined.

Film at home

Marsh's (2005) description of the 'narrative web' of artefacts, toys and clothes of one four-year-old child related to *Winnie the Pooh* as offering opportunities to experience a favoured narrative text in different modes was clearly in evidence in the children's lives. Abbey and her siblings display a 'narrative web' of artefacts particularly in relation to *Winnie the Pooh*. Matilda had her *Harry Potter* corner. Connor had every toy from the *Toy Story* films as well as the Buzz Lightyear pyjamas. All the children in the group told of numerous 'narrative webs' linked to different favoured films experienced at different ages and these films, as Marsh (2005) also describes, clearly permeate family life.

These artefacts had also become important to developing family narratives (Pahl, 2002) about identity. Connor tells a story about his captivation with the *Toy Story* films. This is a story that has been told to him and retold by his mum which he acts out for the camera. All the children shared experiences of books, computer games, clothes, bags, bedding, pens and drinks bottles which relate to films they have seen and particularly films which had become favourites. There were objects parents bought as everyday items and there were also toys used to play games related to films such as wands, figures and soft toys bought as presents or treats. These had a special status, enabling the children to play out their favourite films, but also enabling them to signal their affiliation to a particular film. Popular culture artefacts enabled the children to establish relationships, aligning themselves or distancing themselves from others (Mishler, 1999). As these children approached Year 6 (about to move to secondary school) they admitted being embarrassed about still having and playing with these toys, but the toys were clearly still significant items that formed a part of their memory of childhood and were included in their own narratives about themselves as children. These films elicited strong affective responses from the children and contributed to their developing preferences for other similar texts.

The family was also extremely important to the different ways the children in the group engaged with film. For some of them parents were gate-keepers, keen to limit their *film-viewing*, and not particularly enthusiastic film viewers themselves. For others parents acted as advisors offering guidance, enabling the child to make decisions about which films to watch. In the case of Eve this process was taken extremely seriously and her mum in particular had attempted to widen her experience and encourage her to watch older films as well as contemporary choices. Like the parents in Marsh's (2005) account, Eve's mum was positioning herself as an 'expert navigator of popular and media culture' (Marsh, 2005, p. 30). She was also extremely positive about the role of film in relation to Eve's developing literacy, making links between books and films as well as other art forms. In the case of Connor, he had taken on this role for himself, and had developed skill as a curator of his own experiences.

Parents clearly took up different roles in relation to film at different times. So sometimes going to the cinema was a whole family experience; a treat with a sense of occasion. Sometimes the parent was facilitating but not taking part in the viewing experience. Sometimes the children asked to be able to watch a new film and at other times the parents surprised the child with an unknown film as a gift. For Aaron watching films was, for a time, his main weekly time spent with his dad. For Connor, watching films was a predominantly individual activity, although he had strong memories of earlier shared experiences. For Liam, going to the cinema with friends was a signal of increased independence.

Talk about film

In my preparation for my research I contemplated carefully how best to enable children to talk openly about their experiences of film. As discussed in my methodological rationale (Chapter 5), I was convinced that I needed to develop a range of strategies to initiate talk about film. What I found in practice however, was that the children in the group were very easily able to talk about film. They were used to talking about film because talking about film is already an aspect of their social world; their 'interpretive communities' (Fish, 1980). To some degree I was able to re-create an opportunity for them to share some of the ways they talk about film in their own lives. Although the session was a filmed interview, each child's enthusiasm about their own film experiences led to a higher degree of spontaneity than I expected. So there are a number of stories told that have clearly been told before, for example Aaron's Mum tapping at the window during a scary film and Connor's description of watching *Toy Story* are almost performances of stories that they had clearly previously shared.

Each child also retold aspects of favourite films and this triggered memories of the film that they wanted to share. Matilda told me over five times about Fluffy being a three-headed dog and each time she did, she collapsed with laughter. When she retold the joke she found it freshly funny because she was sharing it with someone who had also watched the films and remembers why it is funny. These film memories or stories are clearly also expressions of identity. Through their talk about film children are able to establish who they are according to the sorts of films they like. They are also able to position themselves according to what it is about the film they enjoyed, the particular way they responded or the aspects or characters of the film they most enjoyed. They are able to become opinion leaders who suggest films to others or share their expertise about a particular film or type of film.

Bromley's description of children drawing on films as part of a 'collective memory', engaging in talk about films because the talk is a familiar discourse within which they are able to position themselves (Bromley, 1996, p. 76), was also in evidence here. It was clear that talking about films was something which happened often socially in school and that such talk regularly led to playing out the fictional world of the films. Although Liam points out that if you have not seen a particular film you can't join in with the conversation, Abbey develops strategies to ensure that she is made familiar with the characters and plot and can join in, at least to some extent.

Like Matilda, Liam enjoys the humour in sharing a moment of a film that he and others found very funny. He re-enacts this moment in the interview and several times later in the research he recounts the same scene with the same gestures and other members of his class join him. Again, this experience is similar to that described by a parent of a child with a particular interest in *Thomas the Tank Engine* transcribed in Marsh's research, (Marsh, 2005). In this case the parent supports the developing interest by talking to the child about Thomas and buying related toys and taking the child to see trains, for example. All the children in the research were able to draw on their home experiences of talking about film into school social spheres.

They support each other in their enthusiastic recounting of particular moments of pleasure developing their role in an 'interpretive community' (Fish, 1980) which extends when they get to school.

Children's film also affords children opportunities to play and there was evidence of the children using play about film to explore identities. The *Star Wars* films offered important opportunities for collective play based on key action sequences and drawing on the characters, narratives and the many and various aspects of the fictional world that marked the text out as distinct, fantasy or science fiction. This was an alternative world which the children could enter whether or not they had seen the films. Play was enriched if the children had experienced the films and these children were more able to access the game and more able to be inventive within it. There were clear leaders, those who knew most about the films, experts who could develop spin off games and new characters. However, all of the children could play *Star Wars* with some level of shared knowledge and pleasure.

Dyson (1997) observes that knowledge of superheroes can act as a ticket for participation for some children and that in play some children have higher status and are able to generate who will be each character and what they will have to do. This was the case both for some of the children in this group and also across a range of media texts, *Star Wars* (Lucas, 1977) for example being a key source and role allocation being extremely important. Dyson observes children use play about superheroes as a space for establishing themselves in the social order. She argues that the children affiliate with others or resist others either by distancing themselves from individuals or by negotiation. The children in my research group reported similar moments where they had either always wanted to be one character, Connor always wanted to be Buzz Lightyear from *Toy Story* (Lasseter, 1995) and would not play unless he was Buzz. Aaron and Liam were much more adept at adapting roles less popular with others and investing them with characteristics that made them more interesting for example Wookies and Yoda from the *Star Wars* films.

The children also clearly played games that were influenced by films but did not have one key film as the source. They described fantasy games and army action games and demonstrated that they knew the conventions of these texts. Eve for example knew that the narrative of her game was to save the world. Matilda knew that lizard robots were the bad guys, and Connor understood that many children's films take clear moral stances conveying particular messages. Thus the children recognise films as having cultural boundaries with familiar conventions and schemas they can draw on in their own play and storytelling.

In their play the children also identify flaws in the texts available to them. There are not enough girl characters and those that are available conform to unappealing stereotypes. Hermione is too boring so no one wants to be Hermione. Playing the films enables children to occupy roles that especially appeal to them that they create for themselves, even if those roles are actually absent in the film itself. Therefore the children can be seen to be reading texts actively, not accepting elements of the texts which do not fit with their own preferred identities.

The children as readers of film

By the age of 10 each child had a considerable repertoire of films to draw on, which they had watched on video, television or DVD at home and at the cinema. These were not only new releases but sometimes older films or films outside of their usual experience. Children's film-viewing is far from homogenous and children have developed preferences which they use as markers of identity and to help them read new texts.

The films we like, our memories and experiences of film, contribute to our sense of identity. Children's films in particular enable children to explore identities through play and by signalling to others their belonging to a group who like a particular film. Play based on film does not reflect an indoctrination of particular ideologies (Tobin, 2000) for example, girls do not opt to be the female characters suggested to them in films. Indeed both boys and girls seek to transform the characters they adopt. Sometimes, this is motivated by wanting to play a more interesting role, and sometimes this is a chance to display knowledge of a particular film.

The imaginative spaces offered by film enabled the children to explore fantasy identities (Buckingham and Sefton-Green, 1994) as well as those closer to their own experiences (Robinson, 1997). Children develop affective relationships with particular significant children's films and these films shape children's emerging tastes and preferences for new narrative texts. Children create opportunities to play and participate in children's films and this reading of films is demonstrably active, social and cultural. These experiences of film do not necessarily relate to the children's orientation towards literacy at school. Levy (2009) highlights a dissonance between children's abilities to read on-screen texts and their perception of themselves as readers of print texts in school. Similarly, all of the boys in the group believed they were not very good at writing and expressed a dislike of reading. In the next chapter I will return to this issue in the light of children's own storytelling in written and oral form.

7
Film in Children's Storytelling

> Well mainly people just start with once upon a time but I think that's a bit boring really. It's what you'd use in a fairytale really. I'd start with something like – say it's like in a film – in an actual film it's come up with all t' writing. And then I'd like think – cos in some films it says the film name and then something like, someone could wake up really fast and then say, 'oh we're late' or something like that. And then you think, 'oh what are they late for?' And then that makes it into a mystery.
>
> But I'm not that good at writing. I can think of a story in my head. I can think it through but then I'm quite slow at writing.
>
> (Interview with Connor)

As he speaks Connor starts to look very animated. He's seeing a story. His eyes become bright and focused on the opening credits that he's imagining. His skill as a storyteller is exhibited in the slightly reverent, hushed tone he uses as he describes an opening title sequence. The idea sounds rather like the opening scene of *Four Weddings and a Funeral* (Newell, 1994), a film which he might well have seen. What he is able to read and then articulate explicitly is an important element of narrative. He notices the way film-makers set up a question in the mind of the audience: What are they late for? Connor then quickly changes the subject, labelling himself as not good at writing. What he is also describing is his dissatisfaction at the way in which his ideas, which are ambitious film ideas, fall short in the written form. As an educator this presented me with a dilemma about whether his teachers should accept that Connor's ideas are moving-image based and give him the opportunity to use film to tell stories or whether they should also attempt to enable him to transform his filmic ideas into the written word. This is an issue that is further addressed in subsequent chapters, but it also illustrates the need to avoid making assumptions about what children know about narrative based only on their school-based writing.

Children have both conscious and unconscious theories about how narratives work (Barrs, 2001) and these are derived from books but also from other media such as film and television (Barrs and Cork, 2001; Willett, 2001). As previously argued, when children read stories they draw holistically (Robinson, 1997) on their previous experiences including their experiences of film (Dyson, 1997; Bearne and Wolstencraft, 2006). However, in their creation of stories we know that children draw on their narrative repertoires selectively, navigating issues of what is appropriate and valued at home and at school. For example, we know that in free-writing children often feel more able to draw on popular culture sources in their stories (Willett, 2001) than in other forms of writing. Despite the proliferation of forms (picture books, film, television, comics, games) and activities (play, playground discussion, figure / toy collection and card swapping) through which children encounter story, when they create stories in school they are most often asked to write them. However, in the current context, as Hilton (2001) argues, opportunities for free or individual writing as opposed to shared and guided-writing are limited. As a consequence, and although writing is not my main focus, it became increasingly important for me to understand contemporary practice relating to the teaching of story-writing as experienced by the children in the research group.

In this chapter I therefore include a description of the Year 5 class teacher's practices in relation to teaching literacy, prior to presenting data from four distinct activities. My analysis of these activities explores the premise that children's engagements with film contribute to their knowledge and understanding of narrative. Data from each activity demonstrate the different ways children draw on their narrative repertoires, including their experience of children's films, when creating their own stories. I focus on the children's understanding of narrative as expressed firstly in interviews, secondly in written form in the classroom, thirdly in a free-writing task and fourthly in an oral storytelling game. This will enable comparisons between the ways in which children draw on their narrative repertoires in written and oral forms (the subject of this chapter) and film form, (which is the subject of the next chapter).

In the context of looking at children's oral and written storytelling, it has been important not to focus on the role of one medium in isolation, and to consider popular children's film as one part of the children's wider repertoire of experiences of narrative texts. I have attempted to describe the provenance of a particular idea about narrative, only when appropriate to do so, that is to say the influence of a film, book or game was evident and confirmed in discussions by the child. My analysis has focused on the children's intuitive and learnt theories about the universal elements of narrative, including character, setting, plot and structure, but also aspects of narrative they draw on which are specific to children's films. I attempt to explore the way in which each activity created a distinct space in which children were able to differently draw on popular culture and children's film to express their ideas about narrative.

Storytelling in the classroom: shared writing

An awareness of the ways in which a class teacher put into practice national policy and strategy in relation to teaching literacy makes it possible to understand the children's particular attempts to draw on their own experiences of narrative in their school-based literacy work. A highly committed and enthusiastic teacher, who had created a vibrant and positive space for learning, taught the Year 5 class. One classroom display included a photo of every member of the class smiling. Another included models and images the children had created of planets and the solar system. This imaginative teacher often used her musical ability to move from one activity to the next, so the children would pack up quickly in order to join in a song accompanied by the guitar. Although she was comparatively young the class teacher was self-confident and assured. She had recently attended a number of courses relating to the teaching of writing, although literacy was not her main area of expertise.

Millard (2006) refers to the way that teachers self-regulate their popular culture preferences, drawing instead on school and curriculum discourses of what constitutes good stories and writing. Having been invited to observe oral and written literacy lessons I also observed occasions where the Year 5 children behaved in a self-regulatory fashion; acting as if what they had thought of would not be approved of. Given that their teacher was certainly not negative about film and popular culture, and had embraced the opportunity to be involved in the research, this was difficult to understand. On further scrutiny it was clear that film was used in two ways in the classroom; film adaptations of literary texts were sometimes shown, although these were often educational films, for example of Greek myths, rather than popular children's films. Additionally, popular films were screened, as described by Goodwyn (2004), as an end of term treat.

Despite her own evident interest and pleasure in film and popular culture, it appeared that the teacher's adherence to a prescribed curriculum and pedagogy restricted her opportunities to engage in what the children's interests in popular culture were (Millard, 2006). The school was under scrutiny regarding literacy attainment and had introduced various schemes and interventions to improve standards of writing particularly.

The national drive to raise attainment in literacy in the UK has led to a plethora of resources being made available to teachers which purport to improve children's writing. A practice that has gained remarkable popularity in primary schools, particularly for Year 5 and 6 teaching, is based on

Wilson's (2002) 'Big Writing' approach. This approach takes a critical view of the way children are assessed in their writing in broad levels and suggests a wide range of interventions to improve writing. Although the scheme proposes activities such as visual stimulus for writing, the two elements that have gained most ground in terms of popularity are the use of V.C.O.P. [see below] and the writing pyramid. V.C.O.P. was in evidence at the research school in the form of boards displaying wow words (vocabulary), examples of ways to join sentence clauses (connectives), examples of ways to start sentences (openers) and examples of interesting uses of punctuation (punctuation). These are also to be found on a pyramid which maps examples against attainment grades. The pyramid explicitly shows children that if they want to get a high level they must use particular examples of each of these elements.

Wilson (2002) recommends these strategies as just one aspect of a wider programme of work to improve writing. Her resources and training for teachers are intricately linked to the curriculum and designated levels of attainment for writing. Although she takes a critical approach to the current curriculum, Wilson clearly views children as having a deficit in terms of reading and language which needs to be addressed. Other forms of cultural knowledge and experiences are not valued:

> We have long believed that if children read well, they will write well, but that is not true for everyone, because around 60 per cent of the population will never read widely enough or regularly enough to absorb more challenging language and we can only write with the language we have in our brain. (Wilson, 2007)

What is more, V.C.O.P., endorsed by and downloadable from the Times Educational Supplement, is used in schools independent of the overall approach to writing advocated by Wilson and as such is problematic. This is perhaps best demonstrated by the post below from a teacher:

> The Ros Wilson scheme, or VCOP as it's known in my school, is a powerful tool for improving teaching and learning in writing across a whole school in a matter of weeks. Ask any child for a checklist of ways they can make their own work better in my institution, and they chant, VCOP! It really is worth checking out if, like us, one of your SIP focuses is writing. (Foldes, 2007)

Apart from the way in which this scheme is perceived to be a quick fix, what is of concern here is the way the children are given lists of things to remember, to chant. As Hilton (2001) points out when aspects of writing are taught isolated from social context, they may not have the desired effect on children's writing. For example, just because a child learns the connective 'in addition' does not necessarily mean they know how or when to use it appropriately. There is not time to enter into a more detailed critique of the way in which Wilson's work has permeated school practice, however it is significant that the children in the research group were quick to chant their knowledge of V.C.O.P. and this was in response to questions about what makes a good story.

Drawing on current primary teaching practices the teacher also consistently gave the children a W.A.L.T. (We are learning to) for each written task, for example:

Write the beginning of a Greek myth.
Retell a story.
Plan a story using a story map.
Write the beginning of a story.
Draw a story map retelling a story.
Start a traditional fairy story in three different ways.

Although all of these activities are potentially useful opportunities for children to develop as writers, they often include additional constraints in relation to the stimulus texts. The style, genre, plot and storyline are often taken directly from the text the teacher has used as a model. Barrs (2001) makes a highly important distinction between a simplistic concept of modelling where children are asked to retell a story they have just heard and the more complex, tacit, longer term, individual process by which children absorb ideas about story and then deploy them in their own creative work:

> Pedagogical approaches which present children with direct 'models' for their stories or which encourage children to base stories on ones that have just been read, depend upon crude theories of how reading influences writing. (Barrs, 2001, p. 32)

These direct 'models' of writing are also models of literary writing, making it problematic for the teacher to include and value children's experiences based on popular culture. As Bearne and Wolstencraft (2006) argue this is problematic for children for whom film or television is their central source of knowledge in relation to narrative. In one particular classroom observation of a directly-modelled writing task I found a distinct absence of popular culture and examples of the children self-regulating the influences they were drawing on.

The first lesson I observed of the Year 5 class from which my research group was drawn was a guided-writing session. The children were asked to look at a close-up photograph of a wolf, displayed on the interactive whiteboard, with a snowy wilderness in the background. As a whole class they were then asked to come up with adjectives to describe the wolf. Their teacher then began to give a structure to their ideas by considering the senses. Many of the children contributed adjectives and what they described as 'wow words' – words that were out of the ordinary and exciting. Ideas were written and re-drafted by the teacher until a description had become a poem. The children were then asked to write their own poem about the wolf.

As I interacted with different children about their work I was looking for examples of the children drawing on popular culture. The most explicit example of this was a girl who had chosen a name for her wolf, which was also the name of a character in the popular superhero film *X-Men* (Singer, 2000). As she wrote her ideas she became aware of my interest and elicited a conversation.

J: I chose that name. [Smiles] I watch too much television I do.

Although she had used Wolverine in the title, her poem was not obviously influenced by popular culture in any other way, but she opted to scribble out the name and try to come up with a new one. I protested that I thought the name was a good opening to her poem, but as an adult in the room, my act of looking at a child's work was enough to prompt her to self-censor. In this activity there was limited evidence of the children drawing on their ideas about wolves from popular culture or fairy stories, despite them having no direct experience of a wolf to draw on. Nor did the teacher elicit ideas from popular culture texts despite the children's subsequent recollection of a class cinema visit to see a film about wolves *Eight Below* (Marshall, 2006). The ideas that came to the fore were about the wolf as a predator in the natural world, which was the same idea as that in the guided-writing poem created with the teacher. Although as an individual activity this appeared to be a perfectly reasonable and appropriate creative writing task, it is possible to argue that the effect of the daily practice of modelled writing might overly shape the boundaries of the children's ideas. As Hilton (2001) argues, shared writing limits children's opportunities to draw on their own ideas and experiences and to explore personal voice, tastes and preferences. During the full fieldwork period the tasks the children were given did not include a free-writing activity, leading to my decision to ask the teacher to include one. Furthermore, the children had to complete these highly boundaried tasks while also recollecting the principals of Big Writing and V.C.O.P.

The array of structures and strategies designed to enable and enhance children's writing gives them a complex set of success criteria to remember during the writing process, shifting the focus away from storytelling, and focusing strongly onto the written form. Willett (2001) demonstrates that children negotiate school discourses of what makes a good story and sometimes deploy them to justify their uses of popular culture. However, if as Barrs (2001) points out children develop theories of narrative based on their previous experiences of texts in a wide range of media, then excluding aspects of their experiences from school storytelling activity, albeit indirectly, limits their ability to participate and progress. To address my research question: 'What do children understand about narrative based on their experiences of children's films?' it was therefore critical to find ways of including and valuing the children's repertoires of narrative across media. Individual, informal interviews provided the children with the first context for sharing their experiences.

Explicit/Taught: theories of narrative

In the interviews I asked the children what they thought were the ingredients of a good story. In an interview, it is extremely difficult to fully explore what children know about narrative. Indeed, I had already decided it would be much more productive to look at examples of storytelling in different forms to gain an understanding of children's narrative repertoires. However, when I asked the children what they thought made a good story it was interesting to observe the process of negotiation of school discourses and personal preferences they undertook. The children initially referred to individual preferences, such as action, excitement, make-believe and surprise, and many of their responses relate to plot. In his interview Connor answered the question about what makes a good story with an explicit link to audience, stating that the story you like depends on the sort of person you are. Connor did not position himself in terms of his own pleasures but recognised that different people seek different pleasures in texts.

Connor suggested starting a film story with the question, 'Oh we are late?' and then anticipated how the audience might begin to ask 'What are they late for?' creating a mystery. He has an understanding from his experience of film that stories must suggest questions to the audience and build expectation. The notion of the storyteller's power to include or withhold aspects of the story became a preoccupation for Connor throughout the research process. Aaron distinguished between not knowing what is going to happen next and 'everyone being excited to know what's going to happen next'. Matilda, clearly in role as both a reader and a storyteller, describes how she likes 'stuff that comes out of nowhere, like a monster comes out of an alley'. Thus, in their consideration of pleasure in stories the children appeared to be focused on plot and were able to articulate understanding of the way a storyteller might hold back information in order to surprise the reader.

When I asked the children to talk about what they had been taught makes a good story in school they were, just as Willett's (2001) class were, quick to articulate school discourses about successful written stories. The children used vocabulary and ideas from contemporary curriculum documents about teaching writing and, as described above, particularly from the Big Writing program. So Eve described being given 'success criteria' since she was in Year 4. They referred to punctuation, wow words, rainbow writing, ('if you use good words, you can't use them twice') speech, exclamation marks, connectives and power openers. All of these they attributed as ideas they had learnt at school to help them write a good story. The children perceived checking their writing against the V.C.O.P. pyramid, as key to gaining higher levels in their writing, although they were not equally motivated to do so. As Matilda commented in her interview, 'All around the classroom there's stuff that you can start off with'. Here she was referring to power openers which were made visible on boards in the classroom. Thus, the children had clearly developed a strong set of explicit ideas about storytelling in the written form which related to the use of language, grammar and punctuation rather than focusing on the content of their stories. In the same interviews the children reiterated the ideas they had been taught, but also used the opportunity to reflect on stories they liked and by doing so opened up questions about the narrative orthodoxies they had encountered at school.

Characters and settings

It was clear the children thought that coming up with characters was an important part of storytelling. Aaron and Liam discussed selecting characters as the first stage in their story-writing and said that devising characters helped them to generate their ideas for a storyline. Abbey said that it was better to stick to a small number of characters to avoid confusion. In the interviews the children were drawing on their previous experience of narratives in different media to demonstrate the range of characters they had previously encountered, including Spiderman (Raimi, 2002), Fluffy the dog from *Harry Potter*, (Columbus, 2002) Dr Who (Davies, 2005) and Woody and Buzz from the *Toy Story* (Lasseter, 1995) series of films. As demonstrated in the previous chapter they each expressed preferences for particular characters or types of characters and referred to games in which they played these characters. They all also referred to many generic fictional characters largely from fairy stories such as witches, princesses, fairies and dragons but also from more everyday stories such as a teacher or a little girl. These ideas appear to be based on schemas learnt from diverse children's narratives and clearly distinctions were being made about roles such as goodies and baddies. There was a marked difference between the many and various characters they referred to from children's films and other media and the school-orientated idea of a small number of characters.

Similarly, Abbey, Liam and Aaron all referred to settings in their interviews and said that 'you have to have an interesting setting'. They found it more difficult to say what an interesting setting might be. Abbey talked about simple settings, like the park, which 'can be good' again referring to a school-based convention. By contrast Liam talked about scenes or places where things can happen. I asked him to say more and initially he answered 'places people can go and be at times' and when asked about what happens in these places he answered 'action, fighting, magic and things'. Liam was attuned to the link between types of settings and different forms of action, and he was clearly drawing on the *Harry Potter* films to help him answer the questions. Again, the simple settings preferred in school stories contrast with the many fantastic, magical, dangerous and eventful settings of the wizarding world.

Plot and structure

It is clear that the structure of stories has been given high priority in the children's school-based learning about stories. They expressed a range of ideas they have learnt in school about story structure. Aaron described a teacher's use of the analogy 'a sandwich story' with a beginning, middle and end saying: 'Our teacher tells us which order to put our story in'. This is demonstrated in a number of tasks in school where the children are asked to write the beginning of a story or the end or several different endings or openings of a story. They also reflect on the function of each stage as Aaron describes: the beginning introduces characters, setting and a problem, the middle is 'to tell you what's happening' and then the end brings about resolution.

The children had also been taught an idea about story structure which Eve expressed as: 'There's sort of a problem in the story'. Abbey also stated that she has always been taught that in a story; 'There always has to be a problem'. This approach to narrative which the children are taught explicitly is based on the structuralist theories of Todorov (1968) which proposes a universal structure in which stories begin with an equilibrium, which is then disrupted resulting in a conflict which must be resolved. Reducing this idea to the notion of a problem to be solved is intended to help children order their ideas and give their story narrative tension. However, some of the children were not entirely satisfied by this theory. Abbey had clearly been contemplating this idea independently and had decided that there was not always a problem for example, that 'toddler's books might not really have a problem' and might just be about a day out to the fun fair. Although the theory in its barest form 'a problem to be solved' was questioned, perhaps this was because it had been oversimplified. However, there was evidence that the children regularly tested out this theory, looking out for the main character and what their problem would be in films and books as well as devising characters with problems in their own stories. Thus, although the children clearly recognised that stories have rules and conventions and patterns and structures they did not necessarily assume that these rules were unbreakable.

The children also described being asked to represent the structure of stories visually. In their use of story maps for example, all the children drew the events or actions of a story about an old man and a talking papaya, as if it was a winding path. They each recorded the same events, using arrows to denote the journey the old man took.

Figure 7.1   Connor's story map

In Figure 7.1 Connor's map indicates key points of the story as a linear journey. In this way, the children were encouraged to make their implicit understandings of narrative structure explicit. Furthermore, in the interviews, they could all refer to other moments in their schooling when they had examined the rules of narrative structure as a coherent series of events and were encouraged to use this knowledge to help them shape their stories. Matilda however, pointed out, that there are alternatives to a linear structure. She commented 'you don't have to put it in that order' and described an example of a nonlinear structure from a book she had enjoyed which used flashback. It is significant that the children drew on recent experiences of narrative texts to challenge the conventions they had been taught.

Aaron gave an example of a story he had recently written about being late for the school and having to give an excuse. He described a possible ending as 'and then the Headmaster might say, "I believe you"'. Here, Aaron shows his understanding of story resolution which incorporates the main characters being restored to favour, having been in trouble. Eve, in the same clip, retold her story of a child who explains to everyone at school that they had travelled through time and met a dinosaur and that was why they were late. When nobody believed the child she took the dinosaur into school and the dinosaur scared the head teacher to death. Aaron's story could be seen as more conventional, fitting with school expectations of what Graves (1994) would describe as appropriate story endings.

Eve's story draws on her love of the supernatural and an emerging interest in subverting audience expectations. Eve laughed at my surprised reaction to the story and enjoyed having upturned the expected, more moderate, outcome. She was also clearly drawing on ideas from children's culture, positioning the adult authority figure as the baddie, who has power over the child, does not listen to them, and does not believe them. The rules she followed here were perhaps less coherent and more transgressive than might be expected in school-based stories. I interpreted Eve's story as another incidence of her attempting to break away from the identity of being 'nice and sensible', giving greater prominence to the more daring of her cultural preferences. Thus, as Willett (2001) describes, children can be resourceful in finding ways to include popular culture preferences in their school-based work.

Both Connor and Matilda introduce discussion of the way in which modern writers and film-makers use fairy story plots but then adapt them and change them. Connor describes how film-makers start with a story like 'The Three Little Pigs' (traditional) and change it and make it better. Matilda talks about using fairy stories but 'changing it'. There is also evidence of the children enjoying the subversion of fairy stories in texts such as *Shrek*, (Adamson and Jenson, 2001) and Roald Dahl's *Revolting Rhymes* (Dahl, 1982). Thus, the children showed their awareness of themselves as readers of intertextual (Kristeva, 1967) stories, recognising this as an approach used by storytellers across media. That is to say, taking a familiar story and playing with it, adapting it and making it work for new or different audiences. In this context familiarity with the texts helps the children to set up audience expectations and then surprise them.

These interviews demonstrate that the children were able to express rich and extensive knowledge of narrative, drawing on many different sources. It was evident that the children had been explicitly taught ideas about narrative, especially to help them with effective writing and to structure their stories, which they were quick to share. Furthermore, their narrative repertoires clearly provided them with resources for storytelling as well as schemas for characters, settings and plots. However, the children did not simply adopt ideas from texts or those they had been taught. They clearly questioned the rules and conventions of narratives in their reflections on encounters with texts which to them did not seem to follow the rules. Connor asked about the moral messages of children's film. Abbey questioned whether all stories for children need a problem. Eve was playful with the resolution of children's stories. Matilda questioned the linear nature of narrative structure.

It should be emphasised that I did not ask questions to elicit these sorts of critical responses. The original purpose of the interviews was to begin to understand the children's individual experiences of children's film, however the interviews became research discussions in which the children shared reflections about narrative. For example, when I asked Matilda why the Roald Dahl version of the 'Red Riding Hood' story was funny she referred back to Fluffy the dog from *Harry Potter* and could articulate that this was because we do not expect Red Riding Hood to have a pistol in her knickers because she is 'nice'. Equally, we do not expect a dog called Fluffy to be ferocious. Matilda made the links between the texts in the context of the interview. The children also recalled being authors of playful texts themselves, upturning audiences' expectations. Having begun to explore the children's repertoires of narrative in the interviews, it was useful to then examine the extent to which they were drawing on these in their school-based written stories.

School-based written storytelling

As previously stated, it became essential to look at the role of children's film in children's storytelling in the context in which they are taught as well as within the research activities. The first substantial writing task the children undertook in Year 5 was to write the beginning of a Greek myth. The children had been reading the myth of Perseus defeating Medusa the gorgon. They watched an animated film version and compared the print and film text. They were then asked to write the beginning of a myth of their own which they would then continue in subsequent lessons. I have reproduced their writing here making minor spelling and punctuation corrections to ensure that the work is equally easy to read. The vocabulary of the stories has not been changed. Each of the children used an introduction to a character to begin their story. Aaron writes:

> When Adjust was born he was very cute. When he was older he looked handsome with brown hair, as brown as chocolate. His skin was as gold as gold with a big smile. People will smile back. He and his mate called Apollo they would ride on horses. Apollo was the king's son. One day the prince got kidnapped by the beast Tinyfig, he was red with two front teeth. And he was ..., tiny! But he was as strong as any man or monster, he was lava-proof. Adjust cried until he said

Connor writes:

> Zenda and the legend of the wind waker
>
> Long, long ago was a boy called Link and he had golden, shiny hair and he was known to be the legend of warriors. The evil gorgon had the power of strength and Link has the power of bravery and the power of wisdom.
> [Loysin] the hands of Zelda. So the journey begins on lagoon island where his grandma lives. His grandma says to go and find his sister.

Abbey writes:

> A long time ago in Greece, a girl called Panthena lived a happy life. Her eyes were like sapphires, and with the golden sun they were like silver. Brave, clever and strong Panthena was a match for anyone and also very kind and beautiful. She loved Prince Pyrah but could not tell him as he

lived too far away. One day she was walking through the market, shopping and talking, when a messenger started yelling the news of a contest.

'The king's son needs to marry! He has decided on a contest! The girl who is brave enough to find, kill and bring back the body of a Chimera will win the prince's hand in marriage!' By the time the messenger had stopped yelling, his horse had nearly flopped on the floor in the heat. Panthena filled a bucket and gave the horse a drink. She loved animals.

The stories are written in the third person and the past tense (although Connor briefly switches to present tense). This would appear to mirror the stimulus story the children were read before commencing writing.

Character and setting

Although the children were clearly paying attention here to the written expression of their story, they were also drawing on a range of resources, including popular culture. Connor's main character is called Link, which is also the name of the main character in popular musical film *Hairspray* (Shankman, 2007) played by Zac Ephron an increasingly popular figure who also stars in the *High School Musical* (Ortega, 2006) films. However, Link is also a heroic character in Nintendo's video game series *The Legend of Zelda* (Miyamoto and Tezuka, 1986). Connor drew on both to invent his own character who was the 'legend of warriors'. Abbey began by establishing a main female character who was beautiful and happy. The market scene she described is similar to the one which appears in Disney's version of *Aladdin* (Clements and Musker, 1992) where Princess Jasmine ventures out of the palace in disguise to experience the world. Jasmine, like Abbey's character, Panthena is brave and clever as well as beautiful. Panthena is also 'a match for anyone'.

Having established main 'goodie' characters the children invented additional characters, continuing to draw on their narrative repertoires. Connor opted for a traditional baddie pitting his warrior against the 'evil gorgon'. Abbey opted for the Chimera, perhaps reflecting her greater experience of texts with mythical creatures in. The characters the children chose steered them into certain trajectories in terms of plot that were to a degree already determined. Link must journey to find his sister and defeat the gorgon. Adjust must defeat Tinyfig to rescue his friend Apollo. Panthena must find a way to win the prince without harming the chimera. Myths, like the folk tales studied by Propp (1968), are populated by characters who occupy a particular function. The children were implicitly aware of the functions their characters should fulfil, even where they adapted the convention in terms of gender, as Abbey did. They also still spent time attempting to invest them with some detail drawn from a wide range of sources.

Clearly the children all draw on existing frames of reference (Goffman, 1974) or schema from familiar texts. However, in the case of Aaron, he pushed the boundaries of the frames of reference of myths in order to incorporate ideas from other experiences of texts. Aaron was able to draw on the traditional characters he had heard about in the introduction to this activity, but his description of Tinyfig is perhaps more reminiscent of a monster from a contemporary animation such as *Pokémon* (Tajiri, 1986). Aaron described Tinyfig as small and red with two front teeth and a super-power – that of being lava-proof. Here, Aaron was making links between monsters in Greek myths and monsters in the Japanese animated programmes he was more familiar with such as *Pokémon*.

Robinson (1997) found in her research that children drew on their closest experiences of texts to understand new ones. In an encounter with a new fairy story, children would draw on previous experience of fairy stories. When approaching a more realist text they drew on experiences of soap operas. Robinson (1997) also argues that children work across media in their interpretations of texts, using similar strategies to respond to both print texts and television. It is useful then to think about how children work across media and genres in their own storytelling. In relation to the myth Abbey, Connor and Aaron all drew on traditional stories to help them with ideas, as these were their closest experiences. The stories they drew on were as likely to be filmed representations as print versions, as can be seen with Abbey's character Panthena's proximity to the character Jasmine. They also looked outside traditional stories to help them with devising particular characters such as Connor's character, Link.

The children were therefore involved in a complex process of character construction in which they imagined the story world, in this case mythical, that the characters lived within. The characters evolved from their experiences of this world, so they introduced princesses, heroes, warriors, gorgons and old wise grandmothers. However, the children also made links across media to help them devise their characters. The children used, transformed or subverted character types in their stories drawn from children's culture including film, games, print fiction, comics and television. Abbey's Panthena, Aaron's Tinyfig and Connor's Link all occupy conventional roles in the plot but have some contemporary ideas incorporated in them. Aaron's monster was a Pokémon type creature who evolved, but he was lava-proof and associated with volcanoes. Abbey's Panthena entirely subverts expectations of the gender role of Princesses and although there are precedents for this in other texts, it is interesting that Abbey includes a link to herself in her character's love of animals. Characters thus became a useful means of making cultural links.

In this context Abbey's writing is highly coherent however, the other children struggle to combine these elements and adhere to the school discourses of good writing. Matilda's mythical story highlights the difficulty in combining contrasting ideas coherently:

> 'Joe, bread and butter's ready', shouted Mrs Jar, Joe's Mum. Joe ran into the hut like house. Mr Jar, Joe's Dad was eating his bread and butter so was Mrs Jar.
>   'So Joe', 'Mr Jar said', 'how are your paper rounds?'
>   'Well after lunch I'm going to get my first payment'.
>   'How much?' Mr Jar said. 'Well you can go and buy us some nice bread and fruit'. 'Yes Dad well! must be off'. Taking 3 slices of bread, he walked off. Joe was a brown haired boy with black glossy eyes. He was kind, handsome, brave, strong, clever but very poor.
>   When he was home the king was there smiling meanly.

Matilda's characters refer to bread and butter and paper rounds situating the story in modern times. The 'hut like house' and arrival of the king situate the story in a slightly more mythical, long ago setting. Although the family seem modern, Joe is a handsome, brave and strong hero and the king is mean. Matilda clearly planned to use a traditional fairy tale plot but was also keen to use modern elements. In their myths the children tried to incorporate modern ideas, even when this produced anachronistic clashes of the modern and the ancient. Many contemporary children's texts play with modern ideas in ancient or imaginary story worlds. The *Shrek* (Adamson and Jenson, 2001) films, for example, include a branch of Star Bucks in the city of Far, Far Away. The children are familiar with post-modern and intertextual story landscapes, however, it is possible to question the extent to which their stories would be considered congruent with school notions of appropriate storytelling. Furthermore, this approach to storytelling is demanding of a writer and requires skilful signalling of authorial intent, a skill that might need to be developed and practised over time.

The task 'write the beginning of a myth' acted as a stimulus to the children who drew on the texts that were closest to myths to help them devise their story. For each of them their previous experiences of narrative texts were different and included children's films as well as other forms of popular media culture. They found it particularly easy to incorporate ideas for characters from films and games in this fictional space and this also impacted on their plot choices. However, they were not all as successful at combining their ideas into a written form that was compatible with school requirements to include descriptive language or complex sentences and punctuation.

Plot

In their mythical stories each child quickly established a happy status quo and then introduced a challenge, in this case in the form of an enemy who causes a disruption or conflict within an otherwise happy scene and who will need to be defeated by the main protagonist. The children understood the function of conflict in a story and the need for resolution. In narrative texts closure is seen as the answering of questions or satisfying of expectations (Porter Abbot, 2002). In stories where there are both kernal (main plots) and satellites (additional events) closure can be partial. There might be the resolution of a particular issue, so the monster might be defeated, but unanswered questions may remain. Children's fiction, both film, print and television, conventionally has a high degree of closure and usually the expectations are satisfied in a morally unambiguous manner. The good guys win; the bad guys lose. The main character is restored to their rightful place. This perhaps relates to adult perceptions of children needing greater security and predictability in stories made for them. In the children's written stories closure was highly visible (even where they had not finished the story), possibly as a result of the explicit notion of a problem that has to be solved at the heart of their understanding of stories. This understanding, again both explicitly taught in school, and implicitly part of the children's experience in relation to children's film strongly influences their storytelling. This raises a question about the extent to which their story would be valued if its ending was elliptical or ambiguous.

Language

All the children drew on visual ideas to establish the main characters, using conventional colour associations. Colour is clearly an important shorthand used to convey meaning. The central characters in these stories are all attractive and associated with being golden. Golden is used here as an unambiguously positive colour, connoting royalty, heroism and goodness. Brown, Aaron's choice of colour, is not so often conventionally used but, as a mixed-race boy, Aaron used it linked to the most unequivocally positive thing he can think of: chocolate. This attention to colour appears to be evidence of the children attempting to produce the descriptive and figurative language they know signals higher attainment. However, although Abbey and Aaron both demonstrate they know what a simile is, the ones they chose are awkward and clichéd. Barrs (2001) argues that the literal approach to writing which requires children to use a simile, is not compatible with a more implicit approach in which children learn to find new ways of expressing ideas, drawing on their previous experiences of stories.

The children's use of language to express the qualities of their characters also reflected influences from their previous experiences of text. Connor used repetition of the phrases 'the power of strength', 'the power of bravery', the 'power of wisdom' and the phrase 'so the journey begins', to build an effective rhythm, drawing on the language and register used to introduce characters in the console games he has experience of. Connor's use of 'He was known to be the legend of warriors' and Abbey's, 'The girl who is brave enough to find, kill and bring back the body of a Chimera will win the prince's hand in marriage!' contrasts with Aaron's more straightforward use of 'When he was older he looked handsome with brown hair'. 'He was known' connotes the fame of the character. Abbey's use of speech also combines a lot of information with the style of a breathless, urgent proclamation. Where Connor is using language he has encountered in games Abbey uses the language of print stories. Aaron seems least comfortable with the language of mythical storytelling preferring to use the word 'mate', to friend for example and 'cute'; both more contemporary, colloquial choices than Abbey and Connor's use of language. In their use of language the children also draw on different sources that they consider appropriate to the task. Abbey's use of literary sources assists her in achieving the highest levels in terms of school-based literacy.

Given that the children are very concerned to use descriptive language it is interesting that they choose to do so in relation to characters. However their language choice in relation to setting is simple and even formulaic. To establish the setting of their myths the children use temporal locators 'A long time ago' and 'Long, long ago' which implies a general other world, other time but little else. We know Aaron's story may involve a scene featuring volcanoes, Abbey's story begins in the market place and Connor's story takes the main character, Link, to Lagoon Island. This perhaps implies that each child has imagined the setting of their story but has not had the space, time or motivation to enrich their descriptions. When children write they are being asked to emulate both the form and the style of print texts:

> To ask children to write is always to ask them to write in a recognisable form … asking children to improve their style means 'borrowing' from other literary texts. (Lensmire, 1994, p. 34)

As a result, when children draw on popular culture they are often moving from one mode to another – from feature film or multiplayer online game to written prose. In doing so, they face a set of challenges. The texts they draw on a scaffold of ideas but not on form or style (although it is interesting that Connor does directly lift some game language). Thus, writing and, in particular, writing tasks which take a form that children may have limited experience of preclude some children's full participation. They are being asked to make big jumps from one media, mode, style or genre to another, and it is possible to argue that teachers need to construct connections so that children can channel their ideas successfully into different contexts.

Free-writing: a tale of two worlds

Although the children said that they first think of the characters in their school-based stories, the nature of the story is often prescribed by the objective set for them by the teacher and this, to some extent, shapes the parameters of children's storytelling. Since I was interested to see what the children would write about given a wider choice, I asked the teacher to include some free-writing tasks. The first of these, included here, was a task to write a short story that could be turned into a film. In setting this task I hoped the children would feel encouraged to draw on their ideas about film freely, enabling me to see aspects of their narrative repertoires previously obscured. On reflection this seems a rather naïve hope, that is to say that in order to fully enable children to draw on their experiences of children's film would have involved a scheme of activity such as the one undertaken by Barrs and Cork (2001) who helped children make connections between literary texts and their own storytelling. However, even in this limited activity it is possible to discern some differences in the children's written stories which are of interest.

Character and setting

In data from this task in particular I found evidence of the way the children made distinctions between the real situations of everyday story-worlds and the fantasy and adventure of imaginary story-worlds. I began to perceive that the characters the children used in each of the research activities could be broadly divided in terms of these two fictional spaces. These story-worlds are found in children's fiction, across media, where sets of rules and conventions determine what might happen in everyday and imaginary narratives. The everyday world features ordinary children in real life situations and does not involve magic or fantasy. These characters include children, their friends, their enemies, their parents, their pets, as well as teachers and head teachers. Sometimes the children directly projected themselves into the fiction they wrote and sometimes they created what might be called semi-autobiographical characters. At other times they used contemporary characters from everyday types of fiction they had encountered before. The imaginary, story-word could be split down into many sub-categories relating to texts types such as folk tales, fairy stories, fantasy, adventure, action and science fiction, however this story-world could involve magical creatures, time-travelling dinosaurs and visiting aliens. The children devised characters in this category including dragons, aliens, and a mysterious old man. Contemporary children's films very often include an imaginary story-world, even when they are set in everyday settings to begin with. Lensmire (1994) argues that children prefer to write fantasy stories so it is interesting that in her story for a film, Eve used an everyday child as a central character who had an annoying cousin and a mediating father:

'Flowers Everywhere'

Jim looked horrified, sweating with fear he stepped into his bedroom. 'Aarhhggg'. His cousin has come to stay.

'Hiya Jim just redecorating our room', said the stranger.
'Miya get out of my room and and what is this? Flowers err'. With frustration he ripped flowers in handfuls, throwing his cousin's things out of his bedroom.

In this story Eve introduced two main characters, cousins, who do not get on well. There are parallels to the *Horrid Henry* (Unwin, 2006) stories except that Eve chose two cousins of different genders, rather than brothers. This allowed Eve to introduce a disruption to the narrative in the arrival of the cousin, Miya, a girl who tries to take over and puts flowers in Jim's room.

Eve established Jim as a main character by beginning the story with his emotional state and although writing in the third person she mainly presents his point of view.

She also introduced dad, a calm character, prepared to meditate between the two cousins rather than the wearied and frustrated parents in *Horrid Henry*. The parent here might resemble Eve's own life experience. Traces of influences on this story from children's fiction are evident but the ideas are not simply imitated, they have been absorbed and transformed and by introducing a gender difference in the initial scenario Eve sets up the possibility of many further storylines. Eve also uses a strong convention of children's films and television drama of a male lead character, rather than female and the female character she chooses to incorporate invades the boy's bedroom with feminine flowers. It is interesting that in her writing of female characters and despite her verbal rejection of 'girlie girl' characters Eve includes one in her own story.

The everyday story-world Eve created generates particular sorts of stories like the *Horrid Henry* stories of being naughty, getting into trouble, and clashes of gender; the imaginary world of fantasy or magic is not expected in these stories. This free-writing environment allowed Eve the space to draw on stories she was extremely familiar with from children's books and television programmes and uses character types and ideas which also helped scaffold storylines. Far from finding the task too open or without structure Eve clearly enjoys drawing on a popular animation and book series. Despite her stated preferences for film and television programmes with magic, supernatural elements and time travel she chose to set her story in an everyday story-world which could be serialised.

By contrast Matilda used the free film-story writing activity as an opportunity to take everyday characters into the imaginary worlds she enjoys and placed herself at the centre of the action:

'Dragon Curse'

Are you sure? Jemima looked around the dark, old cell. Lucie hung onto Jemima, 'let's get out of here …' Lucie's voice echoed in the darkness.
I gulped this wasn't what I'd planned. I saw it – but this cell!' It's too much.

'Let's go back …' Jemima took one step when a blood curdling noise came from above. Lucie looked up, three dragons were flying in the air, (one dragon was green, the other was blue but the last one was red!)

Lucie screamed but as soon as she could the green dragon picked her up and flew off. Jemima was off her feet and carried by the blue dragon and the red dragon was a big softie I could tell! Flew down and nuzzled my hand. I had to do something so I did. I jumped on the red dragon and let the dragon follow the green and blue dragon!

Here Matilda was following a convention of many children's stories in film and print where a group of ordinary children are transported into an imaginary world. In this case these children are Matilda herself and her classmates. In an imaginary world, everyday children can encounter magic (so Matilda can ride on dragons), although they often retain many of their everyday qualities. The rules here are to expect magical characters and events such as talking animals and spells. In her film story Matilda used the dragons she often expressed an enthusiasm for, but she subverts the convention making one of them friendly rather than fierce, rather like Fluffy in 'Harry Potter', an idea she found so amusing. She was clearly trying to give the story tension by making it appear that dragons are to be feared but then showing that they are actually friendly. This technique is used a great deal by Rowling (1997) in the 'Harry Potter' books as was pointed out by Matilda herself. In her story Matilda uses the first person that she has expressed a preference for previously, and there is clearly an enjoyment of projecting herself into a fantasy. This contrasts with her mythical school-based story which she wrote using mainly speech and in the third person.

Everyday or imaginary worlds of stories, adopted by the children, generated rules about the characters which the children applied in their own work. They had internalised a complex set of rules and conventions governing the types of characters and the sorts of plots and setting that the audience might expect of the story world. This knowledge was clearly influenced by a wide range of sources including children's film and television. In her story for a film, Abbey writes:

'Heroes Can Be Big or Small'

Arthur, or ant as we shall call him, was a normal boy, except for one thing — he was only an inch tall.

Now, this strange condition is caused by a disease called Mini-it is which comes from Mars. Ant's dad was an astronaut who had been on a trip to Mars before Ant was born and brought back the disease, which had effected his wife and Ant 18 years later.

Abbey appears to be drawing on an idea that is quite common in children's fiction, that of a small or shrinking character, for example *Stuart Little*

(Minkoff, 1999), *Big* (1988) *Honey I Shrunk the Kids* (Johnstone, 1989). The rules in these stories are that the ordinary everyday world remains the same but just one thing changes or is different. The story interest is generated by the change of size (or one other magical element) and the impact this has on the everyday world. Abbey, who demonstrated the ability to use descriptive language and a coherent storyline in her myth, writes very differently for this activity. Her excitement at being able to write about something potentially for film made her more playful and her story appeared to be far less planned than her other work. She layered one idea onto another rather than knowing the plot beforehand and she did not focus so strongly on the style of her writing. This raises further interesting questions about what happens to children's writing when they make use of film ideas – a question I will return to.

Plots and masterplots

In their free-writing stories the children continued to adhere to the ideas they had learnt about plot and structure. They set up a problem to be solved or a conflict to be resolved and it was clear that they had a plan for how they would continue and complete their story, even when they did not finish writing. Even in serialised stories the need for episodic closure was understood. For example, Eve ends the chapter with the two cousins apologising to each other but there is a hint in the 'mumbled apology' that this was only just the beginning of a series of encounters between the two characters, as if it was the first of a series of chapters. Just as schemas from texts such as fairy stories provided the children with ideas for characters, settings and plots, the conventions of the different story-worlds also helped the children determine the sorts of events that could happen in stories. However, the events were often linked thematically or were concluded to convey a moral message.

When I first met Connor in class, he had quickly absorbed the idea that we would be talking about films and he asked me a question:

Do you think all children's films have messages, Miss?

Like Abbey and Matilda, Connor notices an orthodoxy, in this case in relation to children's films, but he then also questions it. The idea of a film's moral or message was something that came up in group discussions on a number of occasions. The children recognised that children's films often have strong moral messages. Looked at in the light of their free-writing of stories it is possible to infer that the children also linked morals or messages to plot. Porter Abbot (2002) describes stories as following masterplots which are:

stories that we tell over and over in a myriad of forms and that connect vitally with our deepest values, wishes and fears. (Porter Abbot, 2002, p. 42)

His examples include Cinderella (traditional), featuring 'neglect, injustice, rebirth and reward'; a story which is found widely in European and American culture. Porter Abbot (2002) argues that some masterplots are tied to particular cultures, here he takes the 'rags to riches' masterplot as his example of a plot particularly resonant in American culture. In this masterplot the hero is born in poverty and through hard work reverses his fortune. At different times each of the children drew on masterplots. In her myth, for example, Matilda seemed to have a clear story structure in mind and, like the others in the group, she appeared to be drawing on her knowledge of fairy or traditional tales. The main character is poor and has to work to support their family. The king is mean and will perhaps make an unreasonable request. Even though Matilda places modern characters and ideas in an 'old' setting she draws on a master plot, that of uneven wealth, or rags to riches. Liam's written film story follows a highly conventional 'rags to riches' structure despite the modern setting; he writes:

> 'Yours is crap!' said Tim.
> 'It's not', said James.
> 'It is the crappest mobile ever!' shouted Tim.
> 'You go away then', mumbled James. James walked away from Tim and sat on a chair and held his mobile tight.
> The next day James was on his way to school. An old man came up to James and said, 'Give us a look at your mobile'.
> 'Ok but be careful with it', stuttered James. The old man had a good look at it
> and said, 'I will give you £50,000 for it'.
> 'Ok', said James.
> And if you are wondering what James did with the money, he bought a brand new car for his mum and he got a collection of mobiles and Tim was James' butler. And they all lived happily ever after.

As well as the reversal of fortune element there are also traces of the fairy story, Jack and the Beanstalk (traditional). The old man, his identity unknown, resembles the mystery man in Jack and Beanstalk and his offer of money, if more direct than giving magic beans, also fulfils the role of an unknown male who, for reasons never revealed, wants to help James. James, like Jack, lives with his Mum and buying her a new car replaces stealing gold, a harp and a golden egg-laying goose. The changed status of Tim, the boy who criticises James for his mobile, echoes many films where the corrupt, successful baddies who stand in the hero's way are taken down a peg or two. This can be seen most recently in the children's film, *Bedtime Stories* (Shankman, 2008) although there are countless other versions of this storyline. There is also humour in the idea that Tim acting as butler also lives happily ever after in servitude — he does not escape humiliation. Liam is clearly drawing on American cultural masterplots which he sees as resonant of his own experience. He creates a new story but its framework is that of both a traditional fairy story and the reversal of fortune masterplot. There is an absence of merit or hard work, usually a feature of this masterplot in children's films; the reversal of fortune is based on luck. This perhaps indicates to an extent the degree of agency Liam perceived in terms of his own future. The theme and moral of Liam's story links to a masterplot he will have encountered before many times, which acts as a scaffold for his story.

Although children develop a repertoire of experiences of narrative they do not simply copy ideas they have encountered, they transform them according to personal experience and preferences. The existence of schema, story-worlds and masterplots help shape the children's stories, but they do not necessarily help them with the expression of their ideas. Thus, Liam's story includes a power visual image of a boy slumped in a chair clutching his mobile phone 'tight'. However, Liam's choice of language arguably does not do justice to the idea he imagined, although it is (to me) a powerful image. As children undertake free-writing they have to balance their enthusiasm for the ideas they come up with, with a consideration of their use of language, punctuation and grammar. This is especially the case in a context where children are consistently taught to write efficiently in a first draft form, for the purposes of the SATs exam. In their free-writing, ideas and content clearly became more important to the children than language and expression.

Language

In all the children's 'free' stories the characters and settings are sparsely described and remain almost implicit. It could be argued that they rely on what could be termed a visual short-hand or frame of reference. In the case of Liam's film story, he seems to be relying on his audience knowing what a school looks like so feels there is no need to describe a school. Furthermore, although the school is the initial setting of the story he then takes us into a possibly more imaginary story-world but we do not have any information about it other than the two symbolic items mentioned, cars and mobile phones, as signifiers of a change of fortune. Eve similarly simply sets her story in a generic home without giving any further detail. The children assume that the audience would be able to imagine settings.

In Matilda's story the 'dark, old, echoing cell' effectively sets up a number of questions and expectations because we know from the title that dragons are in some way involved in what happens. If Jemima asked her friend 'Are you sure?' in the context of the park or the playground, very different expectations would be invoked. The cell implies possible danger, imprisonment and the need to escape. By adding 'old' Matilda is perhaps implying an uncovered secret or mystery relating to a former inmate. By adding 'dark' and 'darkness' Matilda creates fear and tension; the characters are in the dark, which the audience know is the place where the frightening and the unexpected might happen. By the use of the word 'echoing' Matilda adds a sense of scale and the abandonment of the cell. All of these ideas are evoked effectively but not through detailed description of setting. The words are all concise and familiar, even mundane, they suggest aspects of the story which we can infer because of our previous experiences of story particularly those visually represented. The lack of detail might be because certain words are iconic – highly connotative of the possibilities of the particular story-world. It could perhaps be argued then that the strong schemas in children's stories, such as a dark cell, evoke meaning which the children do not feel the need to embellish.

Connor clearly has sophisticated understandings of how narrative texts work and yet his writing does not always take the reader with him. He assumes the audience have knowledge of the scenario which he has not fully explained in language. He uses master plots and frames of reference as a short-hand. It could be argued that what he misses out are the things the audience would be able to see, hear and infer if watching this story as a film sequence; the stories he can see in his head. Further meaning would be implied by what the audience does not see, the gaps created through continuity editing. This challenge is demonstrated when Connor attempts to write a story of the film he has made in the free-writing task:

'Step to the Challenge'

One day there was a couple of kids speaking to each other on the school yard. One kid called Zak (the big show off and all the others we don't need to discuss anyway). Another kid called Joe (Zak's best friend) was walking up to Zak.

Joe: Hay Zak What's up?
Zak: Have you heard about the talent competition, I'm so going to win.
Joe: Can I enter?
Zak: Yea but it costs £1 to enter
So he entered. The next day the competition started. Joe was first.
Joe: I was ok I got two yeses and one no.
Zak: My turn.
When finished he came out and said,
Zak: Did you see that I was wicked.
Joe: Stop bragging you loser.
The next day Zak was up against Joe in the challenge.
Zak: You may as well just give up Joe.
Joe: What and back down from a loser like you. No way.

This retelling of the story he devised for film relies heavily on dialogue and lacks description. Despite his engagement with the story and the opportunity to make it into a film, the written account leaves out much of richness of the filmed story. Sarland (1991) and Millard (1997) observed differences in the way boys and girls read texts noting girls' greater concern with emotion and causality and the boys' greater interest in action and information. Here the gender differences seem less clear and all of the children focus on action and events with little description in the free-writing. Millard explains this because of the way in which film is edited:

> When pupils, who are already sophisticated consumers of visual narrative, write a story, they often use methods absorbed from these media to convey the action. This gives their writing a filmic quality that may seem jerky and undeveloped in contrast to the writing of those which make use of more literary conventions. (Millard, 1997, p. 124)

In Liam's rags to riches story he also leaves gaps for the audience to fill in. His story is almost entirely plot, with very little descriptive language. Despite this, the elapses in time he uses are typical of the organisation of a unified story with a distinct beginning, middle and end. Abbey, who has most experiences of children's literature and least experience of popular culture, achieves the highest rate of success in the literacy curriculum. Abbey's school-based written stories are more carefully described and her sentences more complex and her ideas more literary. However, even Abbey's free-writing lacks description and is written in simple sentences with a focus on events and including large leaps in chronology, which are reminiscent of film rather than literary texts.

Children move readily between different forms of narrative when reading stories (Robinson, 1997). Writing stories, drawing on different media clearly presents more difficulty. As I have illustrated, when children draw on ideas from films, television programmes and games and transform them into writing their narrative repertoires act as a scaffold for ideas such as characters based on schema or events in story-worlds. These elements do not help them with written expression and indeed because the children share a familiarity with some aspects of children's narratives they use a short-hand that assumes the reader can see what they see as they visually compose their story. Although they clearly do see and hear their stories they do not write them as fully multimodal. For example, in his film of his talent show story Connor took great care choosing appropriate costumes for his character to convey his cool, but show off, characteristics. However, in his written version there is no mention of clothes to imply characteristics, we are just told the character is a show-off. It is therefore possible to argue that children would benefit from opportunities to explore the different and similar ways different types of media tell stories for them to consider carefully when to leave gaps for the audience to fill and when to add detail.

Graves (1994) argues that media-based stories are problematic because of the implausible plots and characters, the reliance on dialogue and lack of description. However, it would be foolish to argue that films (or other popular culture texts) overly rely on dialogue – in fact children's films have comparatively small amounts of dialogue. Nor do children's films intrinsically lack depth or the ability to connote meaning through modes such as colour, lighting, costume, gesture. What Graves (1994) points to are the elements that children focus on when they move from film to the written form. However, since film *is* able to express complex ideas visually, aurally and spatially perhaps what is highlighted is a need to help children draw on these affordances in their writing (something that contemporary children's authors, such as Phillip Pullman, have been doing for some time) that is to say, using the full affordances of film in their writing rather than the surface features that are perhaps easiest to move across to the written form.

It is important to acknowledge that the influence of children's film and other aspects of popular culture enrich children's 'funds of knowledge' (Moll et al., 1992) of the narrative form. Furthermore, that different media offer different experiences which are not equally valued in the classroom. Acknowledging distinct narrative experiences and children's narrative repertoires and recognising their contribution in schools may be the first stage of a longer process of enabling children to draw on these funds in their writing. However, it is also important to recognise that a number of further stages might be involved in enabling children to draw on their rich and extensive narrative repertoires in different forms including writing.

Oral storytelling: a tale of transgression

Oral storytelling was not a strong feature of school-based storytelling, although sometimes the children were asked to retell stories they had just listened to. However, oral storytelling outside the classroom provided a further insight into their engagements with narrative. In the verbal storytelling activity the rules and conventions shaping engagement and behaviour were almost entirely abandoned by the children. I filmed this collaborative activity in which I started a story and the children were asked to verbally complete a new part of a story and then pass it on to the next child. Having observed the distinct roles of everyday and imaginary stories in their writing I drew on these in the story starts I gave them. They dispensed with these story starts especially in the second and third stories and moved straight to introducing specific or generic ideas from popular culture. The number of ideas they had often spiralled out of control and the stories became chaotic and frenetic exchanges of ideas and attempts to out do each other. The children did not stick to the conventions of storytelling that they had described as important to writing and clearly a range of media influenced their ideas, not just in terms of content but also in terms of the form of expression.

Character and setting

In the oral storytelling a wider range of imaginary characters from popular culture emerged including vampires, werewolves, zombies and 'Star Wars' characters. In this context the children were less concerned with rules and more playful so even where everyday characters, such as a doctor, were introduced they were unlikely to 'behave themselves'. The characters also tended to be character types who were more dangerous and action-orientated than those in their school-based writing. The settings were based on similar iconic storyworld elements so that they immediately associated the princess with a castle, for example:

> The other werewolf took princess into this castle thing yeah and then [he pats his leg to pass story on] and that's about it.

Liam did not embellish the castle, indeed he's quick to distance himself from any detail about the castle, but he recognised that the castle is a key place in stories about princesses.

Although Connor took his start from a fairy tale opening, he did not stick to fairy tale storytelling style. To him the cat suggested other possibilities. So he continued 'Once upon a time there was a princess who lived in a magical kingdom with her cat' thus:

Connor: And the cat turned into a big werewolf. And its claws snapped off and then big claws went 'shhhw' [demonstrates growth of claws by cat / wolf with hands]. And it turned into a werewolf and all its, all its. It walked into the shower so its skin went down, er its fur went down again so it wasn't all spiky. And when it came out it went like that [gestures cat/ wolf shaking itself] and went all spiky again and then it went to look for the princess and it found a pea and it ate a pea and it got poisoned [Looks up to finish and passes story on].

As Connor told his part of the story he could clearly see and hear it. His description drew on animations such as *Tom and Jerry* (Hanna and Barbera, 1940) or the more recent 'Itchy and Scratchy Show' which features on *The Simpsons* (Groening, 1987–Current). If we pay close attention to his use of language, it is possible to visualise the cat's benign paws turning suddenly into sharp claws, fur sticking up and then appearing smooth again. It is a convention of animations featuring animal characters to use fur to express a wide range of meanings. The spiking up of fur to make the character look cool, scary or strong is then contrasted with wet or flat fur where the character is made to look silly, reduced to a small, timid version of themselves. Connor paid attention to visual aspects of the story, drawing on animation conventions rather than being concerned with events appropriate to different story worlds. Connor also drew on the Andersen fairy story *The Princess and the Pea* but soon reverted to animation where the rules changed and characters could be flattened, exploded or poisoned, but still live to see another day. The shift from one form of storytelling to another created a fluidity in the role of the characters but also in terms of the action they could take.

The second attempt at verbal storytelling began with an everyday character and both Eve and Aaron initially stuck with this story-world but Abbey introduced a vampire and when Liam continued he introduced a superhero dad and a castle again:

Liam: And then the boy broke out somehow and ran off to his dad and his dad said, 'Don't worry I'll save you'. [Speaks like a superhero]. And then the vampire bit his dad and took the boy's dad to this big, massive castle and then started looking for the boy [passes story on].

This time the castle is described as 'big, massive' but again no detail is provided or perhaps needed. Liam's voice as he says the dialogue is a parody of early superheroes such as Batman. In this context the group suggested characters or settings not in terms of individual qualities or appearance but based on schemas from fairy stories or films to the extent that they were parodying these overly familiar elements.

Plot and structure

When the turn of the story Connor initiated passed to Matilda she was unsure about how to continue because she felt the cat's death ended the story. To her the cat / wolf's death was a permanent closure because she was sticking to the rules of a different story world:

M: It's just that he's told a lot of the story. I don't know what's coming next. It's like the end of the story.

Connor then reflected on the number of events needed to make up a full film:

C: [Interrupts] do you know a film it goes for two hours. You can't just, then the Princess comes back to the wolf and the wolf …

Connor saw no problem with the cat dying and coming back to life. Eventually, Liam intervened by introducing another werewolf to fight with the first one and the story moved away from the animated style that Connor began with. However, distinctions between different story-worlds and different forms of narrative had been blurred; anything could happen and characters appeared in what appeared to be a more random manner.

Game plots

Liam and Aaron both described action as the most important quality of a good story and both shared their enjoyment of guns, weapons and fighting in films and games. This was apparent in their oral storytelling but was not a feature of their school-based written stories. The pleasures in both film and game narratives which feature this sort of action can be seen as an influence on each of the boys' approaches to storytelling:

Aaron: So the King went to the castle to see the witch and the witch were going to turn him to stone when she fired the lasers to turn him to stone. He pulled out red gush and he put it in front of the laser so it blocked it – and it bounces back to turn the witch to stone and he ran back and when he killed the witch things start going wrong. Trees would come to life and things so he had swords on his back and a chainsaw cos he was like a king who does wood, chops and things – he chops wood down – so he's – chainsaw and chops all the trees down and then a monster comes and he pulls out these swords and he's fighting it and the wolf dies but he's badly hurt. He gets home – the princess tries to heal him.

Eve: And then suddenly and then suddenly they, in the princess's castle a troll jumps out and ate the princess. The end [smiles – laughter].

Aaron's detailed account of the protagonist moving from one hazard to the next and needing to find new weapons or a device to assist him in overcoming the opposition feels very much like a game narrative. In games the avatar moves through levels to achieve a final goal and has to defeat many obstacles, gaining tools and tricks to help on the way but also paying the price of any wrong moves by losing life or health. Aaron finished this story with the princess in the role of healer, another common element of games where the avatar needs to return to full health. Eve's ending, by contrast, is concise, if equally violent. Eve was keen to end the story and to move onto a new one, perhaps indicating less enjoyment of the details of the battle, but she also understood how to create humour by defying expectations of her to ensure the story got back on the straight and narrow. Although oral storytelling enabled the children to draw on narrative games structures, they also feature considerable action and often violence which, as Willett (2005b) points out, would not be considered appropriate to school-based stories.

Coherence

Chatman (1989) asserts that 'some principal of coherence must operate' in narrative texts (Chatman, 1989, p. 30). He argues that there must be continuity in identity of the 'existents' of the narrative. So things cannot randomly change or be introduced from one moment to the next. During the oral storytelling activity, rules about character and plot at first appeared to have been abandoned with enthusiasm by the group, with a little reluctance from Matilda. However, it soon became apparent that they were still thinking about the extent to which the story had coherence and could therefore be considered plausible:

Connor: Cos they went from dead and then they turned into vampires [whispers of suggestions] zombies, zombies or vampires, no vampires (cos it won't work with zombies) and then he turned the light switch on and then shone it at him and then he pulled out his mirror to look at his self, cos he took a mirror to his school every day, he shone the mirror and he could see where the light was shining and he shone it at every single vampire there was and they ... [passing on the story].

Connor, as the storyteller, was happy to take the suggestion of zombies rather than vampires as the baddies to be defeated. Connor then realised that the idea he planned to do with light would not fit with zombies so he changed his mind. Then he went ahead with the idea of light but worked out that he needed to introduce a mirror to make the device work. Rather than just allowing his character to find a mirror, Connor suggested that the boy always had a mirror and was known to take it to school every day. In the first case Connor perceived some sort of problem that would mean that zombies were not, according to convention, susceptible to bright lights. This could be described as non-diegetic or intertextual coherence, so the need for coherence comes from outside of the text and lies in what the audience might already know about the nature of zombies. In the second case the coherence is diegetic; Connor was acknowledging that early in the story it would have been good to establish that the boy took a mirror to school so that it was not a surprise later on.

The issue of coherence was again raised by Aaron, who was the principal storyteller, in the final verbal story based on *Star Wars* (Lucas, 2002) characters. This story began as an everyday story but Aaron quickly changed course:

B: Sarah answered the loudly ringing phone, 'oh no' she said.
Eve; She, em her Mum had said. She said 'oh no' because her Mum had been taken to hospital in a serious car crash and she was and she was traumatised when she heard.

Aaron: that Master Yoda was [laughs] taking care of her. [Laughter] He was a small, he was a small green alien with a light sabre what could chop through metal and he was the best doctor there but every patient he operated on died [laughs and passes story on].

Aaron was entirely happy to abandon coherence and take the story in a new direction, furthermore he said entirely contradictory things; Master Yoda is a good doctor but all his patients die. Abbey was happy to take on the *Star Wars* story but was keen to restore some sense of causality:

Abbey: Obviously he wasn't a very good doctor so in the end they decided to put Master Yoda out of his job. [Passes story on].
Liam: So then Master Yoda pulled out his light sabre and chopped up all hospital and [Connor comments] Shut up. Sarah's mum's eye popped out. [Passes story on]

Liam appeared mainly to be concerned here to outdo his peers in terms of how gory and unexpected the events he introduced could be. So the coherence of the story was again abandoned until Connor's final installment:

Connor: Then Obi-Wan Kenobi used sign language. It was a new language that no one had ever heard before and it sounded like this [speaks made up language] and he said it so loud that people in outer space could hear it. Oh well not really people – aliens. The, the aliens came down in a ship like this [produces blu tac space ship-laughter] the dangly bit was just in case it, it ran out of gas – it could stick onto a building and hang on like that and then all the aliens came out and Obi-Wan Kenobi said you need to em you need to help Master Yoda and they all came to Master Yoda and Master Yoda didn't know they were helping them so Master Yoda battled all the.. battled all the aliens and he thought he had won and he walked off to go and kill someone ... one of the humans and one of the aliens come up from behind and jumped on him and then Master Yoda went like that [stabbing motion] and stabbed himself in his stomach and it stabbed the other one and it took it out like that [knife holding action] and the alien fell to the floor.
Aaron: What about Master Yoda?
Matilda: the machine, the machine.
Aaron: It was a hologram. It was a hologram what people could jump on so that's how he did it.

During the course of Connor's narration, Aaron stopped interjecting to make suggestions; he was happy to let his friend take over. However, he listened intently and became increasingly concerned about how Yoda could have stabbed himself in the stomach and not died. He gave this some thought and then suggested a hologram, a device that has been used in *Star Wars* (Lucas, 2002) films before. However, he realised that a hologram would need to have some solidity, not usually a feature of holograms, so he suggested an adaptation. This adaptation might stretch plausibility to the limit, but it is also fair to say that some explanations of events, relationships and technology in the *Star Wars* films require some fairly contrived explanations to regain coherence. What is important is that once Aaron had ownership of story and had established it as a *Star Wars* story he sought the same level of coherence as a *Star Wars* film would have. When the children drew on favoured and significant texts, like Jenkins' (1992) textual poachers they took a high degree of ownership of their own story and used their knowledge of the conventions of that story, avoiding breaking rules which other fans of the text would recognise.

The nature of the oral storytelling task appeared to enable to children to draw on popular culture readily. This led to shifts in form so that live-action and animated children's film characters and settings as well as film and game plots were used as sources. Although this did not satisfy conventional coherence, a coherence in line with the original source texts was constructed. The children paid little attention to audience in terms of carefully explaining their story but the audience, that is to say themselves, and the ephemeral nature of the task did enable them to be playful and transgressive in a similar way to the children in Grace and Tobin's (1998) study of video production.

In school the children had been taught to recognise elements of narrative such as characters, settings and plot. Written storytelling was taught to enable children to improve writing skills in accordance with contemporary curriculum practices, in particular Big Writing. This scheme is predicated on the view that children have a language deficit which can be compensated for using strategies such as V.C.O.P. However, the children's narrative repertoires, accumulated through experiences across media from both in and out of school, equipped them with a rich and complex mix of theories and resources. In analysing their narratives in different forms I became aware that each activity highlighted a small tip of the iceberg of the children's repertoires of narrative. Across the range of activities the children articulated extensive knowledge of narrative, drawing on a wide range of sources including children's books, films, television, cartoons and games.

The children's knowledge and understanding of narrative was not given full expression in their school-based storytelling. Indeed, during the research period I became aware of a dominant staffroom discourse that the children did not have any ideas for stories and that they found it hard to know where to start. On a number of occasions I observed the children sitting, facing blank pages in their books, saying they did not have any ideas. I interpreted this as a reflection of the difficult position the children found themselves in. An approach to writing which favours certain sorts of language, content and structural choices might be problematic for some children. Simple settings, and not too many characters, as occur in everyday stories, are considered appropriate as are stories based on the children's own experiences (Graves, 1983).

> Children who use models provided by popular fiction short-circuit the most valuable aspect of writing process – the opportunity it affords for meaningful self-expression, the chance to explore one's place in the order of things. (Graves, 1983, p. 39)

For some children basing stories on personal experience might be problematic and high risk in the classroom. Moss (1989) suggests that by asking children to write about what they know, teachers are invoking romantic notions of childhood and for some of the children in the research group personal experience may not have been considered appropriate material for school stories. Feeling discouraged from drawing on popular culture sources prevents some children from exploring fully the range of ideas available to them. Children draw on 'what is to hand' in their play and in their story-telling (Kress, 2000) and if what is to hand is not valued in the classroom, it is not surprising that children appear to be stuck for ideas.

In the guided-writing lesson which I observed none of the children drew on popular culture ideas despite having no first-hand experience of the subject. The only child who used a name from a comic strip and film character crossed out her idea, commenting that she 'watched too much television' as an explanation. There were also times when the children regulated their own ideas because they implicitly understood that their experiences of narrative were not compatible with school values. Some UK National Literacy Strategy written tasks also limited the extent to which the children could draw on their knowledge of narrative, for example, a direct retelling of a story did not enable children to adapt and transform ideas to reflect their own identities and preferences. However, opening spaces in which children can draw on popular culture clearly allowed them to become motivated to share their experiences of narrative.

In the interviews the children named a plethora of children's films, which were clearly resources for play and identity formation, but this relationship with film went unacknowledged in school. The focus of the interviews on narrative and children's film enabled the children to draw on their repertoires of narrative and it was clear they were able to explore and question in greater depth what they knew. In so doing they were beginning to make some of their knowledge of narrative explicit. They were also evidently drawing both on taught ideas and those they had encountered in texts and they discussed these holistically, as Robinson (1997) also observed, rather than referring to only one medium.

Giving children time and space to reflect on narratives holistically while drawing on individual experiences, enabled the children to stand outside the individual text and raise questions about the patterns and meanings of stories.

What emerged as important here was not that film (or any other media) was more significant to children but that the children benefited from the opportunity to consider all of their experiences of narrative to develop awareness of the patterns, conventions and constructions of story. If some children are not able to discuss their narrative repertoires, because these are made up of media texts, not literary texts, then those children are excluded from discussion.

School-based writing tasks which placed an emphasis on demonstrating skills, such as use of descriptive vocabulary, for example the mythical story, appeared to limit the extent to which the children could immerse themselves in the story worlds of their texts. However, as Dyson (1997) and Willett (2001) demonstrate, children can be resourceful and determined to include their experiences of popular culture in their own stories. There was evidence here of influences from children's films as well as games and these seemed to suggest themselves to the children, particularly in relation to the characters they devised. Furthermore, where the children did draw on children's films they were not simply copying ideas; they transformed them. In incorporating aspects of children's films and popular culture in their stories, children adapt them to the task and according to their own tastes and preferences. In their written stories the children attempted to produce characters that were a hybrid (Kenner, 2004, 2005); an adaptation or transformation of ideas from their home and school experiences of narrative.

In their free-writing task the children drew much more extensively on children's film as well as other forms of popular culture. They demonstrated sophisticated, implicit understandings of the rules and conventions of the everyday and imaginary story worlds of children's film. Lensmire (1994) argues that children prefer writing fantasy stories because they are pleasurable and they have greater control over them and there was evidence that a distinct fictional world (outside their own immediate context) offered children a safe distance in which to tell stories. The children mostly chose imaginary stories in their free-writing and particularly drew on the schemas offered by children's films in terms of plot and themes. These masterplots provided a structure in which the children could adapt, transform and contemporise story ideas, projecting themselves as characters into their narratives. Far from being overly restrictive then, the familiarity of plots in children's fiction, including those of children's films, can usefully scaffold a structure for children's storytelling.

Although they mainly chose imaginary stories, the fictional worlds they created gave them opportunities to project themselves into the text and 'explore their place in the world' as Hilton (2001) advocates. The children also adhered closely to the child's point of view or invested their lead character with aspects of themselves. Having a child at the centre of the narrative and telling the story from that child's point of view follows a characteristic of children's films, and other children's fiction. The children clearly also favoured telling stories about children, from their own point of view.

In the oral storytelling context the children were much more playful with textual rules and drew far more on their knowledge of film and in particular the visual and auditory elements of film. They showed understandings of setting up and disrupting audience expectations and quickly intervened in a film-based story line when they felt the coherence of the story was threatened. The children's anarchic and transgressive oral stories however, were not compatible with school-based notions of good storytelling and there is a disjuncture between what children know and what they are able to express at school about narrative. This disjuncture relates to the source of their knowledge so that those with knowledge of film, game or television narratives find it harder to make use of that knowledge in a school context. Furthermore, for those children whose experiences of narrative are largely based on visual and auditory popular culture texts, the transference from multimodal form to written form (school stories) presents a challenge. As a consequence, they have gaps in their writing, which are perhaps comparable to the gaps left for the reader to fill in films. So Liam and Connor write stories which are almost entirely plot, with no attention to description. If they are further limited in terms of the sorts of story-writing activities they can undertake then it is easy to see why their self-esteem in relation to writing is impaired.

The final data chapter, Chapter 8, focuses on children's responses to a range of film production activities, exploring how children draw on children's film in this storytelling context. However, given the high status of writing in schools, especially in relation to narrative, I feel it is critical to return to the issue of supporting children to move from one media to another in their production of stories. The relationship between written and moving image production is therefore further explored at the end of Chapter 8.

8
Film in Children's Film Production

Children are resourceful in their attempts to draw on their repertoires of narrative in their storytelling but very often in school this storytelling process is constrained in particular ways by the strong emphasis on writing. Furthermore, current practices relating to the teaching of writing in schools such as direct modelling (Barrs, 2001) can further limit the extent to which children fully express their ideas and understandings, particularly in relation to popular culture (Willett, 2001; Parry, 2010). As Willett (2005b) concludes, looking for children's uses of popular culture in children's writing provides only a partial picture of their narrative repertoires, so it is critical to also look at their production of multimodal narrative texts.

To understand the particular relationship between the children's engagements with children's film and their own storytelling it was important to provide them with appropriate opportunities for film production. The focus of this chapter therefore, is on research activities that brought the children directly into contact with film-making. I include analysis of three film production activities: the first involved the children in the production of a paper animation, the second involved them in creating superheroes in drawn and Plasticine form and the final activity was a live-action short film production. A more detailed explanation and rationale for the inclusion and analysis of these activities is provided in Chapter 5.

I present here my analysis of both the process of production and the children's texts, focusing on their constructions of character, setting, plot and structure and asking the same two questions of the children's responses: what ideas about narrative do the children draw on and what is the particular role of children's film as a part of children's repertoire of narrative experiences. I combine this cultural analysis with attention to the semiotic affordances of the texts the children produced. In particular in the children's live-action film productions I draw on the approach used by Burn and Parker (2003), paying attention to the children's uses of the individual and combined aspects of the kinekonic mode. The social and discursive nature of these activities, especially by comparison to the written tasks, allowed me to reflect on the decisions the children made and the extent to which they were able to draw on their implicit understandings of film in their own productions.

The data below demonstrates experiences of children's film were used as a set of resources for characters, plots, settings and themes which helped the children create their own film narratives. The children also drew on their implicit understandings of the modes and conventions through which films are constructed in their own text production. Furthermore, the children responded distinctly to each of the activities in relation to the form (drawn/Plasticine animation, live-action, short film) but also in terms of the parameters of the task and the anticipated audience for their texts. This data therefore invites further reflection on the way narrative, as an aspect of literacy, is taught in school and how to respond to the needs of children for whom children's film is a highly significant narrative resource, which is the focus of the final section of this chapter.

Paper animation

In the paper animation activity the children drew characters and settings and were asked to film three scenes. Rather than using stop-motion animation, this process resembled puppet-like movement of two-dimensional figures. The children moved the figures and recorded the voices and sounds as they went along rather than editing them. The whole activity was undertaken in one afternoon and involved the children in little pre-planning, relying on the spontaneous ideas they came up with as they engaged with the task. Their response to this activity resembled to a degree how they might play narratives games in the playground.

Character

Spencer's (1988) suggestion that 'given the opportunity' children will draw on all their cultural resources to help them to tell stories was certainly in evidence in the children's responses to the paper animation activity. Just as in the oral storytelling, the characters, suggested by the children, were inventions based on ideas from popular culture including films and there was a plethora of suggestions including:

Pair 1 (Connor and Aaron) a cowboy, a 'Frankenstein' monster, a superhero, a mutant, golfers, a pigeon, and a cloud
Pair 2 (Matilda and Eve) a dream catcher, a girl and a dog
Pair 3 (Abbey and Liam) a bully, a nerd, a lion, and a vampire-hamster.

In drawing on a shared set of ideas from popular culture, including films, the children were able to position themselves in familiar discourses (Bromley,

1996) and schemas (Marsh, 2005). None of the children simply reproduced characters from familiar texts but drew on them as from a generic pool, using them as a resource but adapting them to their own tastes and preferences. Although initially Connor took the lead with both ideas and drawing, Aaron quickly joined in:

> Aaron: You draw ... like a human with bat wings.
> Connor: No you draw a mutant. Cos we'll both have a human and we'll both have a mutant. Yeah?

The social, playful and open-ended approach the children took to the activity also resulted in more playful, hybrid and transgressive characters who were clearly situated in an 'imaginary' story-world. Connor was keen to have a superhero but also wanted to do something both funny and action-orientated. As they worked, they explicitly discussed superhero films, cowboys films and horror films in a way which enabled them to share and extend the expertise they had developed in relation to these genres. They

Figure 8.1   Connor and Aaron: textual poachers

engaged with the rules of the texts they referred to and, like the children Mackey (2002) observed reading and Jenkins' (1992) textual poachers, they also understood how these rules can be provisional and might need adjusting to create new texts.

This pair had the greatest number of ideas in relation to characters and since they were both confident in the medium of drawing they were able to generate pictures of each idea quite quickly. They resisted the school discourse of a small number of characters in this context and tried to amalgamate as many ideas as possible into the five characters they eventually used.

Burn and Parker (2003) refer to the improvised elements of creativity and communication that are part of the messy reality of film-making. Certainly there were elements of the children's drawing which were planned but equally there were drawings which 'just turned out that way'. In creating his first character for example, Aaron was able to tolerate that, even as the co-creator, he did not fully know what was going to happen in his story yet. The Frankenstein head he drew took him in a particular direction. There were some clear influences from horror, a genre he said he did not like, with cross-shaped daggers, bat wings, dripping blood and stitched scars. However, eventually he rejected this character and redesigned it so that it became more closely related to Connor's cowboy character; a hybrid of the cowboy's nemesis the Indian and a superhero who could fly. These characteristics were important to Connor's sense of the emerging story but Aaron retained some elements of horror from his previous draft because he liked how his drawing turned out. Thus, the ideas for the story were part of a process of social negotiation, which included drawing on previous experience of films.

The process of adapting characters was influenced by the improvisatory nature of drawing in this context. However, Kenner (2005) describes children negotiating the different social contexts of home and school by creating cultural textual links through the production of hybrid texts. Although Kenner's work focused on bilingual children, it is clear that a similar process of adaptation and production was taking place here. Given the opportunity to draw on what they knew about children's film in this form the children became motivated, and accessed a rich seam of cultural resources.

As Kenner (2005) goes on to argue, confronted by a monocultural curriculum, without opportunities to make these textual connections, children can become alienated and disengaged.

Connor and Aaron used their drawings like puppets through which they 'played' their ideas for stories, while continuing to negotiate. They redrafted their drawings and developed and adapted their play as new ideas for a storyline emerged. Throughout this time I could regularly hear comments such as:

Connor: And then the cowboy says 'Get out of my home'
Aaron: No then I say ...

These negotiations were evidence of both boys easily stepping in and out of the diegetic world of the story they had invented. Their blurring of themselves and their characters mirrored the way they play, putting themselves into the roles of their characters; something they also described doing in the playground.

Eve and Matilda began with much more benign characters, a 'Dream Catcher' and a girl with a dog. As on other occasions, the girls invested a great deal of effort in their drawings and this was a medium they felt confident in. Matilda's Dream Catcher was a creature that resembled an alien but perhaps also a mythical creature or monster from the *Pokémon* (Tajiri, 1986) genre of animations. The detail on the wings and tail and the tiny stars, fit with the idea that this creature came to children at night and tampered with their dreams. This is an idea Roald Dahl explores in *BFG* (Dahl, 1982) but Matilda decided quite early on that her character would give children bad dreams.

Just as the boys did, Eve and Matilda incorporated sounds and physical gestures in their production of elaborate fight scenes. They argued about what was going to happen next, stepping in and out of the diegetic world, and just as in the written and oral storytelling, Eve, appeared to gain pleasure in enacting roles which took her outside the usual 'nice' persona she played in animal and magic games. Producing or rather 'playing' this text (Mackey, 2002) appeared to offer an opportunity to perform identities outside their conventional childhood identities and outside what would be considered appropriate in school stories. Just as playing popular culture is important to identity exploration in the early years (Marsh, 2005; Pahl, 2006), it is equally important to older children as they begin to construct new versions of themselves.

Due to a lack of social connection between them, Abbey and Liam did not play their story in the same way the other children did. Their idea was strongly grounded in school, 'everyday' stories about bullying. They set a bully against a nerd and then added attributes to each. So Abbey described the bully eating crisps and chocolate as a negative, greedy characteristic. Throughout the process of discussion Liam suggested more transgressive elements but Abbey managed and even limited his input by controlling the process of drawing and filming. Meanwhile Liam watched as Aaron and Connor pushed at the textual boundaries, as they outdid each other with increasingly rule-breaking, hybrid characters.

In the process of creating paper animations Abbey also produced a drawing of a hybrid character that she did not use in the final story. Figure 8.2 is a hamster with bat-like wings. She did not spend too much time on drawing this character but it is of interest as a response to some of the ideas circulating in the group. She wanted to join in the fun that was involved in being inventive with popular culture characters and began drawing on the ideas of the others from horror. In Abbey's transformation of the hamster the

Figure 8.2   Abbey's 'Vampire Hamster'

result looks benign. There are none of the drops of blood or fangs or anything scary which the boys in particular drew on. Abbey created a character that was potentially funny because of the incongruity between the idea of a cute furry hamster and a vampire. In doing so, she also makes this character much more acceptable, rather like the character 'Mona the Vampire', (Holleyman, 1999) an animation on children's television. The vampire hamster is a goodie and is not associated, in this drawing anyway, with sucking blood or evil.

This approach to adapting characters is something Abbey continued to do throughout the project. As can be seen later on by her approach to devising a superhero character based on fruit, Abbey wants to be part of this play, and the key to joining in seems to be knowledge of popular culture and transgressive humour. As someone with much less experience of popular culture Abbey had not developed her own enjoyment of the sorts of violent or gross stories the others in the groups enjoyed, although neither did she reject them. However, she did understand about incongruity and how it can produce amusement and used this in her attempts to join in the fun. The other children tolerate this, but it is clear that they do not really value her contributions, or at least her suggestions are not met with the same exhilarated responses they give each other.

By making the characters more sanitised than violent and only mildly transgressive, Abbey marks herself out as distinct from the others, if not deliberately. This demonstrates the significance of popular culture as a shared or 'collective memory' (Bromley, 1996) which can exclude some children whose home experiences are perhaps closer to those of the formal school curriculum, valuing books and emphasising particular values. While incorporating children's popular culture in school, it is therefore important to remember that children's experiences are not homogenous. It is a pertinent reminder too however, that children whose main experience of narrative is drawn from their experiences of popular culture, may feel just as excluded if they cannot draw on these in the classroom.

Settings/visual design

In Eve and Matilda's film the Dream Catcher, girl and dog feature very large eyes. This has become a signature aspect of Matilda's drawing, one which the other girls emulate. Here, Matilda was also effectively drawing on comic strip and animation conventions which exaggerate some features to create different effects. The eyes make both characters seem 'cute' and 'funny' and

Figure 8.3 Eve's girl with dog

also situate them in the animated film genre and again in an imaginary rather than everyday story-world.

Eve and Matilda also created the setting of an everyday room for their characters, again using the conventions of comic strip to highlight particular items. In this sense they also demonstrated an awareness of audience, making certain elements appear of greater significance through size and use of colour. For example, on the book placed on the armchair in Matilda's Dream Catcher the words 'Dream Catcher' are immediately visible, written as it is in large font. So Matilda had deliberately distorted the scale of the font in relation to the book, chair and room in order for the readers to quickly understand the function of the character. This sense of the audience was quickly abandoned once the two girls started playing out their story. However, it is clear that the drawn form afforded this pair the opportunity to draw on their experiences of comic strips, illustrations and cartoons to enrich their use of colour, and detail such as weather and facial expressions to considerable effect. Furthermore, it is clear that a distinct and collective drawing style was emerging. It is therefore interesting to reflect on Hilton's (2001) suggestion that children need opportunities to find their own voice in their writing (Hilton, 2001) and consider whether they also need opportunities to acquire and develop a style in other forms of storytelling.

Figure 8.4   Matilda's 'Dream Catcher'

Liam and Abbey spent a great deal of time on their school setting calling it 'Skull School' and adding in details such as cobwebs and bats. They choose conventional horror colours such as red and black. They draw bars in the windows and their aim is to make their school seem scary and spooky. An interesting detail appears in Abbey's drawing of the main character who has a Nike tick on his shoes. Both children are aware that Nike is a 'cool' brand but also say that children who have Nike trainers 'might be spoilt'. Later on in the next activity Abbey uses the Nike tick for one of her own characters although she also adapts it by turning it into a banana. This repeat or signature use of ideas in storytelling is usefully made visible in drawings, representing as it does here a sustained adaptation of a popular culture resource. In using it in different context Abbey is also considering its meaning.

Connor and Aaron paid little attention to the drawings of their setting, especially when compared to their drawings of characters. They do however choose distinct and deliberately random settings for example a cityscape, the wild west and a golf course. This reflects the way in which, in some animations, the settings can change sometimes in a rather surreal manner, an affordance of animated texts that would not be a convention of live-action film, for example.

Figure 8.5 Liam and Abbey's characters and setting

This pair also includes some interesting objects such as a golf flag, and a telegraph pole which they designed to function as a high structure the pigeon could escape to. As Pompe (1992a) points out, in children's media text production it is often the unusual or unexpected elements they include which we pay attention to because they are not an element of existing schemas of stories the children use elsewhere. Like many creative processes, the boys cannot remember where these ideas came from but it is clear that these aspects of setting have a function in the narrative structure. The tent Connor made has an opening door for his cowboy, demonstrating inventive use of the affordances of particular materials and adding to the range of ideas the children attempt to express. Although a simple and unadorned device, it does allow the boys to hide characters and create an element of surprise. As Burn and Durran's (2007) work demonstrates, a more sophisticated approach to animation production would enable far more in-depth exploration of the affordances of the medium. However, this simple and accessible activity can emulate some of the processes through which children come to understand how film is constructed. Furthermore, the speed at which this activity can be undertaken and completed and its ephemeral nature had an impact on the nature of the texts produced.

Plot

The plot and structure of pair one and two's stories were quite similar to that of the oral storytelling. Although an underlying linear structure of conflict and resolution can be traced in the stories they perform, other aspects are worked out as they go along. This playful response enables us to glance at the children's 'dialogic imagination externalised' (Spencer, 2004, p. 547). Even when their performance was being filmed, they were still inventing rather than sticking to re-enacting a planned idea. The ideas built on each other and sometimes contradicted each other and coherence was given little consideration. Interestingly, in the planning stages Matilda said that the girl would be the main character and 'have a problem to solve', but this idea is largely forgotten once they begin to enact their ideas.

Aaron and Connor draw on their experiences of animations, which link together one violent interlude after another such as *Tom and Jerry*, (Hanna and Barbera, 1940) *The Simpsons* especially the 'Itchy and Scratchy' sketches (Groening, 1989) and *Roadrunner* (Jones, 1949). Their storyline was based on direct conflict between two of the characters and a pigeon. There was some confusion because both boys wanted the best part, as they perceived it, and so they compromised and were both main characters. For the audience, the adult audience, their storyline becomes rather repetitive with various different scenes of one character trying to kill the other.

Eve and Matilda's story lasts for over six minutes and again it centred on conflict between the two characters. So the Dream Catcher gives the girl in the story bad dreams. The girls did attempt a resolution at one moment in their story, but quickly re-started the conflict. The process was marked out by hysterical laughter, overt self-direction, and little sense of a predetermined storyline. Like the boys in pair one, the girls played through their story rather than enacting or performing a storyline they had predetermined. Also, like the boys in pair one, the girls became exhilarated by their own humour often created by surprise or disgust. They began to experiment with the comic effect of unexpectedly violent behaviour from such 'cute' characters; at one point they started to scribble out the drawn posters on the wall of their setting, something they found hugely funny. On another occasion they used gross things such as 'maggots on your head'. The black and white clarity of a moral children's story is replaced in these texts, not by shades of grey or greater complexity, but by an irreverent parody of these rules and conventions.

Grace and Tobin (1998) liken children's approach to video production to the use of 'fun house mirrors' on the human body, 'exaggerating and distorting for comic effect' (Grace and Tobin, 1998, p. 53). Although the girls started with benign characters and an everyday bedroom setting, their playful approach to the activity led to the plot of their story being driven by conflict and physical action between the two characters. Although the girl was planned as the 'nice' character who would have her dreams 'tampered' with, these ideas evolved, becoming increasingly anarchic. The resolution to the story is temporary and the characters quickly revert back to trying to out-do and annoy each other. This is resonant of many children's cartoons where resolution between the two main protagonists can only ever be temporary to sustain the serialised narrative.

As Liam and Abbey did not play their story but pre-planned it, their final text had a clear a linear narrative with a strong closure although the extreme ending does, like Eve's dinosaur story, subvert the conventional ending of a bullying story. In their story the nerd was going to overcome the bully, drawing on a David and Goliath masterplot. Abbey took on the role of bully and Liam the role of nerd. He sought to find an interesting and surprising way the nerd could beat the bully so he rejected the idea of telling a friend, parent or teacher but came up with the idea of the nerd buying a lion from a pet shop. The lion would not only frighten the bully but would eat him. This was an idea Liam intuitively knew would be funny and unexpected and which challenged what a school narrative about dealing with bullies might suggest.

Sound

What cannot be read from the text below is the performance of the characters using intonation and language from their experiences of film:

Connor (Cowboy): I'm gonna kill this pigeon. Exterminate ... and you're not getting in my way.

Aaron (Bat Mutant): I'm on the same team as you, you dufus.
Connor: I'm gonna end up killing that skinny, little bagga bones.
Aaron: Well I wanna kill the pigeon.
Connor: For some reason that skinny, little bagga bones is my best friend.

Throughout their story, the boys made use of voices, physical action and sound effects, including singing a sound track. They displayed extensive knowledge of the sorts of sounds an animation would use to establish mood, to reveal plot and in particular to create humour. Matilda and Eve used comic style language in their play such as 'Di dum, di dum', (waiting for something to happen) or 'Ha ha' (at having 'got' the other person) or interjections such as 'Arrgh' or 'Ow' (in response to violent action), borrowing ideas from texts such as *The Beano* (Thomson, 1938–Current). Connor and Aaron also used comic language like sound effects such as 'splat' but supplement this with ideas from a range of other sources, 'exterminate' is clearly borrowed from the Daleks on *Doctor Who* (Davies, 2005) and 'dufus' is a common word, meaning idiot, in American drama for children. Both usages could be described as imitation and do not demonstrate any particular inventiveness or playfulness in their use. However, 'skinny, little bagga bones', highlights the way the boys immerse themselves further into the less familiar language and attitudes of cultural worlds outside their experience, such as the cowboy western, and 'gansta' language in this context of parody. They experimented with new accents and uses of dialect and again they were drawing both explicitly and intuitively on the language, content, dialects and accents they have experienced in film. Pair one and two tested out these characters' voices to comic effect.

In the course of devising their ideas and in performing their story Abbey clearly did not trust Liam to tell the story effectively. Twice she talked over him when I asked about their ideas and twice she succeeded in making him stop speaking. Interestingly, when this happens he began to realign himself with the boys, laughing knowingly when Abbey used the word 'nerd'. Later in the filming of their story, Abbey in character as the bully could not resist narrating the plot, positioning herself as the most powerful of the two storytellers rather than batting the story between them. Indeed, Abbey mentioned the idea of the lion from the pet shop, giving away Liam's punch-line and removing any surprise or suspense for the audience. Having found herself at a disadvantage in terms of her knowledge of popular culture, Abbey attempted to appropriate this task and asserted her status by verbally dominating the process. However, she was also aware of the social value of popular culture and was torn between enacting her familiar literacy identity and her desire to join in with her peers' enjoyment of popular culture. Liam found it uncomfortable to be on the receiving end of Abbey's assertions and this was a barrier to full participation for him. In negotiations of status in relation to experiences of popular culture and school-based literacy the stakes are clearly high.

Pleasure at play

In the light of Grace and Tobin's (1998) analysis of children's production work I would argue that the opportunity to play in relation to storytelling enables children to explore aspects of narrative that they have familiarity with and pleasure in. In their use of hybrid characters Aaron and Connor can be seen engaging with familiar rules, understanding that a cowboy and a Frankenstein monster are not conventionally expected in a story together, but they were also responding playfully, 'fooling around' (Mackey, 2002) with ideas to see what happens, which is a response animation makes possible. Quite quickly they wanted to push the boundaries of the task I had set them. Grace and Tobin (1998) draw on Barthes (1975) notion of 'jouissance', pleasure taken in the evasion of social order to explain the similar response they found in children's video production. Both Aaron and Connor and Eve and Matilda gained an exhilarated pleasure, perhaps jouissance, at being able to break textual rules (mixing up genres), behaviour rules (responding spontaneously and noisily) and task rules (changing the guidelines to the task they were given). Initially, they sought my permission to do so. Both boys also wanted a main character and another character, as Aaron asked me:

> Miss, can we have two characters each, like a mutant for both of us and a human for both of us? (Aaron)

I agreed to this because I only set the criteria of two characters to keep the task focused and manageable in the time and I was keen to see where their idea would take them. It was the last time in the process the boys sought clarification or my opinion during that afternoon and they worked entirely independently, completely absorbed for over two hours (and would have continued had we had more time). This is an important observation because the boys' playful approach to the task could have been construed as chaotic and unfocused but was actually a display of intense immersion in the task and in the fictional world of their story.

Grace and Tobin (1998) use Bakhtin's (1984) term 'carnivalesque' to understand the way in which young children used video production to 'invert the usual hierarchies' and take on new roles which allow them to explore 'parody, fantasy, horror, the grotesque and the forbidden' (Grace and Tobin, 1998, p. 48). Certainly there was evidence of the fantastic or the horrific in the children's films, although these were sources of humour. I interpret this as evidence of two distinct pleasures. Firstly, there is the pleasure of displaying knowledge of those texts which you have pleasure and expertise in, something Pompe (1992a) also found. Secondly, there is the process of placing at a distance ideas which are difficult and uncomfortable. The children, like those in Willett's (2005b) study, clearly enjoyed violence and had sophisticated understandings of the textual rules governing the inclusion of violence. They were also placing violence, death, night-time visitors and bad dreams at a distance from which they could laugh at them.

Grace and Tobin (1998) suggest that the carnivalesque approach the children take to telling stories, which draws on popular culture, enabled them to explore complex and contentious issues, not easily dealt with in school. It is important, however, to recognise that many children's texts contain elements of the carnivalesque; the grotesque obsession with the scatological or the authority figures who need taking down a peg or two are regular elements of children's narratives. Thus, while the children might be enjoying their own uses of the carnivalesque in their stories, they are, in so doing, following the conventions of those texts. However, in written stories the children tended to moderate these ideas, they intuitively knew that these elements would not be valued in or appropriate to school. As Luke and Carrington (2002) argue, the texts of the classroom often exclude issues that many children encounter in life such as poverty or violence, whether in close-up or at a distance.

The uncomfortable truth is that for some children, creating violent stories is not exploring the shocking or frightening things that happen to other people, but putting experiences in their own lives at a distance from which they can be both funny and non-threatening. These sorts of experience are distinct from the pleasures children have in on-screen violence. Issues of violence arising in film may make us, as teachers and researchers, uneasy:

> Something about children's delight in mock violence threatens adult authority and disrupts culturally constructed notions about childhood innocence. (Grace and Tobin, 1998, p. 51)

We may wish to heighten critical awareness of the way violence is depicted, but we have to be careful not to inhibit children's expression of this pleasure. Clearly, in interviews Aaron was aware that I might disapprove of his pleasure in shoot-em-up films. However, violence in the boys' lives was a source of distress whereas violence represented in film was a source of amusement. The children may have been able to explore and enjoy ideas about violence in a moving image form, but this did not make them less sensitive to the impact it had in their own lives. It is important to consider this in the light of the storylines they evolved because they would be so easy to dismiss as derivative and of little value. Our inclination to protect children from violence, while entirely understandable, is flawed. By ruling it out of school story-production activities we have to ask who we are protecting. Since children do encounter violence in texts and in life it is something that should not be excluded from discussion or production. In this activity the children navigated the fictional space in which violence recurs, demonstrating their knowledge of textual conventions.

Like the children in studies by Burn and Durran (2007) and Pompe (1992a) the medium of animation, even in this basic form, acted as a space in which children's repertoires of popular culture texts were of value. It is evident that this task afforded the children the opportunity to draw enthusiastically on a range of cultural resources. There was an overflow of ideas that were quickly and spontaneously spoken aloud. Furthermore, these ideas were based on shared knowledge and experience or 'collective memories' (Bromley, 1996) about which the children could speak to each other, in a sort of short-hand, in the knowledge that they would each know how one character or idea might relate to another. The children's status in the social order of the classroom was displaced in this setting because knowledge of popular culture was of greater value than that of the school-based literacy curriculum. As Pompe (1992a) found, some children, used to being the most successful, were disquieted and some, usually accepting of their own lack of success, were highly motivated and engaged. This disruption of the social order was not accepted without question and a struggle ensued involving Abbey and Liam which was difficult to resolve satisfactorily.

The children's playful engagements with telling these stories were distinct from their school-based storytelling. It is clear that encouraging children to draw on animated popular culture influences and creating a space in which they can play with ideas rather than commit to just one idea, provided a rich opportunity for the children to draw on and extend, through social interaction, their funds of knowledge (Moll et al., 1992) about narrative.

Drawn and Plasticine superheroes

In this activity the children worked individually rather than collaboratively and the focus was entirely on the devising of characters in the superhero genre. This was an opportunity to explore ideas about a specific and familiar children's film genre and to compare children's productions in two different forms that of Plasticine three-dimensional and drawn two-dimensional figures. Not all of the children produced drawn versions of their superheroes, preferring to start straight away with their modelling Plasticine version. (Matilda was also absent from school for this activity.) As a consequence, I have selected to present the three characters that were created in both forms to focus on the movement from one form to another.

Character

Abbey's character for a new animation series demonstrates her understanding about the way superhero stories work but also her distance from the contemporary superhero films such as *Spiderman* (Raimi, 2002) or *X-Men* (Singer, 2000) that her peers were more immersed in. In her annotations to her drawings she wrote, 'Main Character', understanding that in most superhero films there is one main superhero who is the central protagonist. Rather than give her superhero powers of physical strength Abbey attributed

Banana Boy with cleverness, a banana gun with the ability to make people happy and shoes 'Kindly sponsored by Nike' which are rocket-powered. Here Abbey was clearly trying to signal her knowledge of a popular sports brand but by drawing the ticks as bananas she moved closer to parody.

In her accompanying written text Abbey draws on her first-hand knowledge of small boys playing by using bananas as guns; she has four brothers. She also explored her ideas about what a 'goodie' should or could be like. Although she draws on the conventional idea that all superheroes have enemies, she is inventive with her original idea of a fruit theme. Rather like children's books series such as *The Munch Bunch* (Bond, 1979), Abbey invests fruits with personalities so that arch-rivals are 'Strawberry Girl's' and 'The Apple Gang' and his friends are 'Cherry' and a pet hamster named 'Lemon'. Abbey was clearly able to imagine storylines being generated as a result of the interaction between the key characters and although she stuck to this particular element of superhero narratives, she did not feel bound to the conventions as her contemporaries did. There was again an altogether younger and less dangerous element to her invented character. 'Have you heard? Bananas make you happy', she wrote as her character's catch phrase.

There are precedents for fruit being given human attributes in children's popular culture and especially in early reading books linked in with the

Figure 8.6   Abbey's 'Banana Boy' drawing

idea of healthy eating. Of course, there is also *Bananaman*, (Bright, 1983) a comic strip and cartoon character with recognisably British use of humour, in particular parody. Although Abbey's ideas are not directly derivative of these texts she would appear to be following a similar creative path. So just as *Bananaman* parodies the rather serious superheroes and gently makes fun of the genre, she enjoyed the process of combining tough guy superhero attributes with the rather more comic idea of fruit and this is similar to her approach to her vampire hamster, demonstrating that when children find an approach to text production that they enjoy they reuse it and extend it.

By contrast Connor's superhero in Figure 8.7 is, in appearance, reminiscent of a traditional Marvel or Thompson comic creation. The posture, a crouching figure disguised and ready to pounce, is far closer to the older character Spiderman than a children's cartoon character. The picture is a night time scene, illustrated by dark shading and a crescent moon, with the character positioned on the top of a line of buildings. Connor included a new new idea about the mutation his superhero had undergone. So he has crab-like claws and radiates a light and this, like the *X-Men* characters, is what makes him distinctive. He is more of a tortured soul than Bananaman, isolated by society by his difference. Connor was able to work with generic conventions, drawing on his knowledge of superhero characters but he understood the

Figure 8.7   Connor's 'Crab Man'

importance of some aspect of originality to his creation. Unlike the previous task Connor takes the superhero genre seriously and does not in this case produce a parodic response.

Like Abbey, Eve's superhero is a distance away from the mutant characters of *X-Men*, for example. Her character, Hugo Hedgehog Man is based on an animal and is comical rather than dark. However, Eve again showed knowledge of superhero conventions, with a 'Di da daaaaaaa' comic strip style use of language as a fanfare for her character. Rather than opt for a morally unambiguous, nice guy, Eve devised some quite strong physical attributes such as the ability to pick up buildings, shoot spines, breathe sleeping gas and, in a twist to the usual fate of hedgehogs, the ability to 'squish' people. As can be seen in her story about the head teacher and the dinosaur in the previous chapter and her contributions to the oral storytelling, Eve is not afraid to include violent action in her stories even if this is unexpected by her peers. Eve also understands the comic strip style and the superhero generic necessity of being able to quickly dispense with opponents and she took pleasure in inventing the hedgehog's unique way of dispatching opponents. The others in the group expected her to continue to produce 'nice' and 'cute' animals so this seemed quite a departure for her. She was still able to draw on the many animals she had encountered in books and popular culture but she enjoyed contrasting these ideas with those from the superhero genre.

Moving mode

When turning their characters into Plasticine model form it was interesting that none of the children were entirely satisfied with the results. They did not have very much experience of Plasticine and so were lacking in confidence in relation to building on their ideas from their drawings. Abbey's Banana Boy replicates her ideas in the drawing but the new mode of working does not represent for her an opportunity to build on those ideas.

Connor invented a whole new range of characters to fit in with his idea of a clawed character but the mode of animation, Plasticine rather than drawn, takes him in a new direction. His characters now resemble characters from Japanese animations such as *Pokémon*, (Tajiri, 1986). As soon as he started to work in this medium Connor began to devise different ideas from those he had drawn.

In Plasticine form Connor talked about the way in which the characters might evolve and what powers they had, drawing directly on Japanese Anime-influenced programmes. Although these programmes are also drawn animation the characters often appear in a three-dimensional form in toys, making the transformation more familiar. Connor's characters still have claws, but they are otherwise unrecognisable from his much more moody and serious drawn image. He devised the characters in a family set with a

Figure 8.8   Abbey's 'Banana Boy' in Plasticine

female in mixed colours such as pink and blue and pronounced eyelashes, a male in all one colour, who gets angry and the smaller baby. (It is noticeable that female superheroes only appear when the children move beyond one character to a group.) Connor adapted his idea in this task to the medium and is therefore influenced by previous experiences of clay-animation. This is more important to him than the detail of his original idea, or at least the medium makes a stronger demand on the style of the text than his original idea can withstand.

Eve's Plasticine model did enable her to move from her drawn idea quite effectively to Plasticine and in doing so her character takes on different physical qualities. He has a cape, like many superheroes, over his spines and a hood although it does not disguise his identity. Although the model itself is not necessarily executed any better than her peers, Eve has used this as an opportunity to work on and develop her original idea. She adds colour and changes the shape slightly. This process is more successful for Eve and this is perhaps because her idea is closer to the sorts of texts in which the clay-mation form is used, for example the films made by Aardman

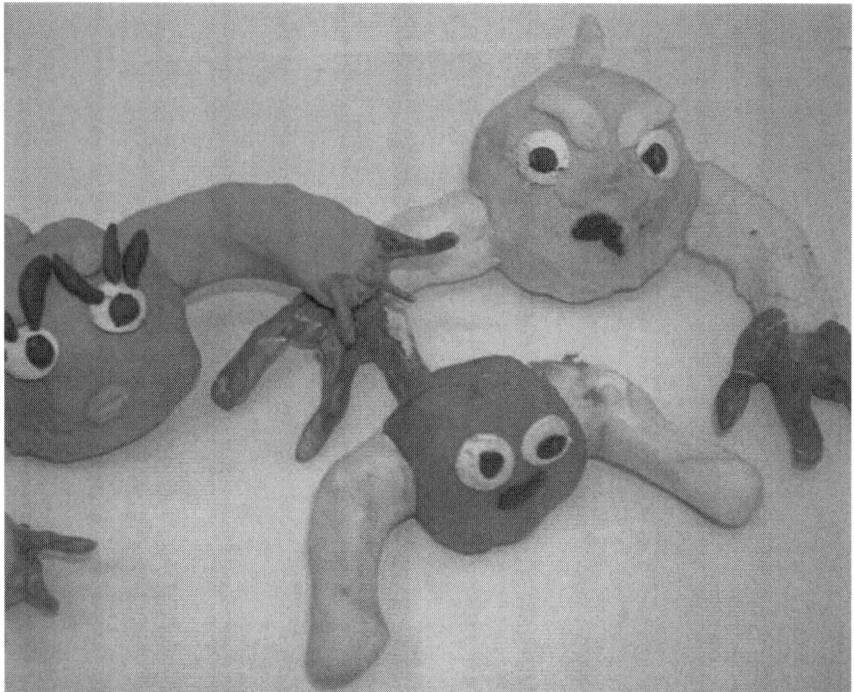

Figure 8.9   Connor's 'Claw Creatures'

and featuring Wallace and Grommit, *A Close Shave* (Park, 1995), and other anthropomorphic characters such as *Shaun the Sheep* (Park, 2007).

In any expression of narrative the medium has a strong impact on the sorts of ideas drawn on. When inviting children to create narratives, it is important to ensure they have opportunities to make them in their familiar forms. That is to say, it is not enough to invite children to write super-hero stories, they also need opportunities to create superheroes in media such as comics, cartoons or live-action films. My selection of drawing as a medium of expression of ideas about superheroes was more effective than my selection of Plasticine, for example. This is an important consideration in the classroom where children might attempt to draw on what they know about narrative in the written form, but in doing so have to also adapt their resources from one medium into another. The animated form, although highly popular is also not the only form of children's film that the children expressed enthusiasm for. Given that many of the research activities had implicitly invited the children to explore imaginary story-worlds, I was inter-ested to see how they would respond to the opportunity to create stories in a film form more associated with everyday story-worlds.

Figure 8.10   Eve's 'Hugo Hedgehog-Man'

Live-action film production

This activity was designed to give the children a sustained opportunity to
undertake each stage of film production:

- Pre-production: the devising, planning, script-writing and storyboarding
  of their film story idea
- Production: the performance and filming of their story idea
- Post production: the editing of their film footage.

The children also organised two screenings of their work and produced
some promotional materials and this aspect of the process has also been
considered in this analysis. (My approach to analysing the children's film
productions is discussed in Chapter 5) At the outset the children were all
given a common set of creative constraints (as outlined in Chapter 5),
including setting the film in school. They worked in same gender, friendship
groups and produced two distinct films. The girls' film was about raising

money for charity to improve the school playground and the boys' story was about two friends auditioning for a talent show. Both included a conflict between friends but the process of decision-making for the two groups led to some noticeable differences in their final texts. That both groups chose an everyday story is almost certainly linked to the everyday setting of the school and the use of live-action rather than animation. Although it is of course possible to add imaginary elements to this setting, the children lacked confidence in their ability to attempt this. Since I was interested in what sorts of everyday narratives the children would draw on, I did not demonstrate to them ways that they could include fantasy elements.

Character

Just as in their written work, the children began the process of thinking about their film ideas with their characters. The children also decided that they would act the main roles themselves and recruit some of their friends to play any additional roles and this had a strong impact on the development of their storylines. The characters were fictional, but they were also versions of themselves. As with their writing, the children drew on popular culture and film sources which linked to their identities. As Potter (2009) illustrates, given the opportunity children use film production as an opportunity for 'self curation', exhibiting and performing aspects of their experience in relation to media:

> The resources from which they made meaning were collected, catalogued and arranged for exhibition. These included practices which were previously unseen, acts of memory and habitualised behaviour which were not previously recorded in this way, but which were part of their everyday, lived experience. As some of the projects showed, this revelation was not unproblematic and was not in itself a process without risk or critical issues. (Potter, 2009, pp. 280–281)

Although in this case the children were creating drama and the children in Potter's study were creating non-fiction films, their close proximity to the characters led to some similar and interesting displays of media preferences and practices.

Connor is seen by the other boys as the ideas person and indeed it was his idea to include a talent show in the film. This decision could be clearly linked to the children's recent viewing of *Britain's got Talent* (Cowell, 2007), but perhaps a better description would be that it was a decision based on a bricolage of experiences. Two of the boys were very interested in street dancing and a street dancer had won the television competition. Connor had also recently watched *Step Up* (Fletcher, 2006) which is an American teen-romance film about street dancers training to be professional dancers. Picking up on this interest a teaching assistant in school had also started a dance group in which both Connor and Aaron took an active role. This had become a significant site for the sharing of dance moves and the types of music associated with street dance. Although by now the boys had rejected *High School Musical*, (Ortega, 2006) as 'cheesy and babyish' they had watched the films with enthusiasm some months before. The boys felt their film would give them the opportunity to dance on film to show off their association with particular sorts of music and dance culture.

It is possible to argue then that their text choices represent an accumulation of their previous experiences of similar children's films but these were mixed up with experiences of reality television, music and everyday life. The close proximity of their film production to their own film tastes and preferences was not without risk (Potter, 2009); the boys were sharing and performing their strong personal interest in dance and that could have made them the target of derision. However, their commitment to the dance theme was stronger than any anxieties they had about peer comments.

Connor and Aaron could not choose who should be the main character so decided to have two main characters and became animated when discussing which costumes, music and dance moves would 'be cool'. They did not make a decision about whose point of view the story would be told from because they both wanted their characters to have equal status, just as they described happened in their film-based games. Liam was very happy to go along with the story ideas of the other two boys, but the dance element was not his choice and as a result he agreed to take on the role of the headteacher.

The girls' group initially had story ideas which included magic and witches but they rejected these before I had a chance to discuss them with them because they 'did not see how it would work'. Meanwhile Eve had suggested an idea about a bun sale to raise money for a charity which the others agreed with. There was some debate about which charity to raise funds for and initially this was planned to be for an animal charity. This idea seemed to come from television dramas although the group could not think of any specific sources. The girls identified the need for a main character but were all keen to be this character. Eventually, on my suggestion, they flipped a coin and Eve was chosen. The other girls, especially Abbey, felt this was the wrong outcome and clearly thought they would have been better in the role. They went on to allocate characters to themselves and to their friends. Once the actors were cast, the characters and the arc of the story also began to change.

Since Abbey and Matilda were not the main character they both became keen to invest their characters with interesting qualities and began to decide independently what these qualities would be. Matilda particularly began to write dialogue for her character which was reminiscent of 'smart' answers given by young female characters in American situation comedies such *Drake and Josh* (Schneider, 2004) and *I Carly* (Schneider, 2007), dramas such as *Zoey 101* (Schneider, 2005) and animations such as *Ben Ten* (Rouleau et al., 2005–Current). Matilda had considerable expertise in the sort of language, dialect and register used by young characters in this programme, which she could immitate. Abbey observed this and tried to emulate this idea in the same way that she appropriated ideas from popular culture in her social engagements with her friends.

At this point the girls did not have a fully planned storyline; they decided they needed a bad character but were not too sure what this character should do. They selected Matilda to play this role and fairly quickly she began to generate further dialogue that gave her character more shape. She became the cheeky one who did not agree with everyone else. Abbey had the least distinctive character to play. She was a friend of the main character with very little narrative function other than to support and agree. As Matilda's naughty character developed, Abbey also played with being naughty and added some new speech and gestures to make her character more interesting.

During the production stage the boys also invested their characters with qualities that they considered distinct from themselves to make the storyline work. Connor's character openly bragged about being the best dancer, something Connor himself would never have done. This was to create a tension in the story, something they were implicitly aware was neccesary to ensure the audience understood the need for this character to learn a lesson. Deciding to play the characters themselves, thus impacted on the development of plot ideas but once a story arc had begun to develop the children were able to distance themselves from their character, changing them in relation to their narrative function.

Both groups found it much easier to make decisions about the role of adults in their films who were sterotypical authoritarian grown-ups who try to spoil the fun of children, like the adults represented in many children's films. In the girls' film, their own teacher played the role of a rather bossy and impatient teacher who has little time for their ideas. In the boys' film it was a headteacher who was the baddie. It soon became clear to the boys that they needed a character whom the friends 'ran into'. This character, the headteacher, was not initially planned to be the baddie but this set of ideas quickly followed. So they decided that the headteacher wanted to fix the competition so that his favourite pupil, a ballet dancer, won and then they decided his motivation for this was that he did not approve of their style of dancing, 'street'. The decisions about characters helped the children develop their ideas for plot iteratively. In performing the characters however, there were further shifts and changes relating to issues of performance.

In the girls' film Abbey's character appears to be a bit mean, gesturing rudely while Eve's character is telling the whole class about the bun sale. This is particularly distracting to the audience because moments before Abbey's character is seen begging the teacher to let them ask the class to do the bun sale, and then she says 'I'm fed up of all this chit chat'.

Abbey performs her role well, but the character was conceived in contradictory ways, distracting attention away from Matlida as the naughty character. Abbey noticed some of the problems arising from the depiction of her character during the editing process. In the written form, Abbey would invest her main character with aspects of her own identity but it is likely she would have little difficulty making the character fit into the context of the story and fulfil the function required by the plot. However, here, because Abbey was not playing the main character, the ideas she invests into the secondary character obscure other elements of the plot. Interestingly this only became visible to her during editing.

During the course of filming it became apparent that while the children had knowledge of the sort of performance style they liked in children's film and television, they were not always able to reproduce it. For example, both Eve and Matilda were very camera shy and became self-conscious when called on to perform. In Matilda's case this led to her abandoning most of the witty dialogue she had written for herself. Matilda's character was written to be mischievous rather than an out-and-out baddie, but an audience might not be able to infer this from the shots the children included. Few shots are from her point of view and we do not hear her voice expressing her emotions until the end. However, when simply acting (without dialogue) she was able to create strong facial expressions and gestures which effectively conveyed some of her characteristics to the audience.

In Eve's case, although she was able to say her lines appropriately they could not film close ups of her at key moments in the film because she giggled so much at this point. For example, when Matilda is discovered by the teacher under the table eating cakes, Eve could not supress her laughter. As we could only work with the teacher for a very brief time, we did not retake this scene so the shot does not convey the emotions of the two characters the children had planned. In fact their laughter, rather than in-character shock can be heard on the soundtrack. The absence of appropriate reaction shots and sounds was a flaw the girls recognised in their footage when they reviewed their film in the editing stage. They also wished they had filmed reaction shots from the two girls at the table rather than the rather clumsy back of heads shot of the teacher catching Matilda.

When playing the headteacher Liam was supposed to be angry and sarcastic like teachers such as Mrs Trunchbull from the film *Matilda* (De Vito, 1996) However, for a number of reasons Liam found it difficult to sustain this character. In his first piece of dialogue he was asked by Aaron's character about the talent competition. In giving simple instructions Liam sounds quite sympathetic.

However, at the end of this speech he finishes by shouting a direct instruction, 'Now!' Liam had a few lines to remember in this scene so he was preoccupied with getting them right, but he was also increasingly aware that the planned dialogue offering information about the talent show to the character Joe, was not consistent with the horrible headteacher they had imagined. If there had been time I think they would have changed the dialogue and shot this scene again. It is an interesting example of the way the boys attempted to incorporate information to help the audience anticipate the plot, that is to say how the competition would work, as well as to enable the audience to be orientated towards who the real 'bad guy' of the story was. This was not apparent until the editing process and the boys just decided to edit those scenes to ensure that the audience could hear the words. So they had several takes in which Liam did sustain an angrier and more sarcastic tone but these were more difficult to follow because of some external sound issues.

While the children found it challenging to perform the characters as they imagined them, they were adept at identifying visual elements that inferred ideas about them. The boys spent a long time choosing their costumes for their film and brought in clothes they would have worn to street dance in. Liam also used an adult suit jacket to signal his authority and elected to hold the school playground bell. Once wearing these clothes and filming the first scene they began to invest their characters with more meaning. For example, Connor and Aaron decided their characters would greet each other using gestures in a similar way to the 'ghetto handshakes' of films like *Step Up* (Fletcher, 2006) to infer that their characters were 'cool' and 'street' but also to show that they were friends who would always greet each other in this familiar way. The girls groups also selected gestures that were appropriate to their characters such as the teacher's folded arms, Abbey's hand gestures and Matilda's throwing down of the gloves she was given to clear up rubbish with. These gestures were directly drawn from experiences of dramatic action whether film, television or theatre. Although they had these clear ideas about physical appearance and actions for their characters, the children had to learn how to film these appropriately.

Early on in the filming Liam was involved in shooting the first of the girls' scenes in the playground. For all the children involved this was a critical point in learning about using the camera. Initially, they used many zooms and moved the tripod over again without noting where it had previously been positioned. They were also trying to work with some rather tricky natural light and had to consider where the microphone was in relation to the characters. Initially, as the camera person, Liam followed instructions from the girls. However, as the one seeing what was being filmed through the lens of the camera, he could also see that fast zooms and sudden moves of the position of the camera 'didn't look right'. Liam was able to identify the problems with the film they had so far and so he began to organise the cast to re-shoot the scene using a much simpler shot. By not zooming in during filming but setting up each shot before recording and using markers so that the actors knew where the parameters of the shot were, he managed to record a much better take of the first scene. Drawing on his intuitive sense of what 'looked right' Liam became very determined that the camera had to be still rather than using too much movement.

Many of the film and television programmes the children watch that are situated in the everyday story-world use quite simple camera shots which, like the rules of continuity editing, aim at fluency and upholding the idea of an intact story-world. In a sense the camera acts as the narrator establishing for example, whose point of view the story is told from. This idea was something they explored in later shots where a smaller number of characters had to be filmed. The children discussed what worked and what did not and when watching back their footage they could see Liam's choices, which followed his intuitive recognition of conventional use of camera shots in narrative films, had been effective.

When filming the opening shots for the boys, Liam, who had by that time gained some experience of filming, chose a medium two-shot to get both characters in as close as possible. Instinctively, the boys were able to work out that close-up shots would 'be better'. Liam continued to use close-up shots wherever possible from then on including the scene where the friends made up. Here, although the dialogue is rather muffled and brief (giggling problems – see outtakes) the camera work is especially effective at capturing the expressions of the two friends, just slightly putting Connor's character into a more important position by giving him slightly more shot space. At that point Liam had become the group expert in using the camera. Later when Connor filmed the bun sale scene for the girls he was forced to film most of it in long-shot because of the angle at which the shot was composed on an awkward corridor. When he could, he used Liam's technique of close-up shots to capture Matilda's character stealing and eating the cakes. This shot is dark and lighting would have made it more effective. Matilda was also very self-conscious about this scene, wanting to 'get it over and done with'. However, significantly Connor drew on what he had learnt from Liam.

Both groups focused their camera work on the characters rather than on setting. They told their stories using point-of-view camera conventions so the main characters were established through close-up and the camera occasionally followed their eye-line or showed them in two-shot or over-the-shoulder and reverse-shot to see the world of the story as they saw it. Both groups achieved this based on a trial and error approach, rather than from any explicit teaching. As Parker argues however, when watching back film productions children see them through the eyes of the audience and therefore can see the gaps:

> The explicit nature of film makes it all but impossible for any filmmaker to ignore anomalies, faults and gaps in composition. (Parker, 2006, p. 156)

After they filmed some scenes early on they looked at them and saw what was wrong and addressed the issues themselves or at least changed their approach when filming the next scene (there was not enough time to re-shoot all the scenes). In a sense they were matching up their own work with that they were familiar with. They began to see the importance of not filming fast zooms for example and they also saw the importance of retaining a consistent position for the camera throughout a scene to create fluency.

An important aspect of the craft of film-making became apparent to the children when the boys' use of costume raised continuity issues. Having filmed on one day and taken their clothes home, they forgot to bring in exactly the same clothes next time. This meant we had to change the shooting order. When I explained this, they did not really understand why it would be a problem, but when it came to editing they started to see how important it was that on one day, as represented in film, their characters would need to be wearing the same clothes unless they actually revealed a reason for changing as part of the unfolding narrative. This led me to reflect that because film-making is such a collaborative and public process, decisions that are made about an issue such as continuity helped the boys to discuss ideas about how they were telling a story explicitly. It was not just that their clothes could reveal a lot about their characters, it was also that in the film the changing of clothes signifies a change in relation to time or place which as the storyteller you must explain to the audience.

Parker argues that characterisation is made explicit in writing but more often inferred rather than told in film (Parker, 1999a). However, the internal thoughts and feelings of characters can be signified in film through dialogue, music, use of colour, costume, body posture, facial expression and lighting. The children attempted to use all of these modes in their representations of their characters although not all of them were within their creative control, for example lighting. Clearly, the children had well-developed understandings that the elements we pay attention to in live-action films are purposefully placed to signify meaning, often about characters. Film offers both similar and different opportunities from written texts to present thoughts and feelings of characters and to establish atmosphere. Some of the children were able to demonstrate greater understanding of this in film form than in their writing. As teachers and researchers it is critical not to make broad assumptions about the scope or limitations of different media. It is also clearly productive for children to have opportunity to create characters in film form.

In their devising and filming of stories the children were able to demonstrate considerable understandings of characters. They were influenced by a range of different popular culture texts including children's films and these helped them devise characters and plan elements such as costumes and casting. They used characters who were central and peripheral and recognised that these characters had particular functions. They particularly drew on everyday children's films in terms of the power relationships between children and adults. The adult characters were the 'baddie' authority figures who tried to control the childrens' actions and the storyline was told from the 'goodie' children's point of view. The role of acting or performance as well as identity projection and the desire to be a prominent character impacted on the final text. The extent to which the film told the story they pictured when devising the script was largely dependent on whether they could act and capture those performances effectively on film. The children were able to draw on their intuitive recognition of film conventions in terms of camera shots, particularly at the stage of watching their footage back and matching it against their previous experiences of moving image narratives.

The process of placing themselves in the story also had a quite different impact from that in writing. It is useful in terms of considerations of movement from one text (a script) to another (a short film) to consider the influence of performance and identity projection and that this works quite differently in a group project by comparison to an individual written project. Some of the changes relating to who played each character and how that character changed meant more meaning was created and the story was the richer for it. Other changes, particularly in the context of a short film, obscured the overall meaning of the text and were confusing. The explicit, collaborative process of production however, enabled the children to usefully discuss the effectiveness of their storytelling.

Settings

Although the overall everyday school setting was selected for them, the children had strong ideas about which places within school would help them to create the locations they were imagining. They were quick to adapt the settings too, either by dressing them in particlar ways, for example the girls created a table of buns brought from home and took considerable care over how these were set out and where the table was positioned. Another way they adapted their surroundings was by using the camera to frame shots to exclude ideas they did not want. For example the girls' group used an extreme close-up of rubbish in their playground shots.

This decision came about after they had taken part in an exercise aimed at ensuring they were confident in using the video camera and tripod to create different shots. Quite quickly they realised that by using close-ups of a stray piece of rubbish for example, they could give the impression of a 'horrible' playground and this led to their idea about raising money for improvements (rather than the original animal charity idea). It is perhaps important to emphasise that the girls did not choose this fund-raising idea because it reflected their feelings about their own school. This decision reflected their recognition that they could give the impression of an improved playground by differently filming their own playground.

The boys also carefully selected some of their settings, framing them in particular ways. For example, they selected the fenced off play area (which is actually for the youngest children) because they wanted to use the fencing behind it which they felt made it seem more real, more 'street' and less like a UK primary school than most of the other settings they had to use. The city-like, urban background the fence connotes, was part of the boys' attempt to convey the fact that these characters were outsiders from the rest of the school. Later in the process the boys wanted to signify that the talent show was a final, and different from the auditions. They decided to have a live audience who could be seen to clap to show how well each child did. They had thought about having a stage and curtains but because we only had one morning session to film this part and because the hall needed to be set up for lunch ten minutes after we were due to complete our activity we had to use the same setting as for the audition scene. Enabling the children to adapt and change their environment to help them tell their story was an important aspect of their meaning making and worth making time and space for. On reflection as this scene was the final climactic scene, it would have been interesting to give the children the possibility to adapt the setting further. However they did use a school trophy and a small platform to signal the difference between this final scene and the audition.

In the filming of the auditions for the talent show Eve made some interesting decisions about where the camera should be. They were constrained by the corridor they were working in but opted for a low angle-shot which would enable the audience to see the children practicing before going in for their audition. They cut the auditions between these shots. The camera acted as a third person observer, rather than representing any one particular point of view although they used close-up to ensure the audience could see the reaction of each auditionee as they succeeded or failed. These are more like the sorts of shots found in reality TV than in drama where the point of view of a lead character would perhaps be followed.

In film form the children considered setting and what it contributed to the overall meaning of their story more than they did in their written or oral stories where they tended not to describe places at all and used existing schemas based on previous experiences of text in short-hand form. Even though the setting was limited by the need to film in school, the children adapted their locations through use of props and attempted to shape meaning by their composition of shots. Clearly, they recognised that setting is an important aspect of narratives with potential to contribute meaning to the story. Perhaps the physical act of having to decide where to film, and then composing an appropriate shot in that space, enabled children to focus particularly on the role of setting in their storytelling.

Plot and structure

Both groups had an everyday school setting and chose to act as the main characters and these elements combined shaped the plot and structure of their stories. However, there were differences in the way each group used their narrative repertoires, particularly their experiences of film, to devise further ideas. Significantly, in the light of their earlier comments about the need for a 'problem', the girls did not initially identify any problem to be solved in their story or any theme. This was perhaps evidence of some of the thinking Abbey had done about not needing a problem and her attempt to work that idea through. It might also be seen as evidence of the influence of the everyday serialised stories Eve enjoys reading and watching on television. These stories keep a core aspect of the disunity of the story unresolved to sustain interest. Tracy Beaker (Wilson, 1991) wants to be, but never is adopted. Horrid Henry is always in conflict with his brother, Perfect Peter (Unwin, 2006). The lack of a problem or any clear source of narrative tension was something the girls did not appear to perceive as a concern in relation to their film story.

In the script-writing session I decided to ask the girls about the issue of the 'problem'. I was keen to see to what extent they had explicitly thought about this. Once the playground improvement idea had developed, I thought perhaps they had identified the element which would give their story a more visible structure and demonstrate a closure or resolution. However, once I began to discuss this issue with them it was clear that the playground was a secondary idea and that it was the bun sale and the relationship between the characters that was of greater importance to them. After some further negotiation they came up with the idea that Matilda's character would try and spoil the bun sale for her friends by stealing some cakes. Once they had come up with this idea the story shape began to form further. They would persuade their teacher to let them have a bun sale, they would organise it and then Matilda's character would be caught stealing and be punished. In the end the children would make up and all play in the new playground together. Their final film resembles a series, having many satellite storylines revolving around different characters, such as the playground needing improvement, punishment of the baddie, the teacher being impatient, and the friendships of the characters. There is a sense that the stories could be picked up and continued episodically. Thus, the girls were perhaps drawing on their experiences of television drama series more than children's films in devising a storyline.

The boys were committed from the beginning to the idea that their film should have a theme or message. The theme of two distinct cultural worlds (ballet and street dance) colliding is also explored in the film *Step Up* (Fletcher, 2006) and a number of other dance-related films which Connor had recently watched. In these films the characters, who represent different social worlds, are usually brought together by their common skill at dancing. Similarly the boys' theme, while not about romantic love, explored the issue of friendship tested by competition. Connor and Aaron decided that the moral of their film would be that 'friendship was more important than winning' a common moral in live-action children's films such as *Cool Runnings* (1993). The idea that a film should have a message is something that Connor had been thinking about from the very first session and it was clearly important to him to incorporate a message he had sympathy with in his own film. Given the strong moral positions of many films and television programmes for children, this is perhaps not surprising. The adherence to a message or theme however, was also an important scaffold supporting decision-making about the characters and the narrative structure. In knowing how their film was going to end, that is to say what the climax of the story would be, the boys were able to plan the events that they would need to show to arrive at this moment.

Theme was not the only organising principle of their film however, and the boys also drew on the now very familiar structure of television talent shows. So they incorporated auditions and then a final performance. They organised their film in a conventional linear structure, over two or three days and with no flashbacks. Parker (2006) found that for some children their film productions demonstrated their understanding of narrative structure far more effectively than their writing, and this would certainly seem to be the case for the boys in this group. In their writing the boys drew on a range of schema to plan the plots of their stories. Each of them discussed the importance of having a story structure and understood about resolution. However, although in their writing the planned structure of their storyline was visible, that is to say, it could be inferred, rarely did they reach the point of resolution. The children's storyboards did not help them to plan good camera shots, they did enable them to divide up the scenes for their film narratives and place them in a manageable structure. Perhaps again the explicit nature of film enabled the children to put their understandings of narrative structure into practice more effectively than in their writing.

All the children used the Apple Mac software, iMovie, to edit shots together to make a coherent story, following continuity editing conventions. This was not because they had been explicitly taught about editing, but because the pre-production and production practices shaped their film footage. Their scripts and storyboards and the shooting in chronological sequence meant that they had a clear sense of when and how to link each shot. So to an extent they had edited in camera, and although they did have some different takes of each scene these were often filmed from the same angle. When selecting which take of each shot to use, many decisions were made because a particular take was the best performance or nothing went wrong, rather than for any other aesthetic reasons. Despite their growing understandings of camera conventions, sometimes there were big movements of camera or changes in the composition of the shot that meant they had to use transitions to attempt to make the scenes flow from one to the other. This process, however, did seem to heighten their awareness of the need for visual continuity in their work. Another tactic the boys used to create continuity was to use a song which starts as sound track then becomes part of the diegetic world of the film and then becomes soundtrack again. This enabled them to link together the scenes of the auditions.

The most challenging element regarding the structure of their films was the spatial arrangements they made to represent the passage of time. Porter Abbot (2002) argues that narrative is the 'principal way in which our species organises its understanding of time' (Porter Abbot, 2002, p. 3). As can be seen in the interviews and previous examples of their work the children had absorbed understandings of the way texts demonstrate time passing and organise events. In their writing and oral storytelling they organised their stories into paragraphs, although often using mundane language such as 'and then' which enabled them to move either slowly or quickly through time. In film they found it particularly difficult to represent longer shifts in time by days, weeks or months.

For example, in the girls' film although most of the action took place across several days which they were able to signal reasonably effectively using simple cuts from one scene to the next, the final scene is supposed to happen some time later. They signal this with the title 'Many bun sales later' to ensure the audience were aware of the passage of time and here they were also paying attention to the coherence of the story, that is to say that one bun sale does not provide a new playground. However, they were not entirely satisfied with this tactic, knowing that it did not mirror what they would see in films. Clearly, the children would have benefitted from being shown how films use transitions, dialogue, lighting and sound to represent the passage of time.

Children's expressions of chronology in their storytelling might also relate to form. For example when the children write a story in school the writing they draw on as a resource to help them is likely to be a children's book, which is not short and is often divided into chapters. In their school-writing then children are being asked to condense their ideas for a children's book into a short story. Similarly, in this activity the children came up with ideas for children's feature films and then had to condense them into short films (a form they have almost no experience of). The rhythms and movement of chapters and scenes, paragraphs and sequences, shots and sentences are distinct in novels and feature films. Short forms such as poetry or the short film or story have different conventions which may be less familiar to children. Children need to have access to a variety of texts, including short films if they are being asked to create films in this form.

Interestingly, at the beginning of the process of film-making the children constantly tried to renegotiate the length of their films. I had set a length at 3 minutes because I believed we would struggle to finish anything longer, but they knew that this was not consistent with the duration of a feature film. Since we often ask children to adapt their stories into different forms it might be useful to explore the ways in which we can help them to recognise the different spatial and temporal conventions of narratives in different media. By doing so we might also make it possible for children to make informed and appropriate decisions about the duration, structure, pace and rhythm of their stories.

Atmosphere/tone/soundtrack

Editing a sound track onto their film was one of the favourite moments of the project for most of the group. Part of this response was the novelty of the experience. It was not one that they had ever encountered before and they loved what music added to their story. They quickly became playful, realising that different music had a very different impact on their film. The children selected to use popular music that they liked as their sound tracks although they sometimes chose things because they 'went better with the story' or inferred something about a character. The professionally produced music also heightened their perception of the quality of their film. So although the school did not exactly match what the boys had in their minds for the setting of their film they tried to make up for this in their use of music so they choose music which they felt contributed to creating a 'buzzy' atmosphere. The boys in particular used the sound track as an opportunity to display their music preferences, contrasting this to the classical ballet music they used for their rival competitor in the talent show.

Burn and Parker (2003) demonstrate the importance of sound as one mode which used in conjunction with others contributes to children's meaning-making. Without having had the opportunity to try out different musical choices on their films and then select when they would come in, whether they were diegetic or non-diegetic, it is unlikely that the children would have gained an understanding of the affordances of music as one aspect of their storytelling.

Institutional awareness

The children used the iMovie titles enthusiastically choosing colours and fonts with care. Both groups chose the same style that was used in the first *Star Wars* films, just because they liked them. Of course, the *Star Wars* rolling titles might not be considered appropriate to the everyday genre of their films but towards the end of the project the playfulness they had exhibited in earlier activities had returned and many of their decisions were motivated by having fun. All the children were also very enthusiastic about the outtakes they had added at the end of the film. These seemed to be the most satisfying decisions they made because the editing of the scenes from their films offered them less choice, whereas the editing of the outtakes involved them in selecting from all of their footage and then experimenting with all the effects available on the software, including playing footage backwards and speeding it up. Their inclusion of the 'giggling' outtakes also mirrors the sorts of material available on film DVDs which show behind the scenes of the film. They were telling a story about the fun they had while filming and this, as in the film industry, is an important aspect of developing a relationship with the audience.

Audience

The children were taken aback by the positive response they received at the screenings of their films. I think by then they had lived with their films for so long they no longer regarded them as anything special. However, seeing them on a big screen, hearing people laugh at appropriate times and anticipating their responses to certain moments, such as when Matilda is discovered or when Connor and Aaron are freeze-framed dancing, provided them with great satisfaction. I think they felt that to other people their films were better than they now thought they were. Having accomplished their first films and learnt something of the film-production process they were more critical of their own work than their peers and teachers who did not have experience of film-making.

Both the audience's positive response and their own more critical response contributed considerably to them developing their skills of film production. Just as having a real audience enhances the writing process, having an audience for film production has a strong impact both on the content and learning process. The children's more ephemeral texts gave them opportunities to explore the more transgressive and playful aspects of narratives they have pleasure in. Film production for a particular audience, including adults, produced different responses from the children. Here, they drew on school discourses of what was suitable in stories, especially those stories that would be shared at a cinema with parents and teachers. There was no moment in the live-action film production when the children asked if they could include violence for example or swearing. However, their choice of content, and the texts they drew on resulted in films which were expressions of identities in practice.

The dialogic and explicit nature of live-action film-production activity enabled the children to make decisions about character, plot and setting which enriched their stories. For some of the children their live-action films enabled them to express greater complexity of understanding of narrative. Furthermore, making films in this way enabled the children to make implicit and intuitive understandings of the semiotic affordances of film explicit. For example, the children learnt a great deal about the way shot composition contributes to meaning-making. Watching films does not necessarily make this understanding explicit to them, but making films helps them to put their intuitive knowledge into practice. Live-action was also an opportunity for the children to draw on children's films and also children's television programmes with everyday settings and they did so, particularly in their representations of relationships between adults and children but also in their use of themes to help them structure their films.

Analysis of the children's responses to the research activities and the texts they produced demonstrates that children's film plays an important role in developing understanding of narrative. In the film production activities the children drew on a wide range of familiar narrative elements from children's films to help them devise characters, settings and plots. Clearly through engagements with children's film narratives children learn about the common characteristics of narrative, however. And through experiences of film they also learn about the specific affordances of texts in different media. When they read stories children draw on their previous narrative experiences holistically; when they encounter new texts they turn to their closest previous experiences of fiction and life to help them (Robinson, 1997). This data implies that in creating texts children also turn to their closest experiences in terms of both content and form. Analysis of the texts and the process of production illustrates that given the opportunity children can draw on repertoires of experience of children's film. However, some aspects of these narratives and some of the modal affordances of film are more visible and as such a more useful and accessible resource than others. It is important to consider the implications of this finding for education, in particular, how best to enable children to make explicit some of their intuitive understandings of narrative.

In the drawn and Plasticine animation activities the children drew on an extensive repertoire of characters, some of which were from what could be called a generic pool, that is to say characters strongly associated with particular genres. The character types were from the imaginary story-worlds of films: vampires, mutants, superheroes, magic dogs and pigeons. The drawn form also enabled the children to make use of their knowledge of comic strip visual and language conventions. The children adapted rather than reproduced these ideas, creating hybrid characters which pushed at textual boundaries. They were able to draw on the particular affordances of animation in their drawings and designs for settings and in relation to plot. In their performances of their stories they paid attention to the different modes of film including colour, sound and music to convey meaning. Individual children could be seen to be developing signature responses to storytelling which relate to form (drawing), such as the use of exaggerated facial features or to wider narrative conventions (plot) such as the use of a subverted and unexpected ending.

The social, collaborative and improvisatory nature of this activity enabled the children to share their cultural capital and extend their expertise. This led to a marked shift in the hierarchy of learners, so that knowledge of popular culture and the ability to take risks and break rules in relation to text production were of high value. The responses were different depending on whether the task was undertaken in a friendship or non-friendship pairing. So that the one pair who was not in a friendship group approached the task in a more conventional and less playful manner from those who were working with friends who shared their enthusiasms. The friendship pairs also projected themselves into their stories leading to the creation of two main characters, which in turn led to their performance of cyclical rather than linear plots.

The context of the paper animation activity, that is to say, that it was not to be presented to an audience and that it was a form of animated 'play', meant the children could fully engage in storytelling without going through the lengthy process of full animation. This created a space for them to distance themselves from school discourses of what makes a good story and immerse themselves in the conventions and characteristics of children's animations and comic strips. Thus, the activity provided an opportunity to explore, from a comfortable distance, and resist regular identities by creating transgressive stories which dealt with ideas that concern children, such as violence, death and sleep, using parody. While this activity invited the children to be playful and transgressive in their texts and their approach to the task their work also reflects their understandings of the conventions of children's cartoons and animations which also incorporate these elements.

Even within the genre of animation, the specific medium, drawn or Plasticine, impacted on the ideas the children could draw on. This related to the children skills and experience at using different media. However, to fully express their ideas about a particular children's genre the children benefitted from opportunities to create them in the form they had encountered them in. For example, the children's drawn superheroes were richer in character than their Plasticine models. The choice of medium for film production activity has a strong impact on the extent to which children can draw on their experiences.

In creating film narratives children draw on existing schemas that are part of a culture they share and can access. The children readily drew on children's popular culture and these children's films, games, comics and television programmes often contain transgressive and playful elements that do not feature in the same way in the literary texts children are expected to read and write in school.

Children need opportunities to share their pleasures in transgressive and playful texts to enable them to share what they know about narratives in the formal classroom setting. If when children engage with film the space that opens up invites them to explore their own knowledge and pleasures then what results may be seen as incompatible with traditional classroom practices. However, as Bearne (2004) argues it is critical that we do find ways of valuing children's competences across a range of text production to 'ensure children's existing capital is not squandered' (Bearne, 2004, p. 102). By inviting into the classroom children's home engagements with film and other media and popular culture we may have to make some uncomfortable adjustments to pedagogic practices including re-evaluating what we value as important in storytelling in the light of what we know about film and other popular media. As Bearne writes:

> Readers, texts and institutions change and so should ways of helping children get a handle on the kind of literacies that are given high prestige. (Bearne, 2004, p. 99)

When devising and scripting their live-action films children started by thinking of ideas for characters, just as they did in their written stories.

Since they also decided to be the main characters the characters became performances of identities.

However, the children used this film production activity to display their popular culture and film tastes and preferences in a similar way to the 'curation of self' Potter (2009) describes. This curation displays both affiliation to particular texts such as street dance music or expertise in texts such as the vocabulary, dialect and register of serialised comedies. Interestingly, once the plots of their stories developed the children were prepared to adapt their characters to fulfil their function in the narrative thus distancing themselves from the role they were playing. Furthermore, when they filmed themselves acting there were further changes to the characters, particularly where the children could not perform in the way they had imagined.

The medium of live-action film and the school setting encouraged the children to opt for characters from everyday story-worlds. The anticipated audience (parents, teachers, peers) influenced the children to draw on school discourses of an effective story that is to say stories which draw on personal experience (Graves, 1983) rather than the fantasy they chose in their animations. In the live-action films the influence of children's films was particularly visible in relation to the representation of relationships and conflicts between adults and children. The children had an intuitive understanding of the need for tension between the 'good' and 'bad' characters and they devised adult authority characters who were peripheral and functional. Like children's films they also followed the point of view of the children rather than attempting to show the adult characters' perspective. Television drama series were also a source for live-action drama particularly in relation to narrative structure and dialogue.

In their live-action films the children paid attention to detail in a way that was distinct from their approach to writing. While in their writing they were made explicitly aware of the need to incorporate specific aspects such as descriptive language, in the film production their attention to visual and auditory detail, such as music, costume and gestures, was driven by their desire to make their story effective for the audience. All the children were able to express meaning through elements such as shot composition, music, titles, costume or casting to enhance the impact of their story. Even where the children could not perform the roles as they imagined them, they demonstrated knowledge of appropriate gestures and styles of performance. They also attempted to adapt the school setting or to frame their shots to show a partial view.

Parker (2006) observes that some children are able to express their understanding of narrative structure in their film production more effectively than in writing. In the boys' case the moral of their story, which was similar to other children's films about dance, acted as an organising structure for the events of their story. However, they also drew on the structure of television talent shows which they were highly familiar with. Through practice and peer learning the children's intuitive use of the conventions of continuity- editing developed. Parker (2006) argues that the explicit nature of film production raises children's awareness of gaps in composition and in the process of filming and reviewing and editing clips the children certainly became aware of flaws and attempted to address them matching their camera shots to what appeared to them to look right. Where it was not possible to re-shoot problematic scenes they attempted to fill what they perceived to be gaps in their expression such as inferring time passing, using titles and diegetic and non-diegetic music. Thus, in film-production plot and structure would appear to be aspects of narrative that the children recognise explicitly and put into practice in their work. The process of filmmaking can clearly help make explicit understandings of narrative that children use in their intuitive readings of film (Parker, 1999b). However, some elements such as those conventions used to show the passage of time seem to be less visible.

Bearne and Kress (2001) argue that children need to understand the affordances of particular modes. Each mode inherently makes some things possible and inhibits others Bearne (2004). Rather than look at the affordances of particular modes in terms of what they do or do not do, I would argue that they should be explored in terms of how they do the same things differently. Parker (2006) and Marsh and Millard (2000) suggest that film as a form is limited in relation to expressing the internal thoughts and feelings of characters. However, the children demonstrated that through music and shot composition they could suggest the emotions and moods of the characters. It is important to be careful not to make assumptions about the affordances of different media, especially in relation to limitations. A productive set of questions might be: 'How does film adopt a character's point of view?' And 'How does film convey the mood of a character or setting?'

In their writing, some of the children paid very little attention to describing their characters or settings. However, in their films they were clearly making decisions about the different modes to make their films have greater clarity, interest and appeal. Where Connor and Aaron decided to choose street clothes for their characters, they invested those clothes with meaning and they also begin to explore how even something as simple as costume can have a role to play in signifying to the audience when a day has passed or a new event is happening. If they were then to consider how in writing they would communicate the same thing this might drive forward their desire to use descriptive language more meaningfully than feeling they need to include a simile to achieve a certain level of attainment.

It is important not to see this as a one-way process; understanding the affordances of film might enrich children's ability to write. Equally, understanding the affordances of writing might help them in their film-making. So a description of particular aspects of a setting, i.e. the colour of the grass in the moonlight, might enable children to think more about how to compose, frame and light their shot of some grass to create a certain impact. Indeed they may decide that to have the same effect they would need to draw on a different mode; to have a certain type of music or sound that would help create the atmosphere of the setting. Film production enables children to pay attention to the distinct modes of film and to combine them to create meaning. By doing so they are making explicit aspects of their understanding of narrative which would otherwise remain under the surface. Film production thus has a vital role to play in the development of children's understanding of narrative, potentially also enhancing their access to school literacy. Recursive opportunities to tell stories in moving image form should be an entitlement for children and in the light of digital technological advances this is both a possibility and an imperative.

9
A Case for Children's Film

Methodological reflections

The nature of this study was a small scale, qualitative research project which drew on the experiences of six children in one school, in a large city in the UK. It was never my intention to produce research which attempted to generalise about the particular experiences of these children to make inferences about the wider population. As Cohen, Manion and Morrison (2007) point out, this would amount to attempting to apply the measures of reliability of quantitative work to qualitative work. I aim to avoid drawing on the rhetoric (Firestone, 1987) of quantitative methodologies, particularly in relation to the making of generalisations. Regardless of scale or paradigm, or claims to be 'evidence-based', as we hear in everyday discussions of education, research can only present data which are particular to the researchers, the context and the research participants at a particular time and context (Wellington, 2000). The limitations and criticisms of qualitative work are often the result of inappropriately applying quantitative criteria. To evaluate qualitative work thoughtfully and rigorously, the tools of appraisal should stem from the qualitative paradigm:

> Qualitative methods express the assumptions of a phenomenological paradigm that there are multiple realities that are socially defined. (Firestone, 1987, p. 16)

As a consequence I would not wish to defend my research in relation to the conventions of a quantitative approach considering generalisability, validity or triangulation, for example. My aim, then, is to find ways to critically reflect on the qualitative data I have produced, rather than attempt to identify the limitations of a qualitative study per se.

In particular it was apparent that where the children were offered a range of means of expression this enabled increased participation in the research. Ensuring a long-term opportunity for research dialogue increased the 'dependability' (Lincoln and Guba, 1985, pp. 108–9) of the data. For example, I asked of written, verbal, drawn and filmed stories what each revealed about the child's understandings of narrative or what aspects of popular culture they draw on. In doing so I was influenced by an awareness of the semiotic affordances of the children's texts, for example: 'Why does Aaron use the colour red in this image?' Rather than offer a semiotic analysis of the discrete texts I treated them as artefacts the children produced with the cultural and material products they 'have to hand' (Kress, 2000) attributing meaning where there was clear evidence that the child themselves had attributed a similar meaning. This led to some checking back and forth asking about decisions such as: 'when you used the colour red here you seemed to be enjoying drawing blood, knowing it would make your friends laugh'. In doing so I was able to explore a range of interpretations for the children's meaning-making. Sometimes I found I had over-attributed and sometimes misunderstood and this process was again a useful insight into the decisions the children made in creating stories.

It is my belief that this research should aim to contribute incrementally to understandings of children's developing literacy in relation to narrative and popular culture. In the context of educational research Simons et al. (2003) establish the possibility of transference of data into other similar contexts:

> Generalisation takes place (that is to say, there is a process of transforming context-bound data into transferable evidence for other contexts), but only if the relationship to the given situation is sufficiently retained for others to recognise and connect through common problems and issues. (Simons et al., 2003, p. 347)

The idea of transferability describes well the reaction I have had when presenting my data at conferences and seminars. For example, when I talked about Connor's experiences in particular, I found lots of heads nodding in recognition and several teachers have commented that they have a boy or girl like that in their class or that they share concerns about the way writing is taught. Similarly, when I have discussed the particular experience of this school it has become clear that the school is perhaps not atypical of schools that are under pressure to improve performance and which draw heavily on government directives and contemporary initiatives about how writing should be taught. I imagine that in another setting where narratives are taught differently, or where popular culture is valued as a core aspect of literacy, then the data I collected would have been quite different. Small-scale studies such as this enable practitioners usefully to compare data from one context with their own. As such I present my conclusions as particular to these children in this context and invite others to relate them to their own experiences and contexts.

Summary of findings

The universality of narrative (Barthes, 1975) in life and in culture is well established. Links have also been demonstrated between early experiences of narratives and children as developing writers and storytellers (Spencer, 1988; Kress, 2000; Barrs, 2001, 2004). Children participate in a 'narrative web' of popular culture texts and artefacts which enhance their literacy and identity practices (Marsh, 2005; Pahl, 2006). Children's films make a distinct contribution to the 'symbolic resources' (Buckingham and Sefton-Green, 1994; Pahl, 2006) children draw on in their talk, play and text production, contributing to children's emerging understandings of narrative in particular ways which are worthwhile to explore. By engaging with films children are also learning about the semiotic affordances of the kinekonic mode. My research attempted to understand what children learn about narratives from children's films and how this relates to their literacy and identity development, particularly in relation to their production of texts.

Children's participation in and engagement with children's film

For some of the children in this research children's films were a primary early source of narrative. The children had extensive experiences of children's films which they watched at the cinema, at home and in their bedrooms. The children expressed strong affective relationships with particular children's films from their childhoods, had watched many children's films, including some from different eras, and they had developed distinct preferences. With a few notable exceptions the films the children discussed were American. Their viewing of children's films was closely connected to family life but also emerging independent social lives with friends. Parents and siblings adopted different roles, including gate-keepers, advisors, facilitators and fellow viewers. For some, watching children's films was a whole family experience; for others, it was largely an individual activity.

The children enjoyed talking about aspects of favourite films, invoking memories they wanted to share. These film memories or stories were also expressions of identity. Through their talk about film the children were able to establish a sense of self according to the sorts of films they liked or the aspect of the film they most enjoyed. The children could clearly be seen to be reading films in the way Rosenblatt (1970) describes the reading of literary texts, that is to say experiencing them aesthetically and developing strong affective responses to them.

All the children described accumulating artefacts extending their experience of favourite films and demonstrating how these 'narrative webs' permeate family life (Marsh, 2005). These artefacts had also become important to developing family narratives (Pahl, 2002) about identity. Socially, in school these artefacts had a special status, enabling the children to play their favourite films, but also enabling them to signal their affiliation to a particular film. Having artefacts, ephemera and film-related toys was also clearly a marker of identity and enabled social alignment (Dyson, 2003) and this was particularly noticeable in this period of transition, Year 6, when the children were about to move on to secondary school.

At home and socially at school the children talked about and played games based on children's films, and knowledge of contemporary films was a valued asset. Particular films had achieved an almost universal status as a forum for play such as *Star Wars* (Lucas, 2002). The children used play about film to explore identities and children with the most knowledge of the film were more able to access games and more able to be inventive within them. Abbey, who had less experience of children's films, had a strategy in place to make sure she was kept up to date with new films. Films clearly often acted as a 'collective memory' (Bromley, 1996) forming an 'interpretive community' (Fish, 1980), linking groups of children. In their descriptions of play based on films it became clear that children were active readers of film, filling gaps (Iser, 1980) formulating their own responses and adapting the resources available to them. Reading and responding to films was clearly a shared, social process through which meaning was negotiated and transformed.

There are parallels between children developing as readers of books and children becoming readers of children's film. The children selected texts based on preferences which became markers of identity; they were associated with the sorts of texts they liked such as 'fantasy', 'animal' 'action' 'superhero'. Just as some children like certain genres or aspects of print fiction, some of the children had developed tastes in narratives in other media which became an aspect of their identity and they had developed expertise about these stories and the forms they take. Furthermore, experiences of previous texts helped the children to select and respond to new texts.

Within the play relating to children's film the children adapted and transformed characters, resisting some of the roles they were invited to play by the texts. The girls in particular resisted the female roles offered to them in children's films, choosing to play more interesting roles instead, demonstrating that we cannot predict the meaning children will construct in response to texts (Tobin, 2000). In their play the children's reading of films was active, rejecting elements of the texts which did not fit with their own preferred identities. The children were also cultural readers of films, playing games which were influenced by generic elements of films but did not have one key film as the source. They described fantasy games and army action games and therefore recognised films as having cultural boundaries with familiar conventions and schemas they could draw on.

The children's experiences of film provided them with resources for talk and play at home and socially at school. Furthermore, in their talk and in their play the children were clearly aesthetic, active and cultural readers of narrative texts. Marsh (2005) recognises that mediascapes or globalised narratives (Appadurai, 1996) of children's popular culture are adapted into family practices, becoming key resources for play and performance of identity. Marsh (2005) questions why films and other forms of popular culture do not permeate school life in the same way. At home and socially at school, film experiences and preferences were important to the children's development of, and orientation to, literacy and identity practices. The children's engagements with children's films resemble the deep play that Spencer (1991) describes in relation to books and similarly enabled them to accrue a set of resources about narrative. It is therefore useful to consider whether the children were able to make explicit and draw on these narrative experiences in school.

Children's films: a source of ideas about narrative in the classroom

The children's experience of narrative in the classroom was the reading and writing of print text. As a result although the children's home experiences as readers of children's films were certainly visible in the social sphere of school, they were less obvious in the classroom. The teacher was very positive about film however the children often regulated their own writing, understanding that ideas from film and television were not compatible with the tasks they were set. Activities undertaken as part of the National Literacy Strategy such as direct retellings of stories also limited opportunities for the children to draw on their knowledge of narrative from outside school. For example even where they were asked to *draw* story maps or *orally* tell stories, these tasks were often the reductive retelling of just-heard stories – the 'direct modelling' Barrs (2001) roundly critiques as being restrictive. Written storytelling was taught to enable children to improve writing skills as prescribed by interventions such as 'Big Writing'. This scheme perceives children to have a deficit of language which must be compensated for.

In their narratives produced in school literacy activities and in the verbal interviews the children were able to explain what they have learnt about narrative in school. They adopted school discourses about what makes a good story, including descriptive writing (language and style) and a problem to be solved (structure). The children had been taught to recognise and begin composing stories with elements of narrative such as characters and setting. Curriculum and pedagogic constraints often led the children to write in particular ways, for example using awkward similes. Furthermore, the focus on guided writing led the children to emulate approved school stories rather than fantasy stories. Overall, some of the children experienced a dissonance between the storytelling experiences they had encountered at home in film and other popular culture texts and what was valued in school.

In particular there was no space in the curriculum to explore how different children's media texts, such as children's film, created tell stories. As a result there was a lack of connection between the children experiences of narrative and what they were experiencing at school.

Dyson (1997) and Willett (2001) demonstrate that, given the space, children can be resourceful and determined to include their experiences of popular culture in their own stories. Despite the tight boundaries implicit to the tasks, in the children's written stories there was evidence of influences from children's films as well as games. For example, the children attempted to produce texts which were a hybrid (Kenner, 2003, 2005), combining their home and school experiences of narrative. They found characters a particularly accessible way of making cultural links across types of texts. Furthermore, they could use the form and style of one medium in another, so they used the language of games, for example, in their written stories. However, these elements of their stories were not compatible with school curriculum and pedagogy relating to narrative. Children's films have some key distinguishable features from adult films, such as the story being told from the child's point of view and the representation of children's relationships with parents. In their regular written stories the children adhered closely to the child's point of view and adults appeared as authority figures or functional characters rather than as central to the story.

In their free-writing task, (outside regular curriculum and pedagogic practice) the children expressed intuitive recognition of the rules and conventions of the everyday and imaginary story worlds of children's film. In this context the children mostly chose imaginary stories and particularly drew on the schemas offered by children's films in terms of plot and themes. These masterplots provided the children with a structure which they could contemporise and adapt. Even though they created fantasy fictional worlds the children took opportunities to project themselves into the text and explore their identities.

Children's films also often include a high proportion of action sequences, and trangressive, carnivalesque and violent humour in which children are empowered to challenge adult authority. Knowledge of these aspects came to the fore in the oral storytelling activities which were ephemeral and not created for an audience. In the oral storytelling the children paid attention to the visual and auditory elements of film while being playful with textual rules. They set up and disrupted audience expectations and had a strong sense of the internal coherence of the stories based on 'collective' texts (Bromley, 1996) such as *Star Wars* (Lucas, 2002). The children's oral stories, however, were again not compatible with school-based notions of good storytelling.

Writing as the main form of storytelling prioritises print texts over other expressive forms and in this form, without further support, children cannot articulate the stories that they play, think, feel, hear and 'see in their heads'. Clearly, a shift in pedagogy and changes to the curriculum, enabling children to make connections between home and school experiences of narrative are critical. However, this shift would result in changes to the sorts of stories children might be encouraged to write. That is to say, elements of the contemporary textual landscape (Carrington, 2005a) children encounter would need to be recognised and valued in school.

For those children whose experiences of narrative were principally based on visual and auditory popular culture texts the transference from multi-modal form to written form, (school stories) was a challenge. Millard (1997) observes that when children draw on film in their writing they write stories which contain too much dialogue and too little description. When the children drew on film in their writing, they were drawing on a familiar set of short-hand storytelling devices, leaving gaps in their writing particularly in relation to setting. Although the children were clearly active, aesthetic and cultural readers of film, in their writing they needed further support to draw on the multimodal affordances of film. Furthermore, they benefitted from the opportunity to express their funds of knowledge (Moll et al., 1992) about narrative in moving image form.

Children's film in children's moving image storytelling

Film production activity encouraged the children to draw on narrative elements from children's films to help them devise characters, settings and plots. In this context the children had an array of ideas and could be seen developing signature responses to storytelling. The drawn and Plasticine animation activities enabled the children to draw extensively on a generic pool of characters, plots and settings. The children demonstrated their familiarity with textual rules in relation to these narrative elements but they also adapted and subverted them, creating hybrid characters and unexpected plots. In their drawings and designs for settings and in relation to plot the children were able to draw on the particular affordances of animation. They also paid attention to the different modes of film including colour, sound and music to communicate ideas.

The children enjoyed sharing their pleasures in transgressive and playful animation texts and this encouraged them to explore and extend what they knew about narratives. In their paper animations where the texts were ephemeral and the audience was themselves they incorporated fantastical, playful and transgressive elements from familiar children's comics, cartoons and animated films. However, just as with their oral storytelling, their resulting texts may be seen as incompatible with traditional classroom practices. Yet, unless we value children's text production across media (Bearne, 2004), including those elements that mirror the distinctly children's texts they encounter daily, we will only ever see a tip of the iceberg of what children know and understand about narrative.

In their live-action films the children began by devising ideas for characters, just as they did in their written stories. They also decided to act as the main roles to the extent that the representation of characters became performances of identities.

Thus, the children used this film production activity as a process of 'self curation' (Potter, 2009), displaying their popular culture and film tastes and preferences to their peers. The children used their films to signal their connection to or expertise in particular texts. However, when the plots of their stories evolved the children distanced themselves from the role they were playing and were able to adapt their characters according to their function in the narrative. The characters the children envisaged in the planning stages did not always match up to what they chose or were able to perform and as a result the characters changed again when the children filmed themselves acting.

Using live-action film and the school setting implicitly invited the children to devise characters from everyday story-worlds. The children drew on school discourses of an effective story, that is to say stories which draw on personal experience (Graves, 1994) rather than fantasy. In making these choices the children were perhaps influenced by the anticipated audience of parents, teachers, and peers. The influence of children's films could be observed in the live-action films, in particular in relation to the inclusion of relationships and conflicts between adults and children. The children devised adult authority characters who were minor and functional, demonstrating their intuitive understanding of the need for tension between the 'good' and 'bad' characters. Rather than present the adult characters' perspectives they followed the point of view of the children, following a convention of children's films (Bazalgette and Staples, 1995).

The moral of the boys' film was similar to other children's films about dance and worked as an organising structure alongside the structure of television talent shows. The girls also made use of ideas from television drama series in their live-action drama particularly in relation to narrative structure and dialogue. These appeared to be closer to the task they were undertaking than the live-action (non animation) children's films they had experience of such as *Star Wars* (Lucas, 2002) or *Harry Potter* (Columbus, 2002). Plot and structure seem to be aspects of narrative that the children recognised explicitly and could apply to their work. Engagements with children's film had developed the children's understandings of the holistic characteristics of narrative, but it is important to also consider what they understand about the specific affordances of moving image texts.

In their live-action films the children incorporated details, making full use of the affordances of the kinekonic mode. They made careful decisions to include visual and auditory elements such as music, costume and gestures, motivated by their awareness of their audience. All the children were able to articulate ideas, using shot composition, music, titles, costume or casting to enrich their stories. Undertaking collaborative practical production enhanced the children's intuitive uses of the conventions of continuity editing. In the process of filming and reviewing clips and editing the children became increasingly aware of what Parker (2006) refers to as gaps in composition and attempted to address them, matching their camera shots to what appeared to them to look 'right', drawing as they did so on conventions of continuity editing. The children also used titles, diegetic and non-diegetic music to address what they perceived to be gaps in their expression such as inferring time passing. Film production activity demonstrates that children are able make their semiotic reading of film explicit. In their films the children made decisions about uses of the different modes to enhance clarity, interest and appeal.

When creating texts the children turned to their closest previous experiences in terms of content and also form. Animation, for example, enabled the children to make use of their knowledge of comic strip visual and language conventions. However, some aspects of narrative and some of the modal affordances of film are more visible and as such a more useful and accessible resource than others. Some elements, such as those conventions used to show the passage of time, seem to be less visible.

It is important to consider the implications of this finding for education, in particular, to explore how best to enable children to make explicit some of their intuitive understandings of narratives and the forms they take.

Implications for policy

Potter (2009) suggests that the shift away from prescribed literacy pedagogy and curriculum in the UK will potentially result in classrooms in which ' closer negotiation and integration with lived media and popular culture' will lead to 'a critical engagement with making and evaluating texts in many modes' including film (Potter, 2009, p. 269). However, in the current context in which subjects such as Media Studies have been singled out for criticism by the current minister for education, it seems unlikely that children's lived media and popular culture will be readily accommodated in the classroom.

It would seem that education policy is perpetually under review but that resulting policy regarding curriculum and pedagogy is increasingly reactionary, particularly with regard to the teaching of literacy. Popular culture is unlikely to be a high priority but if school practices do not move closer in proximity to the texts children encounter out of school (Carrington, 2005a) those children will be excluded from the literacy curriculum. While there has been a considerable focus on new technologies in learning there has been less of a focus on the narratives that they distribute. These narratives are frequently visual or multimodal. Film is not then an old media but is very much at the heart of the 'narrative web' (Marsh, 2005) of new media and associated with an array of online and offline literacy practices and as such should be taken seriously by policy-makers:

> Teaching about moving image is not in itself a panacea but it is transformative, bringing English much more intelligently in touch with lived culture and critical energy. (Goodwyn, 2004, p. 22)

Not only does the inclusion of moving image in the literacy curriculum connect with the textual landscape of children's contemporary lives (Carrington, 2005a), it also ensures that the teaching of literacy moves beyond an isolated focus on the alphabetic texts:

> Literacy and communication curricula rethought in this fashion offer an education in which creativity in different domains and different levels of representation is well understood, in which both theory and difference are seen as normal and productive. The young who experienced that kind of curriculum might feel at ease in a world of incessant change. (Kress, 2003, p. 121)

Vincent (2004) argues that the word literacy has become 'promiscuous' and cautions against blurring the distinction between literacy, reading and writing, speaking and listening and other semiotic practices such as decoding the visual or oral. Whether we use the word literacy generically or define specialist areas of literacy such cine-literacy, media literacy or digital literacy we must be clear that we are describing a distinct but complementary set of capacities, competencies and skills linked to the texts themselves. Kress argues for a theory of text to meet the needs of 'culturally plural societies in a global world' (Kress, 2003, p. 121). The texts children access influence their sense of self and the stories they tell. It is critical then that we have a curriculum that is responsive to the changing textual landscape children encounter.

Children's films have their own distinct conventions contributing to children's developing understanding of story, alongside other forms of popular culture. Children's films are narrative texts and there is a need for further research which raises questions about children's films as a corpus of work alongside children's books, television, comics and games. Children in the UK access films which are predominantly American. Even taking into account the impact of the flows between mediascapes (Appadurai, 1996) and the culturally hybrid texts that are produced, children rarely see films for children that are of British origin. American films with their long histories of production and patriarchal provenance represent children and childhood in particular ways. These films often follow particular conventions governing what is suitable for children, which may not reflect national or indeed regional cultural experiences.

Analysis of children's films often focuses on their ideological content (Giroux, 1995, 1999), however research which engages with children demonstrates that they are active not passive readers of film (Hodge and Tripp, 1986; Richards, 1995; Tobin, 2000), It is not useful to caricature American films as overtly socialising, they are not homogenous, but there are distinct absences which children in the UK might feel. As Carrington (2005a) points out, texts considered suitable for children rarely deal with diversity or children living in poverty or dealing with violence.

As important as education policy, then, is policy in relation to the production of media for children in the UK. If the current policy of inactivity continues, it will not be long before there is neither film nor television made for children in the UK. It is not enough to say that UK children are well served with American product. If we acknowledge that children's films teach children about films and about narrative, it is critical to go further to say that children are entitled to see films made about and within their own culture. It would not be suggested that children are well enough served by American books. While I would strongly argue that American children's films are significant and indeed are of value I would also argue that children in the UK need to see a diverse range of films, including those that tell the stories of the contemporary British childhood.

Children's film production in the UK is not viable without subsidy but there are models, used in the past, which could enable a small number of films to be made each year. In countries such as Norway indigenous children's films regularly boost audience viewing-figures, gaining local success because the films are culturally apt in a way that global mainstream films could not be. For example, the Norwegian Film and Television Fund reported that in 2009 five children's films sold 1 million tickets in Norway and accounted for 40% of all admissions for Norwegian films. These films should be the model of success that the UK aspires to.

Just as with reading books children need access to a range of films including the familiar and the unfamiliar, the generic and the innovative. To extend their understandings of narrative we must build 'ladders' (Protherough, 1983) of opportunities for them to access a diversity of texts. Although policy changes can bring about systemic change to the curriculum enabling the increased inclusion of film and film production, the role of the teacher is also highly important to determining the way film is taught in relation to literacy and the sorts of films that are available.

Implications for pedagogy and research

In the current context of imposed pedagogy, external scrutiny and self-regulation, the role of popular culture in children's lives remains under-explored in the literacy classroom. Making space for the children to reflect holistically on their own experiences of narratives, encouraged them to question the patterns and meanings of stories. Film was not necessarily more significant to children than other media or popular culture forms, but it made a distinctive contribution to their understandings of the nature and construction of narrative texts. Children, whose narrative experiences are predominantly made up of media texts (not literary texts), are all too often excluded from discussion.

Marsh (2005) and Dyson (1997, 2003) demonstrate that an environment where home and school practices can meet and be valued would enable children to reflect usefully on their home literacy and identity practices. Such an environment might enable children, whose primary experience of narrative is moving image, to use their experiences in the classroom. The children in this research attempted to draw on all their resources to help them tell stories but it was only when explicitly invited to that they drew extensively on children's film. In doing so, they revealed considerable understandings both of the characteristics of narrative and the semiotic affordances of film and were also seen to develop further their understandings when the collaborative process of film-making enabled them to make this knowledge explicit.

It is therefore highly important that teachers/researchers make it evident to children the value they place on children's popular culture. This could be manifested as an enthusiasm and interest in popular culture. Having children's film-related artefacts in the classroom, displays and film libraries as well as shared film screenings might also open up a productive and connected dialogue in the classroom. However, the invitation to draw on popular culture including film also extends to the nature of the tasks set as well as the form of expression they take.

Although children are resourceful in their attempts to draw on their own interests in the school-based literacy curriculum (Willett, 2001) they recognise that they are not entirely compatible with their interests from home. It is not surprising then, that they do not fully draw on film in many of their school-based writing tasks. Dyson (1997, 2003) demonstrates that when teachers/researchers do attempt to understand children's cultural practices, through discussion, children reflect on the meaning of their own actions and responses. Opening this space shifts the balance of power away from the prescribed curriculum and the knowledge of the teacher and towards pedagogy of greater dialogue. Making creative and communicative spaces in which children can explore their own literacy practices and enthusiasms enables them to draw on 'a diversity of symbolic and cultural materials' (Dyson, 2003, p. 213).

When children find that these symbolic and cultural materials are valued in official school spaces they increasingly share them but also explicitly reflect on how they are constructed. Working in a medium different from writing, such as film, also disrupts the existing hierarchies in terms of literacy identities. Some children's cultural capital increases in value and this in turn potentially enhances their school-based literacy identity. To make visible some children's knowledge and understanding of narrative then, schools could undertake sharing, analysing and production of narratives in a wide range of forms including explorations of children's popular culture.

The different research activities opened up distinct spaces for children to explore their knowledge of narrative. All too often in film-making activity children are given criteria about the content with restrictive and worthy adult discourses about issues that children should be concerned with. Indeed funding is often given to projects which ask children to create anti-bullying, truancy, crime films or to address health or environment issues in particular ways. These film-making projects neither allow children to fully explore film as a narrative form, nor do they allow them to draw on popular culture. The resulting films are often a representation of an adult's point of view.

The nature of the tasks set, establish parameters for what aspects of repertoires of narrative children can draw on, and the extent to which they can 'play' with what they know. As was seen in the paper animation task the rules of the task became a scaffold but not a barrier. They were there as a guide not to be followed rigidly and this was critical to enabling all aspects of 'playing a text' as described by Mackey (2002). Furthermore, as soon as they had begun to explore ideas about popular culture, even in the formality of a research project in school, the children shed their official school identities and began to play. In so doing, they also began to move beyond what is considered appropriate in school-based narratives in terms of content but also in relation to their own behaviour. The children quickly introduced transgressive ideas to their paper stories, and they giggled noisily throughout the production process, at times shrieking ideas and collapsing into exhausted heaps on the floor at the end of their activity.

Children engage with popular culture in different ways depending on the audience for their work. Just as Grace and Tobin (1998) observed, the children were prepared to go down more risk-taking, transgressive routes in their text production when the audience for the work was themselves or their peers rather than teachers and parents. Grace and Tobin also noticed children conforming more in relation to the videos produced for adult audiences, which had a clear moral purpose, compared to those made for their peers which aimed to 'surprise, amuse and entertain' (Grace and Tobin, 1998, p. 47). These videos contained references to 'drool, burps, blood, dripping mucus, butt jokes, aggression, violence, and an occasional body part' (Grace and Tobin, 1998, p. 47):

> We argue that video production opens up a space where students can play with the boundaries of language and ideology and enjoy transgressive collective pleasures. (Grace and Tobin, 1998, p. 43)

Of course, inviting children to draw on contemporary children's films in these sorts of tasks has consequences for the curriculum and the teacher. The sorts of play Mackey (2002) and Grace and Tobin (1998) describe, demand a tolerance of transgression both in terms of the types of behaviour allowed in school and the sorts of content allowed in stories. The adult authority role is challenged in this context and would need to evolve into a role of a facilitator or mentor who recognises the need for open play and experimentation as a stage in the production of narratives. Bearne (2004) identifies the need for pedagogic change reflecting changes in readers, text and institutions. Further research might usefully address the sorts of stories children produce when they draw on popular culture, not only in their writing which has been the focus of research (Dyson, 1997, 2003; Willett, 2001; Merchant, 2005a), but in their production of multimodal narratives. Only by doing so can we properly address and advance our knowledge of pedagogy in relation to the teaching of contemporary text production.

The social, collaborative and improvisatory nature of film production enabled the children to share their cultural capital (Bourdieu, 2010) and extend their expertise. Marsh (2009) describes this process as an aspect of productive pedagogy, connectedness. The connections the students could make between home culture and school culture in terms of narrative led to a marked shift in the hierarchy of learners. Knowledge of popular culture and the ability to take risks and break rules in relation to text production were of high value. Thus, children can and do draw on these cultural resources, if the context of their storytelling allows it. However, drawing on popular culture often involves children in the challenging task of creating texts from one media or mode into another.

Millard (2005) describes her work with a teacher in which they take as their focus, fantasy and this, like the work of Dyson (1997) on superheroes, represents an important shift away from a focus on specific texts, either popular or literary, allowing children's different experiences of a wide range of texts to be included and explored. It also enables the writing process to be a shared, social and collaborative process rather than an individual one which Dyson (1997) demonstrates is a highly important aspect of the learning process. Millard (2005) emphasises how children's understandings of 'narrative forms in different modalities may support one another' (Millard, 2005, p. 162).

Reid (2003) argues that film (for example) can be used to scaffold writing and that students can learn about narrative by 'shuttling' between film form and print form to engage with the different modes of each. He proposes that print and film studied together help to make explicit what they have in common and what is specific to each form. He refers to a film where there is both ambiguity and no dialogue. The film acts as a scaffold for storytelling, with learners using their own inferences based on their cultural knowledge. Marsh and Millard (2000) suggest that children need to understand how to deconstruct visual texts, recognising the different and similar ways they signify meaning. Parker (1999a, 2006) also found in his study of children adapting from book to film that children were able to infer meaning in their film which they then went on to describe in more detail in their writing. However, when the children in my research group wrote their own film as a story they did not use description but dialogue instead.

It would seem then that children need further support to adapt an idea to a medium in which they are less confident but that their knowledge of one medium might offer teachers a starting point for enabling children to express themselves in another medium. Teaching about different forms of narrative, through comparisons, might enrich children's understanding while drawing on considerable acquired knowledge. That teaching might include a process by which the teacher draws out what students already know, making that knowledge explicit, sharing specialised vocabulary to extend critical capacities and perhaps most importantly enabling students to undertake a range of creative outcomes (not just written ones) which demonstrate their range of responses, finally enabling students to share, reflect and feedback their experiences.

Had I pointed out to Connor that he could describe in written work the clothes, feelings, facial expressions, dance movements of his character, perhaps his writing would have had some of the richness of his film. In doing so I might have asked him, for example, to consider the role of the sound track and how he could create a similar atmosphere in the written form. Furthermore, had I explained more about the different ways film and print fiction create point of view or time elapsing, he might have found ways of creating these elements more effectively. Developing understandings of how different texts are made can enrich children's reading and production of narratives.

Bearne and Kress (2001) point out that children need to understand the affordances of particular modes. For children to fully understand the affordances of a mode or modes, it is critical for them to engage with critical analysis through production. Critical and creative film production enables children to make explicit their intuitive understandings of the semiotic affordances of film (Parker, 2006; Burn and Durran, 2006). Given that within this research it was clear that the children found some elements of the moving image more visible than others, it also important to consider further appropriate iterative opportunities for film-making, which move beyond what a first encounter with film production can teach, and towards confidence and competence in the use of the kinekonic mode as a form of expression.

Each mode inherently makes some things possible and inhibits others (Bearne, 2004). While I would agree that modes shape texts, it is critical not to make assumptions about the affordances of different media especially in relation to limitations. In relation to narrative it might be more productive to discuss how each medium constructs meaning in relation to characters, setting, plot, structure and other elements such as point of view or audience expectations. The application of these questions might allow children to consider their use of sound track in a film and how this conveyed in their writing. This might motivate them to use descriptive language more meaningfully than their current belief that they need to include a simile to achieve a certain level of attainment.

Understanding the affordances of film might enrich children's ability to write; equally, understanding the affordances of writing might enrich their film-making. This proposition generates the possibility of further useful research which focuses on activities deliberately devised to enable children to learn about narrative through a process of adaptation from one media to another; that is not to say that they look at filmed adaptations of literary texts, but that they have opportunities to create narratives in a number of different media.

Morris (2005) describes the difficulty some children have in bridging the gap between 'their visual knowledge and experience and the conventions of written narrative' (Morris, 2005, p. 21). She argues that the gap that exists is not just between print and written texts but also a gap which relates to children's lack of knowledge at what she describes a deeper level of the conventions of the visual text. Morris advocates the need to make explicit children's understandings of the language or grammar of film. She argues that moving image education should be given curriculum time to provide opportunities to connect 'with children's wider literacy practices' and contribute 'to more meaningful and successful experiences of writing' (Morris, 2005, p. 19). Morris goes on to point out the need for teachers and children to understand the similarities and difference between narratives in print and moving image form.

Further research would be useful to explore in more detail how different media construct narratives and how to make these differences useful to children:

> The point would be to foster an understanding of moving image grammar as an ally, as a mechanism for making communication in the modes of the moving image clearer and enabling a more successful engagement with the lexis of production. (Potter, 2009, p. 276)

Just as Spencer (1988) argues that texts teach texts so movies teach movies. Barrs (2004) argues that the reader can be found in the writer, so too the viewer of films can be found in their film productions. Of course, children do not draw on only films in film production or on only books in their story writing. They attempt to draw on all of their knowledge of narrative in their storytelling when given the opportunity. However, the prominence of writing and the relatively marginalised role of film-making in schools mean that some of children's implicit knowledge of film-making is not fully accessed. Furthermore, only through film production activity can children make explicit their intuitive understandings of the affordances of the modes of film. Only through regular opportunities for making narratives in a range of forms, including film, can children access their own knowledge and by doing so potentially use that knowledge to transform their storytelling from one media to another.

There are many compelling reasons for the inclusion of children's home culture including their home experiences of video production in their school-based learning. If we compare Connor's nine-year-old ability to identify patterns in the filmed narratives he watches, his experimentation with in-phone film editing and his school production of a dance movie with Willett's (2009) example of twelve-year-old Jacob, who produced a skateboard film, there is a crucial difference. Connor could be seen as a younger version of Jacob moving towards becoming part of a participatory media culture Jenkins, (2009). There is one key difference between Jacob and Connor; as Willett (2009) makes clear, Jacob has strong family support for his activity. Connor does not. School therefore represents an important space for home interests to be fully explored, potentially also providing greater access to the literacy curriculum. Although children today can often lay their hands on cameras and do also make films at home there is an important role for schools to provide the 'interstitial space' Burn and Durran (2006) describe and which is needed for film-making (Burn and Durran, 2006, p. 275).

> This is the space where the realm of the amateur minority, who have self-trained in more advanced skills, overlaps with the educational realm where similar skills are provided for the many who would not otherwise acquire them. (Burn and Durran, 2006, p. 275)

This space is not only important to secondary-aged students studying Media Studies courses it is critical to much younger children. Watching, analysing, imagining and making films in school provides children with opportunities to share and extend what they know about narrative. Further research focusing on children's film production in both education and informal settings would enhance our understandings of appropriate and productive pedagogy. If popular children's films remain on the periphery of literacy teaching in primary schools the classroom will become a barrier between children's textual landscapes (Carrington, 2005a) outside and inside the classroom. To enable children to 'tell the stories in their head' we must take seriously their need to tell moving image stories.

Following the closure of the UK Film Council, The BFI has launched a plan for 2012–2017: Film Forever. It covers all BFI activity and will be funded by Grant in Aid from the Department for Culture, Media and Sport and an anticipated increased share of National Lottery receipts. The first stated priority is:

- Expanding education and learning and boosting audience choice.

One aspect of this, the 5–19 Film Education Scheme, was recently awarded to Film Nation UK who are charged with implementing a single integrated film education programme with activities and support across the UK which should be available to all 27,600 schools, to cinemas, youth organisations and community groups. This is a new business partnership combining two former high profile national film education organisations which were First Light and Film Club. Despite the politically led narrowing of the curriculum for literacy, there is a broader will to ensure all aspects of film education, the critical, cultural and creative, are embedded in school practice, and this is a cause for considerable optimism:

> Film education will be transformed across the UK with the creation, for the first time ever, of a single unified programme for watching, making and learning about film. (Film Nation UK, 2013)

It must be an aspiration of film educators globally that the work of Film Nation UK further documents the integral role of film in children's lives and learning and advocates for changes in curriculum and film production policy around the world.

I currently have a new favourite film, *Son of Rambow* (Jennings, 2008), which tells the story of two boys; one is often left to the dilatory care of his brother and one is overly controlled by his Plymouth Brethren family. The boys become friends and get their hands on a camera and start to make films based on the 'Rambo' films they had been pirate copying. The director reveals his inspiration:

> When I was about 11, my dad inherited a video camera from a friend. My dad was crap with anything technological so I immediately comman-deered the thing and started making little films with my friends, and the wonderful thing about it was that back then, anything was possible as far as we were concerned. We were influenced by the Spielberg and Lucas movies and the Vietnam films like 'Rambo' and 'Uncommon Valour' and stuff like that. We wanted to capture the time when you are that age, any-thing is possible and you're all pulling together. You have no fear – you're quite happy to do your own stunts, and you become very resourceful, coming up with all these weird and wonderful solutions for your story and your special effects. (Tilly, 2008, p. 1)

In the film the friendship of the two boys is severely tested and the production goes badly awry. The final scene is set in a local cinema the boys' film is shown (plot-spoiler). To their surprise, it had been finished by the tardy brother who is at once redeemed. Family rifts and friendships are repaired. For the boys in the story their film represents a summer-time of 'being resourceful', and com-ing up with 'wonderful solutions' for their stories. It should not be too dif-ficult for us then to imagine children 'commandeering cameras' at school, delighting in their favourite films and telling the stories in their heads.

References

Adamson, A. and Jenson, V. (2001) *Shrek* [Motion Picture] USA, Dreamworks.

Allers, R. and Minkoff, R. (1994) *Lion King* [Motion Picture] USA, Walt Disney Pictures.

Alvermann, D. E., Moon, J. S. and Hagood, M. C. (1999) *Popular Culture in the Classroom Teaching and Researching Critical Media Literacy*. Newark, International Reading Association.

Appadurai, A. J. (1996) *Modernity at Large: Cultural Dimensions of Globalization*. Minneapolis, University of Minnesota Press.

Aries, P. (1998) From Immodesty to Innocence. In Jenkins, H. (ed.) *The Children's Culture Reader*. New York, London, New York University Press, pp. 41–57.

Arthur, L. (2005) Popular Culture: Views of Parents and Educators. In Marsh, J. (ed.) *Popular Culture, New Media and Digital Literacy in Early Childhood*. Oxon, Routledge and Falmer.

Avery, T. (1930–1969) *Looney Tunes* [Animated Television Series] USA, Warner Brothers.

Bahktin, M. M. (1984) *Rabelais and His World* (Vol. 341). Indiana University Press.

Bancroft, T. and Cook, B. (1998) *Mulan* [Motion Picture] USA, Walt Disney Pictures.

Bandura, A., Ross, D., and Ross, S. A. (1963) Imitation of Film-Mediated Aggressive Models. *The Journal of Abnormal and Social Psychology*, 66(1), pp. 3–11.

Banks, M. (2001) *Visual Methods in Social Research*. London, Sage.

Bakhtin, M. M. (1968) *Rabelais and His World*. Trans. Hélène Iswolsky. Bloomington: Indiana University Press, 1993.

Barker, M. (1989) *Comics: Ideology, Power and the Critics*. Manchester, New York, Manchester University Press.

Barker, M. and Petley, J. (eds) (2001) *Ill Effects: The Media Violence Debate*. London, Routledge.

Barratt, A. J. B. (1998) *Audit of Media in English*. London, BFI.

Barrs, M. (2001) Children's Theories of Narrative. *English in Education*, 24 (1) pp. 32–39.

Barrs, M. (2004) The Reader in the Writer. In Grainger, T. (ed.) *Reader in Language and Literacy*. London, New York, Routledge Falmer, pp. 267–276.

Barrs, M. and Cork, V. (2001) *The Reader in the Writer*. London, CLPE.

Barrs, M., Ellis, S., Hester, H. and Thomas, A. (1990) *Patterns of Learning: The Primary Language Record and the National Curriculum*. London, CLPE.

Barthes, R. (1975) *The Pleasure of the Text*. New York, Hill and Wang.

Barthes, R. and Duisit, L. (1975) An Introduction to the Structural Analysis of Narrative. *New Literary History*, 6 (2) pp. 237–272.

Barton, R. (1994) *Literacy: An Introduction to the Ecology of Written Language*. Oxford, Blackwell.

Barton, D. and Hamilton, M. (1998) *Local Literacies: Reading and Writing in One Community*. London, Routledge.

Bazalgette, C. (ed.) (2003) Look Again! *A Teaching Guide to using Film and Television with three- to-eleven-year-olds*. BFI/DfES.

Bazalgette, C. (2010) Extending Children's Experience of Film. In Bazalgette, C. (ed.) *Teaching Media in Primary School. Los Angeles*. London, New Delhi, Singapore, Washington DC, Media Education Association / Sage, pp. 35–45.

Bazalgette, C. and Staples, T. (1995) Unshrinking the Kids: Children's Cinema and the Family Film. In Bazalgette, C. (ed.) *In Front of the Children: Screen Entertainment and Young Audiences*. London, British Film Institute, pp. 92–108.

Bearne, E. (2004) Multimodal Texts: What they are and how Children use Them. In Evans, J. (ed.) *New Ways of Reading, New Ways of Writing: Using Popular Culture, New Technologies and Critical Literacy in the Primary Classroom*. New York, Heinemann, pp. 13–29.

Bearne, E. and Bazalgette (2010) *Beyond Words: Developing Children's Response to Multimodal Texts*. Leicester, UKLA.

Bearne, E. and Kress, G. (2001) Editorial. *Reading, Literacy and Language*, 35 (3) pp. 89–93.

Bearne, E. and Marsh, J. (2008) *Moving Literacy On: Evaluation of the BFI Lead Practioner Scheme for Moving Image Media*. Leicester, Sheffield, UKLA/University of Sheffield.

Bearne, E. and Wolstencroft, H. (2006) Playing with Texts: the Contribution of Children's Knowledge of Computer Narratives to their Story-writing. In Marsh, J. and Millard, E. (eds) *Popular Literacies, Childhood and Schooling*. London, New York, Routledge, pp. 72–92.

Bell, E. (1995) Somatexts at the Disney Shop: Constructing the Pentimentos of Women's Animated Bodies. In Bell, E., Haas, L, and Sells, L. (eds) *From Mouse to Mermaid: The Politics of Film, Gender and Culture*. Bloomington, Indiana, Indiana University Press, pp. 107–124.

Bell, E., Haas, L. and Sells, L. (eds) (1995) *From Mouse to Mermaid: The Politics of Film, Gender and Culture*. Bloomington, Indiana, Indiana University Press.

Bird, B. (2004) *The Incredibles* [Motion Picture] USA, Pixar/Disney.

Bird, B. (2007) *Ratatouille* [Motion Picture] USA, Pixar/Disney.

Blackburn, J., Chambers, R. and Holland, J. (1998) *Whose Voice?: Participatory Research and Policy Change*. London, Intermediate Technology.

Bloor, T. (1979) Learning about Language: The Language Studies Issue in Secondary Schools. *English in Education*, 13 (3) pp. 18–22.

Bond, D. (1979) *The Munch Bunch*. UK, Studio Publications.

Bordwell, D. (1985) *Narration in the Fiction Film*. London, Methuen.

Bordwell, D. (1988) ApProppriations and ImProp prieties: Problems in the Morphology of Film Narrative. *Cinema Journal*, 27 (3) pp. 5–20.

Bordwell, D. and Thompson, K. (2003) *Film Art: An Introduction*. New York, McGraw-Hill.

Bourdieu, P. (2010). "The Forms of Capital" (1986). Cultural Theory: An Anthology, 81.

Boyle, D. (2004) *Millions* [Motion Picture] UK, BBC, UKFC, Pathe.

Boyle, D. (2009) *Slumdog Millionnaire* [Motion picture] UK, India, France, Film 4/Warp Films.

Brice Heath, S. (1983) *Ways with Words: Language, Life and Work in Communities and Classrooms*. Cambridge, Cambridge University Press.

Bright, S. (1983) *Bananaman* [Animated Television Series] UK, BBC.

British Film Institute (B.F.I.) (1999) *Making Movies Matter*. London, BFI.

British Film Institute (B.F.I.) (2005) *Watch This: Top Fifty Films for Children up to the Age of 14*. http://www.bfi.org.uk/education/conferences/watchthis/top50.html (accessed 10 August 2010).

Bromley, H. (1996) 'Did you Know that there's no such Thing as Never Land?: Working with Video Narratives in the early Years'. In: Hilton, M. (ed.) *Potent Fictions: Children's Literacy and the Challenge of Popular Culture*, London: Routledge, 71–91.

Bronte, C. (1847) *Jane Eyre*. London, Smith, Elder and Co.

Bruner, J. (1990) *Acts of Meaning*. Harvard University Press.

Bruner, J.S. and Bruner, J.S. (2009) *Actual Minds, Possible Worlds*. Harvard University Press.

Bryman, A. (2004) *The Disneyization of Society*. London, Sage.

Buckingham, D. (1987) *Public Secrets: EastEnders and its Audience*. London, BFI Books.

Buckingham, D. (1993) *Children Talking Television: The Making of Television Literacy*. London, Bristol, Falmer Press.

Buckingham, D. (1996) *Moving Images: Understanding Children's Emotional Responses to Television*. Manchester, New York Manchester University Press.

Buckingham, D. (2002) *After the Death of Childhood: Growing Up in the Age of Electronic Media*. Cambridge, Polity Press.

Buckingham, D. (2003) *Media Education: Literacy, Learning and Contemporary Culture*. Cambridge, Polity Press.

Buckingham, D. and Sefton-Green, J. (1994) *Cultural Studies Goes to School: Reading and Teaching Popular Media*. London, Taylor and Francis.

Buckingham, D., Carr, D., Burn, A. and Schott, G. (2006) *Video-games: Text, Narrative, Play*. Cambridge, Polity.

Buckingham, D., Burn, A., Parry, B. and Powell, M. (2010) Minding the Gaps: Teachers' Cultures, Students' Cultures. In Alvermann, D. (ed.) *Adolescents' Online Literacies*. New York, Washington, D.C. Baltimore, Bern, Frankfurt, Berlin, Brussels, Vienna, Oxford, pp.183–199.

Buckingham, D., Willett, R. and Pini, M. (2012) *Home Truths? Video Production and Domestic Life*. University of Michigan Press.

Burn, A. (2007) The Place of Digital Video in the Curriculum. In Andrews, R. and Haythornthwaite C. A. (eds) (2007) *The Sage Handbook of e-learning Research*. London, Thousand Oaks, New Delhi, Singapore, Sage.

Burn, A. and Parker, D. (2003) *Analysing Media Texts*. London, New York, Continuum.

Burn, A. and Durran, J. (2006) Digital Anatomies: Analysis as Production in Media Education. In Buckingham, D. and Willet, R. (eds) *Digital Generations: Children, Young People and New Media*. Mahwah, New Jersey, London, Lawrence Erlbaum Associates, pp. 273–294.

Burn, A. and Durran, J. (2007) *Media Literacy in Schools: Practice, Production and Progression*. London, California, New Dehli, Singapore, Paul Chapman Publishing.

Calvert, K. (1998) Children in the House: The Material Culture of Early Childhood. In Jenkins, H. (ed.) *The Children's Culture Reader*. New York, London, New York University Press, pp. 67–80.

Capra, F. (1946) *It's a Wonderful Life* [Motion Picture] USA, Paramount Pictures.

Carrington, V. (2003) 'I'm in a Bad Mood. Let's Go Shopping': Interactive Dolls, Consumer Culture and a 'Glocalized' Model of Literacy. *Journal of Early Childhood Literacy*, 3 (83), pp. 82–98.

Carrington, V. (2005a) New Textual Landscapes, Information, New Childhood. In J. Marsh, (ed.) *Popular Culture: Media and Digital Literacies in Early Childhood*. London, Sage, pp. 13–27.

Carrington, V. (2005b) Txting: The End of Civilization Again. *Cambridge Journal of Education*. 35(2) pp. 161–175.

Carrington, V. (2009) From Blog to Bebo and beyond: Text, Risk, Participation. *Journal of Research in Reading*, 32 (1) pp. 6–21.

Carter, T. (2001) *Save the Last Dance* [Motion Picture] USA, Paramount Pictures.

Cavin, E. (1994) In Search of the view Finder: A Study of a Child's Perspective. *Visual Sociology*, 9 (1) pp. 27–42.

Central Advisory Council for Education (CACE) (1963) *Half our Future* (The Newsom Report) London, HMSO.

Cerezo, M. Martinez, A. and Ranera, P. (1996) Tres antropologos inocentes y un ojo si parpado. In Garcia, M., Alonso, A., Martinez, P., Ranera, P. and Fores, J. (eds) *Antropologia de los Sentidos: La Vista*. Madrid, Celeste.

Chandler, D. (2004) *Semiotics for Beginners*. http://www.aber.ac.uk/media/Documents/S4B/ (accessed 10 December 2010).

Chatman, S. (1989) *Story and Discourse: Narrative Structure in Fiction and Film*. Ithaca, Cornell University Press.

Chatman, S. (1990) *Coming to Terms: The Rhetorics of Narrative in Fiction and Film*. New York, Cornell University Press.

Chelsom, P. (1998) *The Mighty* [Motion Picture] USA, Miramax Scholastic.

Children's Film and Television Foundation (CFTF) (2010) *About Children's Film and Television Foundation. http://www.cftf.org.uk/about.html* (accessed 19 August 2010).

Christensen, P. (2004) Children's Participation in Ethnographic Research: Issues of Power and Representation. *Children and Society*, 18 pp. 165–176.

Christensen, P. and James, A. (eds) (2000) *Research with Children: Perspectives and Practice*. London, Routledge Falmer.

Clandinin, J. D. and Connelly, M. F. (2000) *Narrative Inquiry: Experience and Story in Qualitative Research*. CA, Jossey-Bass.

Cleese, C. and Cleese, J. (1975–1979) *Fawlty Towers* [Television Series] UK. BBC.

Clements, R. and Musker, J. (1989) *The Little Mermaid* [Motion Picture] USA, Walt Disney Pictures.

Clements, R. and Musker, J. (1992) *Aladdin* [Motion Picture] USA, Walt Disney Pictures.

Clements, R. and Musker, J. (2009) *The Frog Princess* [Motion Picture] USA, Walt Disney Pictures.

Clough, P. (2002) *Narrative Research*. Buckingham, Open University Press.

Cohen, L., Manion, L. and Morrison, K. (2007) *Research Methods in Education*. Oxon, New York, Routledge.

Collinson, P. (1969) *The Italian Job* [Motion Picture] UK Paramount Pictures.

Columbus, C. (1990) *Home Alone* [Motion Picture] USA, Twentieth Century Fox.

Columbus, C. (1992) *Home Alone 2: Lost in New York* [Motion Picture] USA, Twentieth Century Fox.

Columbus, C. (2002) *Harry Potter and the Chamber of Secrets* [Motion Picture] UK, USA, Warner Brothers Pictures.

Connolly, P. (1998) *Racism, Gender Identities and Young Children: Social Relations in a Multi-ethnic, Inner-city Primary School*. London, Routledge.

Cowell, S. (2007) *Britain's Got Talent* [Television Programme] UK, ITV.

Craven, W. (1996) *Scream* [Motion Picture] USA, Dimension Films.

Crichton, C. (1947) *Hue and Cry* [Motion Picture] UK, Rank Organisation.

Cunliffe, J. and Wood, I. (1981–1996) *Postman Pat* [Children's Animated Television Series] UK, Woodland Animations, BBC.

Curtiz, M. and Keighley, W. (1938) *The Adventures of Robin Hood* [Motion Picture] USA, Warner Brothers.

Dahl, R. (1961) *James and the Giant Peach*. London, Alfred A. Knopf Inc.

Dahl, R. (1982a) *Revolting Rhymes*. UK, Perma-Bound Books.

Dahl, R. (1982b) *The BFG*. UK, Penguin Books.

Dale, E. (1946) *Audio-visual Methods in Teaching*. New York, The Dryden Press.

Dante, J. (1984) *Gremlins* [Motion Picture] USA, Amblin Entertainment.

Davies, R. T. (2005) *Doctor Who* [Televised Series] UK, Cymru Wales.

Davies, J. (2006a) Escaping to the Borderlands: An exploration of the Internet as a Cultural Space for Teenaged Wiccan Girls. In Pahl, K. and Rowsell, J. (eds) *Travel Notes from the New Literacy Studies: Instances of Practice*. Multilingual Matters, pp. 57–71.

Davies, J. (2006b) "Hello newbie! **big welcome hugs** hope u like it here as much as i do!" An exploration of teenagers' informal on-line learning. In Buckingham, D. and Willett, R. (eds) *Digital Generations, Children, Young People and New Media*. New York, Lawrence Ehrlbaum, pp. 211–228.

Davies, J. (2009) A Space for Play: Crossing Boundaries and Learning Online. In Carrington and Robinson (eds) *Digital Literacies, Social Learning and Classroom Practices*. London, Sage, pp. 27–42.

Davies, J. and Merchant, G. (2009) *Web 2.0 for Schools: Learning and Social Participation*. New York, Peter Lang.

Deary, T. and Hepplewhite, P. (1993–present) *Horrible Histories*. London, Scholastic.

Department for Children Schools and Families (DCSF) (2006) *Primary Framework Literacy Year 1*. http://nationalstrategies.standards.dcsf.gov.uk/primary/primaryframework/literacy/planning/Year1 (accessed 4 June 2010).

Department for Education and Skills (DfES) (1999) *English: The National Curriculum in England (Key Stages 1–4)* (Online – www.nc.uk.net accessed 10th June 2008).

Department for Education and Employment (DfEE) (2000) *The National Literacy Strategy: Grammar for Writing*. London, The Stationery Office.

De Vito, D. (1996) *Matilda* [Motion Picture] USA, Jersey Films.

Dickens, C. (1838) *Oliver Twist, Or, The Parish Boy's Progress*. London, Richard Bentley.

Dobkin, D. (2005) *Wedding Crashers [Motion Picture] USA*, New Line Cinema.

Dyson, A. H. (1997) *Writing Superheroes: Contemporary Childhood, Popular Culture, and Classroom Literacy*. Williston, Teachers College Press.

Dyson, A. H. (2003) *The Brothers and Sisters Learn to Write: Popular Literacies in Childhood and School Cultures* (Vol. 64). New York, Teachers College Press.

Dyson, A. H. and Genishi, C. (1994) *The Need for Story: Cultural Diversity in Classroom and Community*. Illinois, National Council for Teachers of English.

Ebert, Roger (2005-03-18) Millions. *Chicago Times* [Newspaper]. http://rogerebert.suntimes.com/apps/pbcs.dll/article?AID=/20050317/REVIEWS/50309002/1023 (accessed 4 August 2010).

Eco, U. (1994) *Six Walks in the Fictional Woods*. Harvard University Press.

Edwards, D. (1952) *My Naughty Little Sister*. London, Methuen Children's.

Eisner, E. W. (1993) Forms of Understanding and the Future of Educational Research. *Educational Researcher*, 22 (7) pp. 5–11 (Online http://links.jstor.org/sici?sici=0013189X(199310)22%3A7%3C5%3AFOUATF%3E2.0.CO%3B2-U) (accessed 16 March 2010).

Elkonin, D.B. (1978) *The Psychology of Play*. Moscow, Pedagogika.

Epstein, P. (1998) Are you a Girl or are you a Teacher? The 'Least Adult' Role in Research about Gender and Sexuality in a Primary School. In Walford, G. (ed.) *Doing Research about Education*. London, Falmer Press.

Erikson, E. (1968) *Identity, Youth and Crisis*. London, Faber and Faber.

Fals-Borda, O. and Rahman, M. A. (eds) (1991) *Action and Knowledge: Breaking the Monopoly with Participatory Action Research*. New York, Intermediate Technology / Apex.

Film Nation UK (2013) Launch Press Release / Website Holding Page http://www.filmnationuk.org/index.html (accessed 13 May 2013).

Finch, B. (2008) Children's Film Viewing Practices: A Qualitative Investigation into Engagement with a Feature Film. *Unpublished PhD thesis, Massey University*.

Firestone, W. A. (1987) Meaning in Method: The Rhetoric of Quantitative and Qualitative Research. *Educational Researcher*, 16 (7) pp. 16–21.

Fish, S. (1980) *Is there a text in this Class? The Authority of Interpretive Communities*. Cambridge, MA, Harvard University Press.

Fleming, V. (1968) *The Wizard of Oz* [Motion Picture] USA, Metro Goldwyn Meyer.

Fletcher, A. (2006) *Step Up* [Motion Picture] USA, *Touchstone Pictures*.

Flewitt, R. (2006) Using Video to Investigate Preschool Classroom Interaction: Education Research Assumptions and Methodological Practices. *Visual Communication*, 5 (1) pp. 25–50.

Foldes, R. (2007) http://www.teachingexpertise.com/blog/ros-wilson-and-improving-writing-at-ks1-and-ks2-1799. Post submitted on 26/6/07 (accessed 29 June 2009).

Foote Whyte, W. (ed) (1991) *Participatory Action Research*. London, Newbury Park: California, Sage.

Forgacs, D. (1992) Disney Animation and the Business of Childhood. *Screen*, 33 pp. 361–374.

Foster, H. and Jackson, W. (1946) *Songs of the South* [Motion Picture] USA: Walt Disney Pictures/RKO.

Foucault, M. (1977) *Discipline and Punish: The Birth of the Prison*. Harmondsworth, Penguin.

Frater, G. (2000) Observed in Practice. English in the National Curriculum: some Reflections. *Reading*, 34 (3) pp. 107–12.

Friere, P. (1970, 1993) *Pedagogy of the Oppressed*. Revised Edition London, Penguin.

Fry, D. (1990) *Children Talk about Books: Seeing Themselves as Readers*. Suffolk, St Edmundsbury Press Ltd.

Gauntlett, D. (2005) *Moving Experiences: Media Effects and Beyond*. Second Edition Eastleigh, John Libbey Publishing.

Gauntlett, D. and Holzwarth, P. (2006) Creative and Visual Methods for Exploring Identities: A Conversation Abridged version of a Forthcoming Interview for *Visual Studies*, the Official Journal of the International Visual Sociology Association (IVSA), in 2006. (ONLINE – http://www.artlab.org.uk/VS-interview-2ps.pdf) (accessed 16 March 2010).

Gee, J. P. (2003) *What Video Games have to Teach us about Learning and Literacy*. New York, Palgrave Macmillan.

Genette, G. (1980) (trans) Lewin, J. E. *Narrative Discourse: An Essay on Method*. Ithaca, Cornell University Press.

Geronimi, C., Jackson, W. and Hamilton, L. (1953) *Peter Pan* [Motion Picture] USA, Walt Disney Pictures, Buena Vista.

Geronimi, C., Luske, H. and Reitherman, W. (1961) *101 Dalmations*. [Motion Picture] USA, Walt Disney, Buena Vista.

Gibson, O. (2008) *A One-off Quirky Thing*. http://www.guardian.co.uk/media/2008/jul/21/television (accessed 19 August 2010).

Giddens, A. (1991) *Modernity and Self Identity: Self and Society in the Late Modern Age*. Cambridge, Polity Press.

Gillen, J. Accorti Gamannossi, B. and Cameron, C. A. (2005) 'Pronto, Chi Parla?' ('Hello, who is it?') Telephones as Artefacts and Communication Media in Children's Discourses." In Marsh, J. (ed.) *Popular Culture, New Media and Digital Literacy in Early Childhood*. London, Routledge Falmer, pp. 146–162.

Gillispie, J. (1996) American Film Adaptations of the Secret Garden: Reflections of Sociological and Historical Change *The Lion and the Unicorn*. 20 (1) The John Hopkins University Press, pp.132–152.

Giroux, H. (1995) Memory and Pedagogy in the 'Wonderful World of Disney' in Bel, E.S., Haas, L. and Wells, L. (eds) *From Mouse to Mermaid: The Politics of Film, Gender and Culture*. Indiana University Press

Giroux, H. A. (1995) Animating Youth: the Disnification of Children's Culture. *Socialist Review*, 24 (3) pp. 23–55.

Giroux, H. A. (1999) *The Mouse that Roared: Disney and the End of Innocence*. Oxford, Maryland, Rowman and Littlefield Publishers Inc.

Glebas, F. (2003) *Piglet's Big Movie* [Motion Picture] USA, Walt Disney Pictures.

Goffman, E. (1974) *Frame Analysis*. Harmondsworth, Penguin.

Goodson, I. and Sikes, P. (2001) *Life Histories in Educational Settings: Learning from Lives*. Buckingham, Open University Press.

Goodson, I., Biesta, G. J. J., Tedder, M. and Adair, N. (2010) *Narrative Learning*. London, New York, Routledge.

Goodwyn, A. (2004) *English Teaching and the Moving Image*. London, New York, Routledge Falmer.

Grace, D. and Tobin, J. (1997) '*Carnival in the Classroom': Making a Place for Pleasure in Early Childhood Education*. New Haven, London, Yale University Press

Grace, D. and Tobin, J. (1998) Butt Jokes and Mean-Teacher Parodies: Video Production in the Elementary Classroom. In Buckingham, D. (ed.) *Beyond Radical Pedagogy: Teaching Popular Culture*. London, Routledge, pp. 42–62.

Graves, D. (1983) *Writing: Teachers and Children at Work*. Exeter, NH, Heinemann.

Graves D. (1994) *A Fresh Look at Writing*. Oxford: Heinemann.

Grimm, W. and Grimm, J. (1815) Zipes, J. (trans) (2007) *The Complete Fairy Tales*. London, Vintage.

Groening, M. (1987–Current) *The Simpsons* [Animated Television Series] USA, Twentieth century Fox.

Haase, D. P. (1988) Gold into Straw: Fairy Tale Movies for Children and the Culture Industry. *The Lion and the Unicorn*, 12 (2) pp. 193–207.

Hand, D. (1937) *Snow White and the Seven Dwarfs* [Motion Picture] USA, Disney.

Hanna, W. and Barbera, J. (1940) *Tom and Jerry* [Animated Television Series] USA, Hanna Barbera/Metro Goldwyn Mayer.

Hannerz, U. (1990) Cosmopolitans and Locals in World Culture. *Theory, Culture and Society*, 7 (2) pp. 237–51.

Hanson, S. (2000) Children in Film. In Mills, J. and Mills, R. W. (eds) *Childhood Studies: a Reader in Perspectives of Childhood*. London, Taylor Francis, pp. 145–160.

Hardy, B. (1975) *Tellers and Listeners: The Narrative Imagination*. London, The Athlone Press.

Hart, R. A. (1992) *Children's Participation: From Tokenism to Citizenship*. Innocenti Essays No.4 UNICEF (Online http://web.gc.cuny.edu/che/cerg/documents/Childrens_participation.pdf) (accessed 10 March 2006).

Hay, C. and Marsh, D. (eds) (2000) *Demystifying Globalisation*. Basingstoke, Palgrave Macmillan.

Heath, S. B. (1983) *Ways with Words: Language, Life, and Work in Communities and Classrooms*. Cambridge, Cambridge University Press.

Hickner, S. and Smith, S. (2007) *The Bee Movie* [Motion Picture] USA, Dreamworks.

Hill, T. (2007) *Alvin and the Chipmunks* [Motion Picture] Twentieth Century Fox.

Hillocks, G. Jr (1995) *Teaching Writing as Reflective Practice*. New York, Teachers College Press.

Hilton, M. (1996) *Potent Fictions: Children's Literacy and the Challenge of Popular Culture*. London, Routledge.

Hilton, M. (2001) Writing Process and Progress: Where do we go from here? *English in Education*, 35 (1) pp. 4–11.

Hodge, B. and Tripp, D. (1986) *Children and Television: A Semiotic Approach*. Cambridge, Malden, Polity Press.

Hodges, A. and Haines, T. (2007–2011) *Primeval* [Televised Series] UK, ITV.

Hodgson Burnett, F. (1993) *The Secret Garden*. Ware, Wordsworth Editions Limited.

Holland, A. (1993) *The Secret Garden* [Motion Picture] UK, USA, Warner Brothers.

Holleyman, S. (1999) *Mona the Vampire* [Animated TV Series] Canada, YTV Radio-Canada.

Hollindale, P. (1992) Ideology and the Children's Book. In Hunt, P. (ed) *Literature for Children: Contemporary Criticism*. London, New York, Routledge.

Hymes, D. H. (1996) *Ethnography, Linguistics, Narrative Inequality: Towards an Understanding of Voice*. London, Bristol, Taylor Francis.

Iser, W. (1980) The Reading Process: A Phenomenological Approach. In Tompkins, J. P. (ed.) *Reader-Response Criticism from Formalism to Post Structuralism*. Baltimore, London, The John Hopkins University Press, pp. 50–69.

Ito, M. (2006) Japanese Media Mixes and Amateur Cultural Exchange. In Buckingham, D. and Willett, R. (Eds) *Digital Generations: Children Young People and New Media*. New Jersey, Lawrence Erlbaum Associates, pp. 49–66.

Jackson, P. (2001–2003) *The Lord of the Rings Trilogy* [Motions Pictures] USA, New Line Cinema.

James, A. (1998) Confections, Concoctions, and Conceptions. In Jenkins, H. (ed.) *The Children's Culture Reader*. New York, London, New York University Press, pp. 394–405.

James, A. and James, A. (2004) *Constructing Childhood: Theory, Policy and Practice*. London, Palgrave Macmillan.

James, A. and Prout, A. (eds) (1990) *Constructing and Reconstructing Childhood*. London, Falmer Press.

Jenkins, H. (1992) *Textual Poachers: Television Fans and Participatory Culture*. New York, London, Routledge.

Jenkins, H. (ed.) (1998) *The Children's Culture Reader*. New York, London, New York University Press.

Jenkins, H. et al. (2009) *Confronting the Challenges of Participatory Culture: Media Education for the 21st Century*. The J. D. and C. T. MacArthur Foundation Reports on Digital Media and Learning.

Jennings, G. (2008) *The Son of Rambow* [Motion Picture] UK/France, Optimum Releasing.

Johnson, M. S. (2007) *Ghost Rider* [Motion Picture] USA, Marvel Studios.

Johnstone, J. (1989) *Honey I Shrunk the Kids* [Motion Picture] USA, Walt Disney Pictures.

Jones, C. (1949) *Roadrunner* [Animated Television Series] USA, Warner Bros.

Juluri, V. (2003) 'Ask the West if the Dinosaurs will Come Back?' Indian Audiences/ Global Audiences Studies. In Murphy, P.D. and Kraidy, M. (eds) *Global Media Studies: Ethnographic Perspectives*. New York, Routledge, pp. 215–33.

Kendeou, P., Bohn-Gettler, C., White, M. J. and Van den Broek, P. (2008) Children's Inference making across different Media. *Journal of Research in Reading*, 31 (3), pp. 259–72.

Kenner C. (2004) *Becoming Biliterate: Young Children Learning different Writing Systems*. Oakhill VA, Stoke on Trent, Staffordshire, Trentham Books.

Kenner, C. (2005) Bilingual Children's uses of Popular Culture in Text-making In: Marsh, J. (eds) *Popular Culture, New Media and Digital Literacy in Early Childhood*. Ed Oxon, New York, Routledge Falmer, pp.73–87.

Kenner, C. and Kress, G. (2003) The Multisemiotic Resources of Biliterate Children. *Journal of Early Childhood Literacy*, 3 (2), pp. 179–202.

Kenway, J. and Bullen, J. (2001) *Consuming Children: Entertainment, Advertising and Education*. Open University Press.

Kincheloe, J. L. (1998) The New Childhood: Home Alone as a Way of Life. In Jenkins, H. (ed.) *The Children's Culture Reader.* New York, London, New York University Press, pp. 159–77.

Kline, S. (1998) The Making of Children's Culture. In Jenkins, H. (ed.) *The Children's Culture Reader.* New York, London, New York University Press, pp. 95–109.

Kress, G. (1995) *Writing the Future: English and the Making of a Culture of Innovation.* Sheffield, NATE (National Association for the Teaching of English).

Kress, G. (1997) *Before Writing: Rethinking the Paths to Literacy.* New York: Routledge.

Kress, G. (2000) *Before Writing – Rethinking the Paths to Literacy.* London, Routledge.

Kress, G. (2003) *Literacy in the New Media Age.* London, New York, Routledge.

Kress, G., Jewitt, J., Bourne, J., Franks, A., Hardcastle, J., Jones, K. and Reid, R. (2005) *English in Urban Classrooms: A Multimodal Perspective on Teaching and Learning.* London, New York, Routledge Falmer.

Kristeva, J. (1967) Bakhtine, le mot, le dialogue et le roman. *Critique* (239), pp. 438–465.

Lambirth, A. (2003) They Get Enough of that Home: Understanding Aversion to Popular Culture in Schools. *Reading.* 37 (1), pp. 9–13

Lambirth, A. (2004) 'They get Enough of that at Home': Understanding Aversion to Popular Culture in Schools. *Children's Literacy and Popular Culture* ESRC funded seminar series. Seminar 6–11 February 2004, University of Sheffield (Online http://wwwshef.ac.uk/content/1/c6/05/06/97/EG_11_2.pdf) (accessed 10 May 2008).

Lasseter, J. (1995) *Toy Story* [Motion Picture] USA, Pixar Animations/Walt Disney Pictures.

Lasseter, J. (1998) *A Bug's Life* [Motion Picture] USA, Pixar Animations/Walt Disney Pictures.

Lean, D. (1946) *Great Expectations* [Motion Picture] UK, General Film Distributors.

Lensmire, T. (1994) *When Children Write: Critical Re-visions of the Writing Workshop.* New York, Teachers College Press.

Levin, D. E. and Kilbourne, J. (2008) *So Sexy So Soon: The New Sexualized Childhood and What Parents Can Do to Protect Their Kids.* London, Ballantine Books.

Levy, R. (2009) 'You have to Understand Words...but not Read Them'; Young Children becoming Readers in a Digital Age', *Journal of Research in Reading,* 32 (1), pp. 75–91.

Lima, K. (2007) Enchanted [Motion Picture] USA, Walt Disney Pictures.

Lincoln, Y. and Guba, E. (1985) *Naturalistic Inquiry.* Newberry Park, London, New Delhi, Sage.

Livingstone, S. and Bovill, M. (2000) *Young People, New Media* (Online – http://www.lse.ac.uk/collections/media@lse/pdf/young_people_report.pdf London pp. 1–54 (accessed 24 September 2006).

Lucas, G. (1977) *Star Wars* [Motion Pictures] USA, Twentieth Century Fox.

Lucas, G. (2002) *Star Wars: Attack of the Clones* [Motion Pictures] USA, Twentieth Century Fox.

Luke A. and Carrington, V. (2002) Globalisation, Literacy, Curriculum Practice. In Fisher, R., Lewis, M. and Brooks, G. (eds) *Raising Standards in Literacy.* London, Routledge Falmer.

Mackey M. (2002) *Literacies Across Media: Playing the Text.* London, New York, Routledge Falmer.

Mackey, M. (2004) Children Reading and Interpreting Stories in Print, Film, and Computer Games. In Evans, J. (ed.) *Literacy Moves On: Using Popular Culture, New Technologies and Critical Literacy in the Primary Classroom.* London, David Fulton, pp. 48–58.

Mackey, M. (2006) Digital Games and the Narrative Gap. In Buckingham, D. and Willet, R. (eds) *Digital Generations: Children, Young People and New Media*. Mahwah, New Jersey, London, Lawrence Erlbaum Associates.

Mackey, M. and Robinson, M. (2003) Film and Television. In Hall, N., Larson, J., and Marsh, J. (eds) *Handbook of Early Childhood Literacy*. London, Thousand Oaks, New Delhi, Sage, pp. 126–142.

Malone, K. (1999) Growing up in Cities as a Model of Participatory Planning 'Place Making' with Children. *Youth Studies Australia*, 18 (2), pp. 17–23.

Marsh, J. (2000) Teletubby Tales: Popular Culture on the Early Years Language and Literacy Curriculum. *Contemporary Issues in Early Childhood*, 1 (2), pp. 119–125.

Marsh, J. (2003) Early Childhood Literacy and Popular Culture. In Hall, N., Larson, J. and Marsh, J. (eds) *Handbook of Early Literacy*. London, New Delhi, Thousand Oaks, CA, Sage, pp. 112–125.

Marsh, J. (2004) *The* Techno-literacy Practices of Young Children. *Journal of Early Childhood Research*, 2 (1), pp. 51–66.

Marsh, J. (2005) Ritual, Performance and Identity Construction: Young Children's Engagement with Popular Cultural and Media Texts. In Marsh, J. (ed.) *Popular Culture, New Media and Digital Literacy in Early Childhood*. Oxon, Routledge and Falmer, pp. 28–50.

Marsh, J. (2006) Popular Culture in the Literacy Curriculum: A Bourdieuan Analysis. *Reading Research Quarterly*, 41 (2) pp. 160–173.

Marsh, J. (2009) Productive Pedagogies: Play, Creativity and Digital Cultures in the Classroom. In Willett, R., Robinson, M. and Marsh, J. (eds) *Play, Creativity and Digital Cultures*. New York, London, Routledge, pp. 200–218.

Marsh, J. (2010) Young Children's Play in Online Virtual Worlds. *Journal of Early Childhood Research*, 8 (1) pp. 23–39.

Marsh, J. and Millard, E. (2000) *Literacy and Popular Culture: Using Children's Culture in the Classroom*. London, Paul Chapman Publishing.

Marsh, J., Brooks, G., Hughes, J. Ritchie, L., Roberts, S. and Wright, K. (2005) *Digital beginnings: Young Children's use of Popular Culture, Media and New Technologies*. Sheffield, Literacy Research Centre University of Sheffield.

Marshall, F. (2006) *Eight Below* [Motion Picture] USA, Walt Disney Pictures.

Marshall, G. (1990) *Pretty Woman* [Motion Picture] USA, Touchstone Pictures.

Mayall, B. (2000) Conversations with Children: Working with Generational Issues. In Christensen, P. and James, A. (eds) *Research with Children: Perspectives and Practices*. London, Routledge.

McKean, D. (2005) *Mirror Mask* [Motion Picture] USA, Jim Henson Pictures.

McKee, D. (1996) *Not Now Bernard* [Picture Book] London, Red Fox.

Meadows, S. (2007) *This is England* [Motion Picture] UK, Film 4 Warp/Films.

Merchant, G. (2005a) The Electric Connection: Identity Performance in Children's Informal Digital Writing. *Discourse*, 26 (3) pp. 301–314.

Merchant, G. (2005b) The Dagger of Doom and the Magic Handbag: Writing On-Screen. In Evans, J. (ed.) *Literacy Moves On: Using Popular Culture, New Technologies and Critical Literacy in the Primary Classroom*. London, David Fulton, pp. 59–75.

Messenger Davies, M. (1997) *Fake, Fact and Fantasy: Children's Interpretations of Television Reality*. Hillsdale, NJ, Lawrence Erlbaum.

Messenger Davies, M. (2001) *Dear BBC: Children, Television-storytelling and the Public Sphere*. Cambridge, Cambridge University Press.

Metz, C. (1974) *Film Language*. Chicago, Chicago University Press.

Millard, E. (2005) Writing of Heroes and Villains: Fusing Children's Knowledge About Popular Fantasy Texts With School-based Literacy Requirements. In Evans, J. (ed.) *Literacy Moves On*. Portsmouth, NH, Heinemann, pp. 161–184.

Millard, E. (1997) *Differently Literate: Boys, Girls and the Schooling of Literacy*. London, Washington D.C., The Falmer Press.

Millard, E. (2006) Transformative Practioners, Transformative Practice: Teachers Working with Popular Culture in the Classroom. In Marsh, J. and Millard, E. (eds) *Popular Literacies, Childhood and Schooling*. Oxon, New York, Routledge, pp. 221–240.

Miller, S. and Rode, G. (1995) The Movie You See: The Movie You Don't. In Bell, E., Haas, L. and Sells, L. (eds) *Mouse to Mermaid: The Politics of Film, Gender and Culture*. Bloomington, Indiana, Indiana University Press, pp. 86–106.

Minkoff, R. (1999) *Stuart Little* [Motion Picture] USA, Columbia Pictures.

Mishler, E. (1999) *Storylines: Craftartists' Narratives of Identity*. Harvard University Press.

Miyamoto, S. and Tezuka, T. (1986) *The Legend of Zelda* [Console Game] Japan, USA, Nintendo.

Moje, E. B. and McCarthey, S. J. (2002) Identity Matters. *Reading Research Quarterly*, 37 (2) pp. 228–238.

Moje, E. B., McIntosh Ciechanowski, K., Kramer, K., Ellis, L., Carrillo, R. and Collazo, T. (2004) Working toward Third Space in Content area Literacy: An Examination of Everyday Funds of Knowledge and Discourse. *Reading Research Quarterly*, 39 (1) pp. 38–71.

Moll, L. C., Armanti, C., Neff, D. and Gonzalez, N. (1992) Funds of Knowledge for Teaching: Using a Qualitative Approach to Connect Homes and Classrooms. *Theory into Practice*, 31 (2), pp. 132–141.

Morley, D. (1980) *The Nationwide Audience: Structure and Decoding*. London, The British Film Institute.

Morley, D. and Robins, K. (1995) *Spaces of Identity: Global Media, Electronic Landscapes and Cultural Boundaries*. New York, London, Routledge.

Morris, H. (2005) Seeing the story… What is the impact of moving image on motivation and competence in narrative writing at the end of Key Stage Two? MA Thesis The University of Sheffield (Unpublished).

Morrow, V. and Richards, M. (1996) The Ethics of Social Research with Children: An Overview. *Children and Society*, 10 (2) pp. 203–214.

Moss, G. (1989) *Un/Popular Fictions*. London, Virago.

Murphy, J. (2006) *All in One Piece* [Picture Book]. London, Walker Books.

Neff, H. (1996) Strange Faces in the Mirror: The Ethics of Diversity in Children's Films. *The Lion and the Unicorn*, 20 (1) pp. 50–65.

Newell, M. (1994) *Four Weddings and a Funeral* [Motion Picture] UK Polygram Film Entertainment / Channel Four Films / Working Title Films.

Niesyto, H., Buckingham, D. and Fisherkeller, J. (2003) VideoCulture: Crossing Borders with Children's Video Productions. *Television and New Media*, 4 (4) pp. 461–482.

Nikolajeva, M. (1996) *Children's Literature Comes of Age: Towards a New Aesthetic*. New York, London, Garland.

Nixon, J. (ed.) (1981) *A Teachers' Guide to Action Research: Evaluation, Enquiry and Development in the Classroom*. London, Grant McIntyre.

Nodelman, P. (1992) *The Pleasures of Children's Literature*. New York, Longman.

Ofsted (2007) Inspection Report: (Anon) Primary School, 22 February 2006 to 23 February 2006.

O'Kane, C. and Thomas, N. (1999) The Ethics of Participatory Research with Children. *Children and Society*, 12, pp. 336–348.

Ortega, K. (2006) *High School Musical* [Television Film] USA, Disney Channel.

Pahl, K. (2002) Ephemera, Mess and Miscellaneous Piles: Texts and Practices in Families. *Journal of Early Childhood Literacy*, 2 (2) pp. 145–165.

Palmer, S. (2007) *Toxic Childhood: How The Modern World Is Damaging Our Children and What We Can Do About It*. London, Orion.

Pahl, K. (2003) Children's Text Making at Home: Transforming Meaning Across Modes. In Jewitt, C. and Kress, G. (eds) *Multimodal Literacy*. New York, Peter Lang Publishers, pp. 139–154.

Pahl, K. (2005) Narrative Spaces and Multiple identities: Children's Textual Explorations of Console Games in Home Settings. In Marsh, J. (ed.) *Popular Culture, Media and Digital Literacies in Early Childhood*. London, Routledge/Falmer, pp. 126–145.

Pahl, K. (2006) Children's Popular Culture in the Home: Tracing Children Cultural Practices in Texts. In Marsh, J. and Millard, E. (eds) *Popular Literacies, Childhood and Schooling*. London, New York, Routledge Falmer, pp. 29–53.

Pappasa, C. C. (1993) Is Narrative 'Primary'? Some Insights from Kindergarteners' Pretend Readings of Stories and Information Books. *Journal of Literacy Research*, 25 (1) pp. 97–129.

Park, N. (1995) *A Close Shave*. [Short animated film]. UK, Aardman/BBC.

Park, N. (2007–2010) *Shaun the Sheep*. [Animated Television Series]. UK, Aardman/BBC.

Parker, D. (1999a) You've Read the Book, Now Make the Film: Moving Image Media.

Parker, D. (1999b) *Moving Image, Media, Print Literacy and Narrative*. www.bfi.org.uk/education/research/teachlearn/nate.html (Accessed 09 December).

Parker, D. (2006) Making it Move, making it Mean: Animation, Print Literacy and the Metafunctions of Language. In Marsh, J. and Millard, E. (eds) *Popular Literacies, Childhood and Schooling*. London, New York, Routledge Falmer, pp. 149–159.

Parker, D. and Stone, S. (1997) *South Park* [Animated Television Series] U.S.A., Comedy Central.

Parry, B. (2009) Reading and Rereading Shrek. *English in Education*, 43 (2) pp. 48–161.

Parry, B. (2010) Helping Children Tell the Stories in their Heads. In Bazalgette, C. (ed.) *Teaching Media in Primary School*. Los Angeles, London, New Delhi, Singapore, Washington DC, Media Education Association/Sage, pp. 89–100.

Pink, S. (2001) *Doing Visual Ethnography*. London, Thousand Oaks, New Delhi, Sage Publications.

Polkingthorne, D. (1995) Narrative Configuration on Qualitative Analysis. In Hatch, J. A. and Wisniewski, R. (eds) *Life History and Narrative*. London, The Falmer Press, pp. 5–24.

Pompe, C. (1992a) When the Aliens Wanted Water': Media Education – Children's Critical Frontiers. In Styles, M., Bearne, E. and Watson, V. (eds) *After Alice: Exploring Children's Literature*. London, New York, Cassell, pp. 56–70.

Pompe, C. (1992b) He Quickly Changes into his Bikini: Models for Teacher-Pupil Collaboration. In Alvorado, M. and Boyd-Barrett, O. (eds) *Media Education: An Introduction*. London, BFI, pp. 303–311.

Porter-Abbott, H. (2002) *The Cambridge Introduction to Narrative*. Cambridge, Cambridge University Press.

Potter, J. and Wetherell (1987) *Discourse and Social Psychology: Beyond Attitudes and Behaviour*. London, Sage.

Potter, J. (2009) *Curating the Self: Media Literacy and Identity in Digital Video Production by Young Learners*. PhD Thesis, Institute of Education, University of London (Unpublished).

Print Literacy and Narrative. *English in Education*, 33 (1) pp. 24–35.

Propp, V. (1968) *Morphology of the Folktale.* Second Edition Indiana University Research Center in Anthropology, Folklore and Linguistics Publication 10 / Revised Edition /1968.

Prosser, J. (ed.) (1998) *Image–based Research: A Sourcebook for Qualitative Researchers.* London, Falmer Press.

Protherough, R. (1983) *Developing responses to Fiction.* Milton Keynes: Open University.

Pullman, P. (1995) *His Dark Materials.* UK, Scholastic Point.

Raimi, S. (2002) *Spiderman* [Motion Picture] USA, Marvel Entertainment.

Rapper, I. (1942) *Now Voyager* [Motion Picture] USA, Warner Brothers.

Reason, P. (1994) Three Approaches to Participative Inquiry. In Denzin, N. K. and Lincoln, Y. S. (eds) *Handbook of Qualitative Research.* Thousand Oaks, C.A, Sage, pp. 324–339.

Reid, M. (2003) Writing Film: Making Inferences when Viewing and Reading. *Reading,* 37 (3) pp. 111–115.

Reid, M. (2009) Reframing Literacy: A Film Pitch for the Twenty First Century. *English, Drama, Media.* June NATE.

Reid, M., Burn, A. and Parker, D. (2002) *Evaluation Report of the Becta Digital Video Pilot Project* http://www.bfi.org.uk/education/research/teachlearn/becta.html (Accessed 1 December 09).

Reiner, R. (1987) *The Princess Bride* [Motion Picture] USA, Twentieth Century Fox.

Reitherman, W. (1967) *Jungle Book* [Motion Picture] USA, Disney.

Reitman, I. (1984) *Ghostbusters* [Motion Picture] USA, Columbia Pictures.

Richards, C. (1995) Room to Dance; Girl's Play and The Little Mermaid, In (eds) Bazalgette, C. and Buckingham, D. *In Front of the Children.* London, British Film Institute, pp. 141–150.

Richmond, J. (1990) in (Ed) Carter, R. *Knowledge about language and the Curriculum.* London, Hodder and Stoughton, pp. 23–38.

Riessmann, C. K. (2008) *Narrative Methods for the Human Sciences.* LA, London, New Delhi, Singapore, Sage.

Robinson, M. (1997) *Children Reading Print and Television.* London, Falmer Press.

Robinson M. and Mackey, M. (2006) Assets in the Classroom: Comfort and Competence with Media among Teachers Present and Future. In Marsh, J. and Millard, E. (eds) *Popular Literacies, Childhood and Schooling.* New York, Oxon, Routledge, pp. 200–220.

Rose, G. (2001) *Visual Methodologies.* London, Thousand Oaks, New Delhi, Sage Publications.

Rosen, M. (1992) *The Hypnotiser.* London, Lions.

Rosenblatt, L. M. (1970) *Literature as Exploration.* London, Heinemann.

Rouleau, D., Casey, J. and Seagle, S. (2005–Current) *Ben 10* [Animated Television Series] USA, Cartoon Network.

Rowling, J. K. (1997) *Harry Potter and the Philosopher's Stone.* London, Bloomsbury.

Ruby, J. (1980) Exposing Yourself: Reflexivity, Anthropology, and Film. *Semiotica,* 30 (1.2) pp. 153–179 (Online – http://astro.temple.edu/~ruby/ruby/exposing.html (Accessed 16th March2010).

Saban, H. (1993–1996) *The Mighty Morphin Power Rangers [Animated Television Series]* Japan, USA, 20th Century Fox.

Sarland, C. (1991) *Young People Reading: Culture and Response.* . Milton Keynes, Philadelphia, Open University Press.

Sarup, M. (1998) *Identity, Culture and the Postmodern World.* Edinburgh, Edinburgh University Press.

Sax, G. (2006) *Stormbreaker* [Motion Picture] UK, USA, Germany, UKFC/The Weinstein Company.

Schneider, D. (2004) *Drake and Josh* [Television Series] USA, Nickolodeon.
Schneider, D. (2005) *Zoey 101* [Television Series] USA Nickolodeon.
Schneider, D. (2007), *I Carly* [Television Series] USA Nickolodeon.
Seaton, G. (1947) *Miracle on 34th Street [Motion Picture]* Twentieth Century Fox.
Shankman, A. (2007) *Hairspray* [Motion Picture] USA, New Line Cinema.
Shankman, A. (2008) *Bedtime Stories* [Motion Picture] USA, Walt Disney Productions.
Sharpsteen, B. (1941) *Dumbo* [Motion Picture] USA, Walt Disney Productions.
Siberling, B. (2004) *A Series of Unfortunate Events* [Motion Picture] USA, Disney.
Silverman, D. (2007) *The Simpsons Movie* [Motion Picture] USA, Twentieth Century Fox.
Simons, H., Kushner, S., Jones, K. and James, D. (2003) From Evidence-based Practice to Practice-based Evidence: The Idea of Situated Generalization. *Research Papers in Education*, 18 (4) pp. 347–364.
Singer, B. (2000) *The X-Men* [Motion Picture] USA, Twentieth Century Fox/Marvel Entertainment Group.
Slade, D. (2007) *30 Days of Night [Motion Picture] USA*, Columbia Pictures.
Snær Erlingsson, G. (1995) *Benjamin Dove*. Iceland, Icelandic Film/Zentrope Studios.
Snicket, L. (1990) *The Bad Beginning: Orphans*. London, Harper Collins.
Soep, E. (2003) Learning about Research from Youth Media Artists Penn GSE Perspectives. *Urban Education*, 1 (2.1) pp. 1–6.
Spencer, M. M. (1982) *Learning to Read*. London, Bodley Head.
Spencer, M. M. (1988) *How Texts Teach What Readers Learn*. Stroud, Thimble Press.
Spencer, M. M. (1991) *On being Literate*. London, The Bodley Head.
Spencer, M. M. (2001) Foreword. In Barrs, M. and Cork, V. (eds) *The Reader in the Writer*. London, CLPE.
Spencer, M. M. (2004) What more needs Saying about Imagination? *Reading Research Quarterly*, 38 (4) (Oct–Dec 2003) pp. 546–551.
Spielberg, S. (1982) *E.T. The Extra Terrestrial* [Motion Picture] USA, Amblin Entertainment.
Spielberg, S. and Lucas, G. (1981) *Indiana Jones: Raiders of the Lost Ark* [Motion Picture] USA, Paramount Pictures.
Stanton, A. (2003) *Finding Nemo* [Motion Picture] USA, Pixar/Walt Disney Pictures.
Street, B. (1984) *Literacy in Theory and Practice*. Cambridge, Cambridge University Press.
Sturridge, C. (1997) *Fairytale: A True Story* [Motion Picture] UK: Icon Productions.
Tajiri, S. (1986) *Pokemon* [Console Game] USA, Japan, Nintendo.
Tandon, R. (1989) Participatory Research and Social Transformation. *Convergence*, 21 (2.3) pp. 5–15.
Thomson, D. C. (1938–Current) *The Beano*. [Weekly Comic] UK, D.C. Comics.
Tilly, C. (2008) Son of Rambow Feature. *Time Out Magazine* http://www.timeout.com/film/features/show-feature/1642/ (Accessed 9 September 2010).
Tobin, J. (2000) *Good Guys don't Wear Hats: Children's Talk about the Media*. New York, Teachers College Press.
Todorov, T. (1968) La Grammaire du recit. *Languages*, 12, pp. 94–102.
Todorov, T. (1977) *The Poetics of Prose* Trans. Howard R. (trans) Ithaca, Cornell University Press.
Turtletaub, J. (1993) *Cool Runnings* [Motion Picture] USA, Walt Disney Pictures.
Turtletaub, J. (2004) *National Treasure* [Motion Picture] USA, Walt Disney Pictures.
Tyner, K. (1998) *Literacy in a Digital World: Teaching and Learning in the Age of Information*. Mahwah, New Jersey, Lawrence Erlbaum Associates.

United Kingdom Film Council (UKFC) and Stimulating World Research (2007) *A Qualitative Study of Avid Cinema-Goers*. London, UK Film Council (Accessed 1 December 2009).

United Kingdom Film Council (UKFC) (2008) Statistical Year Book. http://www.ukfilmcouncil.org.uk/publications (Accessed 4 June 2010).

United Kingdom Film Council (UKFC) (2009a) *Top 200 films at world box office 2001–2008*. http://www.ukfilmcouncil.org.uk/theatrical (Accessed 4 June 2010).

United Kingdom Film Council (UKFC) (2009b) *Film in the UK: A Briefing Paper*. Version 3.0. Draft dated: 21/8/09 http://www.ukfilmcouncil.org.uk/research (Accessed 12 August 2010).

Unkrich, L. (2010) *Toy Story 3* [Motion Picture] USA, Pixar/ Walt Disney.

Unwin. D. (2006) *Horrid Henry* [Animated Television Series] UK, Novel Entertainment / ITV.

Van den Broek, P. (2001) The role of television viewing in the development of reading comprehension. 1 Online-http://www.ciera.org/library/archive/2001-02/04OCT99-58-MSarchive.html (Accessed 23 September 2008).

Vincent, D. (2004) *Literacy Literacy* ESRC Research Seminar Series, Children's Literacy and Popular Culture, University of Sheffield, 2004.

Vygotsky, L. (1978) Interaction between Learning and Development. *Readings on the Development of Children*, pp. 34–41.

Walker, A. (1988) *Living by the Word*. London, The Women's Press.

Walker, J. (2004) *Distributed Narrative: Telling Stories Across Networks*. Paper presented at AoIR 5.0, September 2004. http://jilltxt.net/txt/distributednarratives.html (Accessed 10 June 2010).

Watson, R. (1990) *Film and Television in Education: An Aesthetic Approach to the Moving Image*. New York, London, Philadelphia, The Falmer Press.

Wedge, C. (2002) *Ice Age* [Motion Picture] USA, Twentieth Century Fox.

Weitz, C. (2007) *The Golden Compass [Motion Picture]* USA, New Line Cinema.

West, M. I. (2009) *The Japanification of Children's Popular Culture: From Godzilla to Miyazaki*. Lanham, MD, Scarecrow Press.

Whitely, D. (1996) Reality in Boxes: Children's Perceptions of Television Narratives. In Hilton, M. (ed.) *Potent Fictions: Children's Literacy and the Challenge of Popular Culture*. London, Routledge, pp. 47–70.

Willett, R. (2001) *Children's Use of Popular Media in their Creative Writing*. Institute of Education, University of London PhD thesis (Unpublished).

Willett, R. (2005a) Constructing the Digital Tween: Market Forces, Adult Concerns and Girls' Interests. In Mitchell, C. and Reid-Walsh, J. (eds) *Seven Going on Seventeen: Tween Culture in Girlhood Studies*. Oxford, Peter Lang, pp. 278–293.

Willett, R. (2005b) 'Baddies' in the Classroom: Media Education and Narrative Writing. *Literacy*, 39 (3) pp. 142–148.

Willet, R. (2009) Young People's Video Productions as New Sites of Learning. In Carrington, V. and Robinson, M. (eds) *Digital Literacies: Social Learning and Classroom Practices*. London, NY, TA, New Delhi, Singapore, UKLA/Sage, pp. 13–27.

Williams, R. (1989) *Raymond Williams on Television: Selected Writings*. New York, Routledge.

Williams, R. (1963) *Culture and Society*. New York, Columbia University Press.

Wellington, J. (2000) Educational research: Contemporary issues and practical approaches. Continuum International Publishing Group.

Wilson, J. (1991) *The Story of Tracy Beaker*. UK, Doubleday.

Wilson, J. (2007) *Jacky Daydream: The Story of her Childhood.* London, New York, Toronto, Sydney, Auckland, Doubleday.

Wilson, R. (2002) *Raising Standards in Writing.* CHYPS, Learning.

Wojcik-Andrews, I. (2000) *Children's Films: History, Ideology, Pedagogy, Theory.* New York, London, Garland.

Wilson, R. (2007) Quirky Literacy Campaign. Wakefield Express Campaign http://www.wakefieldexpress.co.uk/reading-campaign-news-articles/Quirky-literacy-crusade.2840262.jp 20/4/07 (Accessed 29 June 2009).

Wojcik- Andrews (1996) Introduction (Special Issue: Children's Films) *The Lion and the Unicorn,* 20 (1) 1996 The John Hopkins University Press, pp. v–vi.

Wood, N. (1996) Domesticating Dreams in Walt Disney's Cinderella. (Special Issue: Children's Films) *The Lion and the Unicorn,* 20 (1) The John Hopkins University Press, pp. 25–49.

Young, L. and Barrett, H. (2001) Adapting Visual Methods: Action Research with Kampala Street Children. *Area,* 33 (2) pp. 141–152.

Yuyama, K. (1998) *Pokemon* [Motion Picture] Japan, USA, Toho/Warner Brothers Pictures.

Zipes, J. (1995a) Breaking the Disney Spell. In Bell, E., Haas, L. and Sells, L. (eds) *From Mouse to Mermaid: The Politics of Film, Gender and Culture.* Bloomington, Indianapolis, Indiana University Press, pp. 21–42.

Zipes, J. (1995b) Once upon a Time Beyond Disney: Contemporary Fairy-tale Films for Children. In Bazalgette, C. and Buckingham, D. (eds) *In Front of the Children.* London, British Film Institute, pp. 109–126.

Zipes, J. (1997) *Happily Ever After: Fairy Tales, Children and the Culture Industry.* New York, London, Routledge.

Index

Printed in Great Britain
by Amazon